RED QUEEN?

MICHAEL ASHCROFT

RED QUEEN?

THE UNAUTHORISED BIOGRAPHY OF ANGELA RAYNER

Lord
Ashcroft
@LordAshcroft

\Bb\
Biteback Publishing

First published in Great Britain in 2024 by
Biteback Publishing Ltd, London
Copyright © Michael Ashcroft 2024

ISBN 978-1-78590-856-9

10 9 8 7 6 5 4 3 2 1

A CIP catalogue record for this book is available from the British Library.

Set in Minion Pro and Futura

Printed and bound in Great Britain by
CPI Group (UK) Ltd, Croydon CR0 4YY

FSC
www.fsc.org
MIX
Paper | Supporting
responsible forestry
FSC® C171272

CONTENTS

AUTHOR'S ROYALTIES

Lord Ashcroft is donating all author's royalties
from *Red Queen?* to charity.

INTRODUCTION

In May 2021, the *Observer* columnist Barbara Ellen asked: 'Is Labour's deputy leader, Angela Rayner, resting on her working-class laurels rather too much?' While acknowledging that she has a 'powerful' life story and that 'working-class visibility in Westminster is important', Ellen then wrote: 'Still, Rayner doesn't half bang on about it or let others do it for her.' She wondered whether 'overawed, middle-class politicos, have been cowed into unquestioningly gulping down Rayner's self-mythology or whether she herself feels that her righteous background makes her untouchable'. She went on to assert that Rayner's 'snaky' reaction that month to Sir Keir Starmer's botched shadow Cabinet reshuffle 'outed her as untrustworthy and slippery'. She pondered if her appeal to working-class voters was as strong as is assumed. And she concluded that 'class credibility is always valid, but as a starting point. Sooner or later, the question will always be: what else have you got?'[1]

It is a question worth asking. Though Angela Rayner has been ready to speak about herself at every opportunity, little independent research into her background or early career has ever been published. For this reason I decided that it might be revealing – and perhaps important – to find out more about a politician who has become so prominent in Westminster in such a short space of time.

Barely a year after Rayner's first election to the House of Commons in May 2015, she had been appointed by Jeremy Corbyn as his shadow Education Secretary. Less than four years after that she was elected as the deputy leader of the Labour Party. And by September 2023, she had been promised the post of Deputy Prime Minister in a future Sir Keir Starmer government. Most would agree that such a rapid rise is remarkable. But how did Rayner achieve it? And what does it say about British politics one quarter of the way through the twenty-first century that she did not have to wait longer to reach such heights, as would once have been the case?

Like anybody with an interest in politics, I was aware that Rayner was raised in very tough circumstances, that she had left school with no qualifications, and that she was a mother aged sixteen before becoming a Home Help and then a trade unionist. I also knew that, having cleared these various hurdles and arrived in Westminster, she was immediately regarded by many as a lively addition to the House of Commons and to the political scene more broadly. Those who are not afraid to speak their mind tend to find a way to get their message across, after all. Yet thanks to things that she has said about her political opponents, she is not an uncontroversial figure either. She has certainly made enough inflammatory comments to attract plenty of attention.

I wanted to find out more about who she is personally, what she believes in politically, what drives her and what she is like to work with and for. Does she get on with Starmer? Can she unite the factions of her party to endorse his project? How would she cope with the pressures of high office if Labour did form the next government? Which policies would she push particularly if she were in a position to do so? And does she harbour ambitions to serve as Prime Minister one day?

Many journalists have spoken to Angela Rayner over the past decade or so, yet few have been willing to challenge her. The large number of interviews that Rayner has given equips her biographer with a valuable means of doing so: by testing statements she has made or by using those statements as a starting point for further inquiries.

Whatever anybody who reads this book thinks of Angela Rayner – and she does divide opinion and is capable of generating strong reactions – she is now close enough to power to be taken seriously.

Michael Ashcroft
March 2024

A NOTE ON THE TEXT

I have chosen to refer to Angela Rayner as 'Rayner' throughout this book. Although she used her maiden name, Bowen, until September 2010, it was not until after that date that she became a public figure and she has almost always been referred to by her married name on official documents and in media reports since then.

ACKNOWLEDGEMENTS

Among the many people who kindly agreed to be interviewed for this book, most asked not to be named publicly. For this reason, it is not possible to identify here everybody who deserves thanks. They know who they are, however, and I want to express my gratitude to them for providing the various background briefings that proved so useful.

Thanks must also go to the formidable Angela Entwistle and her team, as well as to those at Biteback Publishing who were involved in the production of this book, and to Syd Lloyd, Simon Trump, David Wharton and the staff of Stockport Local Heritage Library. And special thanks to my chief researcher, Miles Goslett.

CHAPTER 1

GIRL GUIDE

A familiar complaint made of Westminster's MPs by some voters has been that too few of them have truly working-class origins and too many of them have insufficient experience of 'real life'. Instead, it is claimed, a disproportionately high number of Britain's elected representatives have rolled off what is in effect a production line limited to just three phases: after leaving university they work for a politician or party; eventually they are parachuted or otherwise helped into a winnable parliamentary seat to contest themselves; and finally they take their place in the House of Commons, having barely broken into a sweat. It has been said that the prevalence of this cycle has further damaged the link between everyday people and those who speak for them. There is undoubtedly some truth in this idea. In the post-war years more parliamentarians – particularly on the Labour benches – were likelier to have walked one of various hard roads before seeking national office, thereby insulating them from accusations of belonging to a remote political class. Since the 1990s, however, the backgrounds of many MPs have become more uniform, perhaps as a consequence of deindustrialisation and the expansion of tertiary education. Inevitably, though, there are exceptions to the new rules. In 2024 it is generally agreed that Angela Rayner's tough upbringing makes her the most prominent example of a politician who has overcome a variety of challenges to reach the top of a political party without having enjoyed the start in life that most people might assume is necessary.

Angela Rayner was born Angela Bowen at the Stepping Hill Hospital in Stockport on 28 March 1980. Her father, Martyn, married her mother, Lynne Ingram, in Stockport Register Office in June 1977 when he was a 21-year-old storeman and she was an eighteen-year-old bookbinder. At the time of Rayner's birth, they already had a son, Darren, who was born in 1978. A younger sibling, Tracey, was born on Christmas Day in 1982. Both the Bowen and Ingram families hailed from the north-west of England, and according to census records they had been involved in manual labour and skilled trade there for generations. Tracing Rayner's paternal line back to the beginning of the twentieth century reveals that her great-grandfather, Thomas Bowen, was a printer in Stockport. Her grandfather, who was also called Thomas Bowen, was a machine operator in the same town. On Rayner's mother's side, her great-grandfather, Oliver Ingram, was a wire weaver in Manchester and her maternal grandfather, Harold Ingram, made wooden boxes before becoming a toolmaker in and around Manchester.

In the various interviews Rayner has given over the past decade or so, she seems to have pulled no punches when it comes to discussing her personal life, explaining with candour that her childhood was materially deprived and emotionally fractured. Although her parents each listed an occupation on their marriage certificate in 1977, and despite her father changing his profession to 'warehouseman' at the time of their youngest child's birth five years after that, Rayner has never publicly suggested that either of them held down a steady job when she was a girl. Instead, she has been open about the fact that the family lived in council-owned properties and relied on welfare payments and Giro cheques. As to the lack of love and support shown to her by her parents, which she has also discussed in some depth, she has always maintained that their complicated personalities, the explosive nature of their marital relationship, and their own bleak childhoods meant they were not in the habit of indulging their own children with so much as a hug or a kiss. As she told Times Radio in September 2021: 'I'm sure my parents loved me, but they didn't know how to *show* they loved me. It was implied that you didn't get cuddles.'[1]

Rayner has also acknowledged that her mother was raised in what sound like even more difficult circumstances than she herself endured. In Britain in the middle of the twentieth century, it is fair to say that poverty bore a stronger link to what had been suffered during the Victorian era than many people today might imagine, and Rayner's mother apparently lived through the worst of it. She was one of twelve children and grew up on a housing estate in Wythenshawe, just south of Manchester. Two of her siblings were simply 'given away' to a neighbouring Christian couple, according to Rayner, presumably because they could not be cared for. By the age of twelve, Rayner's mother had dropped out of school having never learnt how to read or write. She also suffers from bipolar disorder. Formerly known as manic depression, this condition of extreme mood swings can strike anybody at any time, though it is often believed to manifest itself first in those aged fifteen to twenty.

Less is known of Rayner's father's early life, but Rayner has revealed that the foundations of her parents' marriage were shaky from the start. 'One of the stories was that he got with my mum because the person who was the love of his life ran off with somebody else and he knew my mum would never leave him,' Rayner explained to the BBC in 2017.[2] Her father was not an easy man to live with, according to Rayner. She has spoken many times of his quick temper, his disciplinarian nature and his habit of shouting menacingly. In October 2023, a *Guardian* interviewer even reported for the first time that her father 'scared her so much she would wet the bed'.[3] She has also indicated that it was not unusual for him to be absent from home without explanation. Others who contributed to this book but who did not wish to be identified claimed that, during her childhood, Rayner's father was 'a ducker and a diver' who dabbled in various moneymaking schemes, including driving a taxi. But he is said to have paid little attention to her mother and shown scant interest in helping her to deal with her mental health problems. Politics was not a feature of the household, but Rayner has recalled that, although her father read the Labour-supporting *Daily Mirror* regularly, he also had instincts that are more often associated with the political right. She told Nick Robinson of the BBC in 2018: 'I used to have a phrase: "council house Tory". My dad was one.' She then went on to point out what she considers to be the irony of her father having railed against 'scroungers' when he was himself a recipient of regular welfare payments.[4]

In fact, the MP for Stockport between 1983 and 1992 was Tony Favell, a Conservative who was also an ardent Thatcherite. It is impossible to know whether his status as the town's elected representative at Westminster, or whether any of the policies pursued by Mrs Thatcher's governments, played any part in shaping Martyn Bowen's opinions. Favell, however, who retains a link to the area via his presidency of the Stockport Conservative Association, says that he can recall canvassing for re-election in 1987 and being surprised by the depth of support there for his party:

I remember going to a terraced house in a working-class area in Stockport and a man answered the door and said: 'I'm going to vote for you.' When I asked him why, he said: 'I can't bear the woman [Margaret Thatcher], but she's right.' It made me realise that my own party underestimates the nous of the British electorate,

says Favell. He adds: 'Knowing the kind of situation that Angela Rayner was brought up in, I think what she's achieved is remarkable and I applaud it, whilst regretting her failure to change her political outlook.' Stockport, incidentally, did change its political outlook, and has been represented by Labour MPs since 1992.

Stockport is one of the ten metropolitan districts that make up Greater Manchester. It lies about six miles south-east of Manchester city centre. Like many towns in Britain, it has a proud industrial past, in its case thanks to being on the canal network and having strong links to the nineteenth-century textile industry. Indeed, it became famous around the world as a centre for hat-making. Yet the poverty of some of its inhabitants has long been acknowledged. In his 1845 book *The Conditions of the Working Class in England*, Friedrich Engels wrote of Stockport being 'renowned throughout the entire district as one of the duskiest, smokiest holes', going on to say that it 'looks, indeed, especially when viewed from the viaduct, excessively repellent'. He added that he found the cottages and cellar dwellings of the working class there 'repulsive'.[5]

As the textile industry declined during the twentieth century, Stockport reinvented itself. However, if the Community Care Plan report produced by Stockport's social services division in October 1991 is to be believed, it did so with mixed success. Using statistics stretching back to the early 1980s, this report acts as a useful outline of the town's prospects during Rayner's formative years.

It stated that by the early 1990s, the borough's population was steady at about 290,000, with a 'relatively low' number of ethnic minority residents. 'Within Stockport, wards vary greatly in their social group composition and there are areas where residents experience considerable socio-economic deprivation,' it noted.

Several localities (eg Adswood) are contained within more affluent wards and their degree of deprivation thus obscured. Cale Green, Edgeley and South Reddish together with Brinnington are the most deprived in the Borough. Economic and social problem areas tend to be clustered around the town centre and are mostly contained in Brinnington, South Reddish, Edgeley, Manor and Cale Green.

The report also asserted that Stockport had 'relatively good quality housing stock compared with the rest of the region'; an acceptable communication and transport network; a strong services sector; and decent electronics, plastics, engineering, printing and foodstuffs businesses. In September 1991 its average unemployment level stood at 6.5 per cent – 2 per cent below the national rate – though in its most depressed areas such as Brinnington, the figure was getting on for three times higher than that.

At the time of Rayner's birth in 1980, her parents and brother lived at 108 Bangor Street, a two-bedroom mid-terrace council house in South Reddish, one of those areas considered to be 'most deprived'. By 1982, the family had moved to 46 Alvanley Crescent, a three-bedroom semi-detached house on the Bridgehall housing estate less than a mile south-west of the town centre. Built in the 1930s on former farmland and situated between two more of Stockport's most disadvantaged areas, Adswood and Edgeley, this estate was apparently scarred by antisocial and criminal behaviour throughout Rayner's childhood, so much so that the police maintained a regular presence there.

Doreen Cartwright is a well-known figure on the Bridgehall estate, where she has worked in a grocery store, as a school caretaker and as a dinner lady since she and her late husband moved there in 1968 and brought up four sons. 'I've also worked as a machinist and I had a veg stall in the market,' Mrs Cartwright says. 'My husband was in the Merchant Navy and when he left that he worked as a painter and decorator. There was work if you wanted it.'

Mrs Cartwright accepts that in the many years she has lived on Bridgehall it has had its peaks and troughs, but she maintains that there were even worse estates in Stockport. 'It was a nice place in those early days,' she says.

Our house was not brand new, as the first homes were built here about thirty years before. Things started to change when they built more homes. At its worst, probably in the 1980s and early 1990s, there were certain families who terrorised the whole estate. There were a lot of assaults, some quite serious, and shop windows being put in. The police got involved and slowly they squeezed those troublemakers and things got better again. It has never been that bad, though. Here has never been anything like [the nearby] Gorsey Bank estate. That place was notorious.

At the time of writing, Mrs Cartwright is eighty years old and she says she remembers Rayner's family.

I knew her mother, Lynne, as she used to come in the grocery shop where I worked. People around here used to refer to her as

'Persil White', after the washing powder, because, not to put too fine a point on it, she was never very clean. None of them were. It was a bit unkind. But let's be honest, a bit of soap and water doesn't cost very much. Angela and her brother and sister were always a bit scruffy and dirty, even for round here.

She adds:

Lynne might not have been able to read or write, but she could certainly count her pennies. She was pleasant enough. I don't remember her ever working, but there were a lot of people in the same boat. I knew of Angie by sight, but I can't say I knew any of the Bowens very well. They tended to keep themselves to themselves.

By 1986, Rayner's family had moved again, this time to 23 Baguley Crescent, a slightly larger semi-detached house two streets away on the Bridgehall estate. Life at home was far from comfortable, according to Rayner. She has spoken of the house's threadbare carpets exposing its concrete floors and said it was usually very untidy, a chaotic situation worsened by the fact that her parents bred German Shepherd dogs, which tend to shed their coats year-round. Not only was the house invariably a mess, but, Rayner has said, it was cold, too; her parents could not afford to pay the bills generated by their immersion heater.

It is difficult, almost forty years later, to estimate what the family survived on financially at this time. For one thing, their circumstances were unique to them and would have been strictly private in any case. However, thanks to figures quoted in a parliamentary speech given in June 1985 by Norman Fowler, the Secretary of State for Health and Social Services, it is possible to establish how much money from the state was potentially available to those families in need of it. In his speech, Fowler said that from November 1985, the basic rate of unemployment benefit would increase to £49.25 per week for a couple. The supplementary benefit excluding housing costs – which were met separately through housing benefit – was increased to between £47.85 and £60 per week for a couple. Payments of £10.10 per week for each child under eleven were also available. And people could apply for extra weekly payments to cover items such as heating and special diets if required.[6] It is therefore conceivable that by the time they had moved to 23 Baguley Crescent, this family of five could expect approximately £150 per week on top of their housing benefit, assuming neither of Rayner's parents had a job. That would equate to about £7,000 per year. Rayner told Times Radio in 2021 that her family was in many ways fortunate compared with anybody in their position in the twenty-first century: 'We didn't have money, and yes by today's standards we had a council house and we had a Giro that covered [us],' she said. 'So by today's standards actually we were ok, because the welfare state supported us.'[7]

Hunger was a problem for Rayner, for she has said consistently that her mother's abilities in the kitchen were negligible. She has also explained that her mother's illiteracy made for some memorable meals, including one occasion when her mother mistook a can of shaving foam for whipped cream because she couldn't read its label, and another when she served dog meat thinking it was stewing steak. She has often spoken of feeling hungry as a child.

In Lynne Bowen's defence, it should be noted that in other interviews Rayner has admitted that her mother was not entirely without domestic skills. Indeed, in 2017, for example, Rayner told the *Huffington Post* that her mother's culinary competence had been vital to ensuring that she and her two siblings were not pushed into the care system. 'My mum did a cookery course at adult learning,' Rayner said.

> She wouldn't have been able to cook for us had she not done that course. What value do you put on that? I was able to stay within my parents' home, which is better for young people rather than being in looked-after care, as well as the cost of putting me in looked-after care. Actually the fact that my mum was able to do a cookery course was tremendous for us as children because my mum was able to cook Tatty Hash, as we called it, and things like that – potatoes and corned beef and gravy.

She returned to this theme two years later when speaking to students at Oldham Sixth Form College, telling them:

> My mum did a cookery course. If she hadn't have done that cookery course I would have probably gone into care because my mum couldn't cook … If she hadn't have had that opportunity then we probably would have ended up in care and I probably wouldn't have thanked the state for it.

According to Rayner, her life outside of home was no easier than it was in it, but she felt compelled to take to the street nonetheless. She told the BBC in 2017:

> We'd go out all the day to avoid being in the house because there would be shouting or something so we'd be frightened as kids to stick around. I'd go out on the street on the estate. The in-crowd kids would beat me up. And then if I went home and told my dad

I'd been beaten up, he'd tell me off, ground me and smack me for being so weak and allowing [myself] to be beaten up. So it was pretty tough at times.[8]

Fortunately for Rayner, there were some stabilising influences to help keep her on a smoother path. All four of her grandparents – and, indeed, her great-grandmother, Mary Bowen – were alive at the time of her birth and living either in Stockport or close by. At least one of them, her paternal grandmother, Jean, was a figure from that generation who was a mainstay in her life and that of her siblings. From the earliest stages of her political career, Rayner has acknowledged the kindness and love shown to her by Jean, whom she refers to as her 'nana', even telling prospective voters on her official website in 2014 when she first became a Labour candidate: 'For the most part, I was raised by my Grandma who worked at three jobs to put food on the table.'[9]

She has explained in interviews that Jean would help to buy and wash their clothes. She, her siblings and their mother would also go to Jean's high-rise flat, No. 11 Pendlebury Towers and, latterly, 77 Millbrook Towers, each weekend for lunch and to have a bath, taking it in turns with the eldest child going first.[10]

Jean would also help to look after Rayner's mother when necessary. Sadly, her mother's bipolar disorder meant that her behaviour became increasingly unpredictable as Rayner grew up. Owing to Rayner's father's absences, Rayner has said that she was frequently left to attend to her needs, including bathing her. 'By the age of ten, I became my mum's main carer,' she told the BBC of this role reversal in 2017.

I became the adult ... she's been in and out of psychiatric care. I remember at ten my mum being suicidal and me sleeping like a dog on the end of her bed just to try and stay next to her so she didn't do any harm to herself.[11]

As well as having to help Rayner's mother, Jean's own life was not straightforward and was ultimately blighted by tragedy. Having divorced her first husband, Thomas Bowen, she married a widower, Harold Towers, in 1985. Mr Towers therefore became Rayner's step-grandfather. According to a report from the *Manchester Evening News* published in May 1987, he crashed his Hillman Avenger into a parked Mercedes in Newbridge Lane in Stockport that month. His car overturned, exploded, and witnesses were powerless to help as he burned to death. He was fifty-nine and, according to his death notice in the *Manchester Evening News*, he had ten children.

By this point, Rayner was a pupil at Bridge Hall primary school, which was a short walk from her front door. In adulthood, she has concluded that being brought up in a house that contained no books (she had never even been read a bedtime story) meant she was not ready for school when she first went there. As a result, she did not progress academically. 'Apparently, my mum said that I needed speech and language therapy as well,' she told LBC's James O'Brien in 2021. 'There's a reason why I've got a lisp, thank you very much.' She added that her reading and social skills were less well-developed than those of her peers.[12]

Even if she did not take to school easily, however, there were, mercifully, other pursuits laid on by members of the community that must have acted as a much-needed distraction and in which she is said to have shown a great interest. For example, the Girl Guides was a big part of her life for several years. Kathleen Potts, who was ninety at the time she gave an interview for the purposes of this book, was the leader of No. 9 Stockport Girl Guides, better known as the St Mark's, Edgeley unit. Everyone called her 'Captain'. She remembers Rayner as an earnest child who joined the troop in 1990, when she was ten years old, and who remained a member of it for about three years. 'She was a pretty little girl with the most glorious head of red hair,' says Mrs Potts.

> She was never a nuisance and was unfailingly polite towards me. In fact, if any of the other girls were being a bit naughty she would put them right. Guiding is not about girls who are badly behaved. It's about girls who come in the right spirit, behave and want to learn and do new things.

Mrs Potts knew at the time that Rayner's background was complicated but adds: 'That was not unusual to us.' She goes on:

> One of the first things I remember learning from her was that her mother could not read and write. Nobody ever mentioned anything about her father and clearly she was the one looking after her mum. I would often take Angie home and not once did I ever meet her mum. You would have expected her to at least come to the door, to wave or have a word. I don't think she was capable of social interaction. Lynne didn't understand things very well. In fact, I think Angie had to explain everything for her. I think she would be called special educational needs these days. That probably explains why Angie was so mature for her years. I remember she had an older brother and a younger sister. She seemed to look after all of them. She didn't really have a childhood.

She says:

We would meet every Thursday at St Mark's church hall in Edgeley and Angie would walk across from Bridgehall either on her own or with other members of the unit who were coming. I think she loved it. She would throw herself into the community work we did, and the first aid courses. Once a month we would go on church parade and she would come to that regularly. There was also the Remembrance Parade once a year, and something she said after her first one stuck in my mind. We would march to the war memorial and stand in silence, making the Guide salute for three minutes. Being able to stand still without talking for that length of time is quite a challenge for young girls, and Angie said it was the longest three minutes of the year for her.

Mrs Potts goes on to say that on a couple of occasions the troop went on trips to the Peak District, where they stayed in a house in the High Peaks between Chinley and Castleton. 'Angie could not afford it, so we paid for her,' she explains.

Given the length of time that Rayner was a Girl Guide, it is surprising that when describing her undeniably challenging past she has never chosen to speak about her involvement in this positive extracurricular activity. It is quite clear from Mrs Potts's well-stocked bank of memories that she believes the Girl Guides brought out the best in Rayner by helping to forge her strong personality, her willingness to learn, to say nothing of a range of practical skills. Regrettably, it seems as though the negative aspects of Rayner's childhood dominate her thoughts even today, to such a degree that the Girl Guides has been overlooked when she speaks of her past. As she told Times Radio in 2021: 'The abuse, the neglect, the circumstances of my childhood – I grew up thinking that's normal.'[13] Her teenage years were to prove no less demanding.

CHAPTER 2

LITTLE SHADOW

In September 1991, aged eleven, Rayner began her first term at Avondale School, a comprehensive in Cheadle Heath about a mile from her house in Baguley Crescent, on the Bridgehall estate. Since entering Parliament, Rayner has been characteristically upfront about this period of her life, never trying to disguise the fact that she did not succeed academically and offering a host of reasons as to why this might be so. In July 2017, for example, she told *The Guardian* that she felt the disarray in which she was brought up guaranteed that she faced problems when it came to her schooling. She explained: 'School was the place where I hung about with my mates and got a meal. My mum didn't understand that education was an important thing. She couldn't do my homework with me. I was helping her read stuff.'[1]

There is no question that her mother's lack of formal education and history of psychological disturbance would have had a profound effect on Rayner, so it is unsurprising that she believes these disadvantages hampered her own chances in the classroom. Indeed, some might conclude that when her complicated upbringing is considered, it was almost inevitable that she would not thrive academically. She even told *The Observer* in September 2019 that instead of leaving school aged sixteen like most of her contemporaries, she effectively dropped out a year early. 'My school, we affectionately nicknamed it Avonjail, but it was called Avondale, Avondale High School in Stockport. I left with no GCSEs above a D. I kind of left at 15,' she told the newspaper.[2] She has also suggested that it was an inadequate place, giving the impression that her own chances of doing well there were lower still. Proof of this comes from a talk she gave to students at Oldham Sixth Form College in March 2019, in which she remarked: 'My school was a failing school. And I was a failing pupil. But look at me – I'm sat here as one of the most successful female politicians of my time.'

In discussing this pivotal stage of her childhood, it seems important to learn from other sources what Avondale was like generally and to hear more of Rayner's experiences there. Given her understandable frustration at having left with a poor set of GCSE results, it is certainly worth exploring to what extent it is accurate for her to have described it as a 'failing' school during the five years that she attended it.

Anybody who has read *A Kestrel for a Knave* by Barry Hines or seen Ken Loach's 1969 film of the same story, *Kes*, is unlikely to forget the bleakness of the school attended by its protagonist, Billy Casper, a shy, working-class teenager from a dysfunctional South Yorkshire family who has no academic inclinations and is destined to work in a coal mine.[34] Hines, a former teacher who, like Rayner, grew up in a house with no books, is said to have written his novel as a howl of rage against the British education system as it was organised in the 1960s. At that time those, like Billy Casper, who failed the eleven-plus exam and so did not go to a grammar school were shunted into a secondary modern school, with little or no choice as to which one they attended. There, they might well encounter un-caring staff members who were as interested in meting out corporal punishments as they were in teaching. While Hines's grim inter-pretation of certain state schools was seen by some as having been exaggerated for effect, it is certainly true that many children who went to such institutions were effectively consigned to the scrap heap at an appallingly young age.

Fortunately for Rayner, by the comparatively more enlightened 1990s most state secondary schools could not be accused of oper-ating along such brutal lines. Thanks to national education reforms in 1980 and 1988, parents throughout Britain were given greater freedom than had existed before to decide which school their child entered. This was intended to create a sense of competition, which, it was hoped, might raise standards. One aspiration was that the ele-ment of parental choice would convince mothers and fathers to take a more active interest in their child's education, helping to usher in a positive environment for the wider community.

Avondale High School was a coeducational, non-selective estab-lishment for pupils aged eleven to sixteen. It had been founded in September 1940 and by 1991, when Rayner arrived, it occupied two neighbouring sites in Stockport – one adjoining Avondale Road and St Lesmo Road; the other off Heathbank Road. This second site included a modern recreation centre that boasted a 25-metre swimming pool, a sports hall and an all-weather games pitch. It was the only school in Stockport with such facilities. Records show that 626 pupils were on the school roll during Rayner's first term, making it relatively small when measured against other urban com-prehensives. It was split into a Lower School, consisting of those in their first two years, and an Upper School, catering for those in their final three years. Pupils received twenty-five hours of tuition per week and were streamed in Maths, English, History and Modern Languages during their second and third years before preparing for GCSEs and other public exams in their final two years. The school's social make-up when Rayner arrived at Avondale can be better understood by considering the lunch that was on offer to pupils each day. It cost less than £1 per person to buy and was served in the school canteen. According to an Ofsted report dating from 1994 – two years before Rayner left – 39 per cent of pupils were entitled to this meal free of charge because of low parental income and were given a token to cover the expense. All pupils were allowed to go home to eat lunch if they preferred.

Under Ian Tunnard, the headmaster of Avondale throughout Rayner's tenure, an ethos of focussing on the value of people as individuals was very much at the fore. Pastoral care was taken seriously as well, with a tutor assigned to oversee the academic, social and personal development of each girl and boy. Reflecting Tunnard's respect for traditional teaching methods, discipline was paramount. He knew the name of every pupil in the school and they were all expected to wear a uniform. He also tried to keep a tight grip on bullying, truancy and antisocial behaviour. He made a point of actively recruiting new parents as a way of lifting the calibre of the school.

Tunnard explains that Avondale had been troubled when he became its headmaster in the late 1980s and, despite his best efforts to reinvigorate it, some problems were harder to overcome than others. Moreover, he believes that Rayner personally bore the brunt of some of these difficulties.

'When I arrived in January 1989, Avondale was the smallest school in Stockport because no one wanted their children to go there,' remembers the now-retired headmaster.

I probably didn't realise before my appointment just how poor its reputation was. In those early days, I would drive in to work past bus stops thronged with children in my catchment all waiting to get on the bus to another school away from the area where they lived. A local councillor spoke out and challenged me to deal with all the issues, the bullying, the bad behaviour, and in my first two years there I did my best to turn it around with the help of some very able deputies. I made it clear the school was under new management.

One of the first things to be introduced in 1989 was what were known as 'warning' assemblies. These were the idea of Tunnard's deputy, Beth Mottram, who was already in post when he took over. 'We got them in and told them the way things were going to be,' says Tunnard.

We told those children their behaviour in the past had not been acceptable and it was going to improve. I remember I probably overstepped the mark, because I told them that otherwise I was going to cancel Christmas. Those pupils knew what to expect from me, though, and my staff knew too. I always tried to make Avondale as pleasant a place as possible. My door was literally and metaphorically always open. I tried to be a constant presence. I was straight talking. I would not pull my punches and I was not afraid to permanently exclude those who clearly were never going to change their ways and were ruining our chance to educate others. I would visit parents in their own home if necessary.

Tunnard says that neither he nor Rayner has ever discussed publicly the important role he played in her school career before now, but he has strong recollections of her that have nothing to do with her subsequent political prominence or, indeed, with her academic performance in the 1990s. Poignantly, when talking about her as a schoolgirl he refers to her as a 'little shadow', because she was a semi-permanent fixture by his side during lunch and break times, particularly, he believes, from when she was thirteen or fourteen years old. The reason for this was that she needed to be protected from other children. 'Things were difficult for her,' he recalls.

> She was bullied. She came to tell me, though, and I gave her a place of safety. I wasn't aware who I was protecting her from. She never told me that. Professionally you would have wanted to know, but I understood why children wouldn't always want to disclose information like that. In her case, there was a very real possibility that she would have had to walk home with those same protagonists, and I wouldn't be there to protect her then. I could not make sure she was safe around the clock. She was clearly vulnerable, because she came from a very difficult, deprived background.

Tunnard's plea for parents to participate more fully in the school did not always generate the results he sought. Some didn't even bother to attend parents' evenings. He says he can remember one such event when thirty-eight members of staff were present, but only about twenty parents turned up. 'I wrote to every single one of the parents who did not come asking what possible excuse they could have for not putting their child's education first. Some of the excuses they gave were absolutely pathetic,' he says. Rayner's parents were in this camp.

I never met her father, Martyn. From what I recall I don't even remember him being on the scene at all. I knew her mother was Lynne, although I never met her either and I heard she was trying to hold things together on her own. I have no memory of her brother or sister, either. The Bowens were not a difficult family as such. Some families are like that – they almost slip under the radar, in a manner of speaking. Others were etched on your memory. I could give you the names of families who had been problematic on the Bridgehall estate before I got there, while I was there and I bet some of them still are today. Angela was probably what you could call a loner in school.

Rayner has spoken frankly of her instinct to keep a low profile as a child, not helped by her belief that she was 'ugly' and an 'outcast'. Despite her hitherto unknown reliance on Ian Tunnard's protection, she has also said she was wary of authority figures such as teachers – certainly when it came to discussing her home life with them. She has said that when growing up she saw such people as the 'enemy'.[5] This arguably makes it all the more notable that she turned to Tunnard for help, if his recollection is accurate.

In 2021 she told LBC's James O'Brien that Sue Travis, her English teacher, was conspicuous as an adult in a position of power who took the trouble to try to help her, once staying behind after school hours to work on what Rayner has described as her 'dreadful' spelling.[6] But she has never had much, if anything, to say about Avondale or any other members of its staff that is favourable, least of all her apparent defender, Ian Tunnard. Instead, she has spoken about being persecuted by others, both at school and on the Bridgehall estate, maintaining that her ginger hair made her a target, as did her footwear. 'I never got a brand-new pair of shoes when I was a kid,' she told Nick Robinson of the BBC in May 2018. 'My nana got me a pair of steel toe caps because she said they'll last longer at school and I got absolutely bullied from it when I was younger.'[7]

While she and Tunnard may have similar recollections of the intimidation she experienced there, her description of Avondale as a 'failing school' – as she claimed when speaking at Oldham Sixth Form College in 2019 – may have been something of an exaggeration. Ian Tunnard certainly believes that the various changes implemented by him over several years successfully boosted academic results across the school. 'When I arrived, the percentage of children obtaining five A to Cs in their GCSEs was about 10 to 15 per cent,' he says. 'By 1994, that was well into the thirties.' This sense of advancement is borne out by a relatively positive Ofsted inspection report that was published in May 1994, the year that Avondale switched to operating from just one site at Heathbank Road. It described Avondale as 'a caring, happy school which makes good provision for its pupils.' It went on: 'The school enjoys the confidence and esteem of its parents. Strong pastoral support for pupils and good behaviour contribute directly to learning. This is a school in which the community can show justified pride.' It acknowledged that a 'majority of pupils achieve standards generally below national norms in public examinations' but detailed year-on-year improvements. It noted the school's 'broad and balanced' curriculum and paid tribute to the 'excellent extracurricular activities, drama and personal and social education [that] extend the curriculum provision.' Tunnard's 'strong leadership' was highly praised, painting an overall picture of a well-run school that provided 'good value for money'.

Furthermore, according to a report in the *Manchester Evening News* the following year, Chris Woodhead, the chief inspector of schools in England, singled out Avondale High School and another school in the north-west, Hazel Grove High School, complimenting the teachers for their 'vision, commitment and expertise' and for the way they had achieved improvements in the performance of their schools. Nowhere in Ofsted's 1994 report does the word 'failing' appear and it is hard to believe that by the time Rayner left Avondale in 1996, standards had suddenly plummeted. Certainly the subsequent Ofsted report, published in November 1998, two years after Rayner left, made no mention of any overall decline.

Tunnard's experience of Rayner during this phase of her school career may have been of a meek girl, but as an MP she has often spoken of her wayward tendencies, first hanging around at the local bus station and sometimes catching a bus for fun to Manchester Airport with a friend, before giving in to the temptations of Manchester city centre. Far from being a 'little shadow', to use Tunnard's phrase, Rayner has explained that out of school she was something of a wild child from the age of thirteen, talking of how she frequented nightclubs in order to spend time with members of the opposite sex, many of whom were older than her.

In May 2018 she told Nick Robinson of the BBC that because she looked mature for her years she was able to get into nightclubs including the Hacienda, Sankeys Soap and 21 Piccadilly's.[8] And in 2018 when a journalist called Linda McDougall interviewed her for a book of political profiles, *The Honourable Ladies*, Rayner was quoted as saying that as a schoolgirl 'I was already going out clubbing meeting men – not boys, men – and being out with my friends. I was quite feral. I use that term deliberately.'[9] In September 2020, she told Cathy Newman of Times Radio:

Certainly by the age of thirteen, fourteen, I'd decided that it was much more fun to be involved in the Manchester music scene and going out and having fun. I looked a lot older as well and I was more mature because of my life experience. I used to go out with people who were a lot older than me and go to clubs in Manchester and things like that and I was a bit of a rebel.[10]

And when speaking to Paul Brand of ITV about this period of her life in 2020, she referred to 'getting into scrapes' and 'going clubbing at the age of fourteen' and of 'getting involved in all sorts of stuff that could've been really risky behaviour'.[11]

The picture is further confused by an interview Rayner gave to the LBC presenter James O'Brien in 2021, in which she said that her father – whom she has usually described as an absent parent – grew concerned by her trips to Manchester. She told O'Brien that she was a rebellious child: 'My dad used to have to pick me up from nightclubs when I was fourteen because he couldn't stop me from going. So it got to the point where he said: "I will pick you up outside and then I know you're getting home safely."'[12] If nothing else, this suggests that Martyn Bowen's interest in his eldest daughter's welfare was no less distant than any concerned father's would be. Incidentally, although Rayner has also used some interviews to describe her relationship with her father as poor, it may not have been entirely without bright spots. For instance, she told Cathy Newman of Times Radio in September 2020 that she would sometimes help him during her spare time, painting a picture of something approaching a functioning father–daughter relationship. 'I used to fix cars with my dad,' she recalled. 'He used to have me holding the torch in the freezing cold rain while he's fixing the car, or I'd be cutting out a rocker box gasket out of a Cornflakes box.'[13]

As mentioned in the previous chapter, Kathleen Potts was Rayner's Girl Guide leader for three years in the early 1990s. She also had links to Avondale High School. She recalls:

Angela left [the Girl Guides] in about school Year Nine, I think, when she was thirteen. I am not sure why, but someone said to me they thought she probably discovered boys, which is not uncommon. I lost touch with her after that. But I was also the chair of governors at Avondale, and she must have behaved herself there, too, because if children were disciplined, they would come in front of me. She never did. The previous head had been a bit wishy-washy, and he wanted everyone to be pals and call one another by their first names. He also didn't want times tables on the walls or learning by rote. I disagreed. How on earth are you supposed to memorise things like the National Anthem or literary texts without learning through repetition? When Mr Tunnard arrived I was pleased. He tightened things up quickly.

She adds: 'I was surprised to hear Angie was bullied, because she was very articulate and sometimes the best way to disarm a bully is with a lightning-quick riposte. I would have thought she would have responded like that.'

As noted, Rayner told *The Observer* that she 'kind of left [Avondale] at 15', but this claim cannot be literally true.[14] During the summer term of 1996, when she was sixteen, she was entered for a raft of GCSEs and she has said she received grades in at least seven subjects.[15] She did not achieve a grade C or above in any of them, prompting her to look back on this period of her life with what sounds like an understandable sense of regret, perhaps wondering what might have been had she knuckled down to her books. In 2017 she told the *Huffington Post*:

The reason why I did so badly at secondary and primary [school] was not because I wasn't intelligent enough – I'm a bright spark,

I can get what goes on in Parliament very quickly. The difference for me was I was already way behind my peers. So therefore by the time I got to secondary school it wasn't the thing I wanted to do because I already felt inferior to those who'd had a head start on me, so it left me behind.[16]

What Rayner may not have realised as she sat those exams as a sixteen-year-old schoolgirl was that she was in the very early stages of pregnancy. By the time the summer holidays were underway a few weeks later, however, there would have been no doubt in her mind. The father of her child was Neil Batty, a car valet who was a little more than three years her senior. They are said to have met in a nightclub earlier in 1996. When Rayner first realised she was pregnant, her accounts vary as to what happened. She told Cathy Newman of Times Radio in 2020 that when she learnt the news herself she felt frightened; and when she told her father he was 'bitterly disappointed'.[17] Despite his fearsome reputation, he was not violent. Her mother was, apparently, more sanguine. Yet nine months later, Rayner admitted to the same broadcaster, Times Radio, that the consequences of her unplanned pregnancy were far more tumultuous for her personally. 'My dad threw me out when I was pregnant at sixteen,' she said.[18]

It must have been a shattering blow to her to realise that while her contemporaries were embarking on new adventures, she was facing up to the heavy responsibility of motherhood – without the support of her own father. Worse still, according to Rayner, her father was not alone in having shown disapproval. She has said that she was six months pregnant by the time she went back to Avondale High School to collect her GCSE results, which would have been in late 1996. In February 2017, she gave an interview to the UNISON trade union, which it ran on its website under the headline 'From a council estate to the Houses of Parliament: a UNISON member's extraordinary journey into politics'. Of this trip to her former school, the interviewer wrote: 'Angela remembers people looking and judging her.' Rayner was then quoted as saying:

> They all said that I'd amount to nothing, and I'd be on benefits all my life and have kids with different dads and live in a council house. Which I was upset about. Everyone just thought that I was a write-off, but I wanted to be a good mum, and I wanted to prove them wrong.[19]

This is a claim that she has made in other interviews, though it has never been clear whether the uncharitable prediction of her 'never amounting to anything' was made to her by a teacher or by somebody else. Neither, based on Rayner's words, is it certain when or in what context these words were said, for in a BBC interview in 2018 she stated that a school careers adviser had once told her that she would end up working as a nursery nurse or in catering. 'People had low expectations of what I could achieve,' she said.[20]

Whenever the remark was made, Ian Tunnard's shoulders are broad enough to admit that his staff could have been responsible for it. He explains:

> I have to be honest and say I can't describe her as a star. I would never say anything like that to a pupil, though. To get the best out of them you have got to respect them, otherwise they will never respect you. I had one ex-head of department who would dismiss some children as beyond helping. He would say: 'You can't make a silk purse out of a sow's ear.' I took him to task for that. So I can well believe Angela might have been told that by a member of staff at my school. Several of them would have had that attitude.

He adds: 'Some pupils were not well behaved. Some could be incredibly difficult. A lot of them did not have any parental backing.'

It appears that when Rayner's grandmother, Jean, learned of her pregnancy, she stepped in to help her, possibly allowing her to stay at her flat in Stockport for a while before her baby was born. In view of the support that Jean provided, it is not without relevance to explain briefly why her own upbringing in the 1930s and 1940s was not entirely straightforward, for her childhood experiences may have made her sympathetic to this unplanned chapter in Rayner's life. Having studied various genealogical records, it seems that Jean's father, Thomas Wilson – Rayner's great-grandfather, therefore – had two families at the same time. He married first, in Stockport in 1914, a woman called Sarah Whittaker. Of the children they had together, only one, Agnes, survived. In the 1939 Register, the national census compiled by the British government on the outbreak of the Second World War, Sarah and Agnes were recorded as living at 22 Brunswick Road in Altrincham in Cheshire. Sarah was a cop winder, operating a machine used in jute processing. Her husband, Thomas Wilson, meanwhile, was listed in the 1939 Register as living at 28–30 Queen Street in West Stockport with the unmarried Doris Quinn and four children, all of whom had his surname. It therefore appears that Jean, whose mother was Doris Quinn, was herself born out of wedlock in 1936, a situation that would have been frowned upon at the time. Jean's mother, Doris, did eventually marry Thomas Wilson, in 1941, following the death of his first wife, Sarah.

It should also be noted that Neil Batty, like Jean, did not shy away from his responsibilities to Rayner. One of Batty's relatives said in 2021:

Neil was good for [Rayner] because he gave her a lot of stability and an escape from her situation. He was a bit older and working.

His family background was also very different and a lot more settled. They were a lovely young couple. She got pregnant within a few months of them meeting and then they moved in together.[21]

Since becoming an MP, Rayner has spoken of Batty infrequently in public, though when LBC's James O'Brien asked her in 2021 whether she was surprised that the relationship had not, ultimately, stood the test of time she insinuated that Batty was not mature enough for fatherhood. She replied: 'Neil was twenty B&H [cigarettes] and a Ford Fiesta, so that was never going to last, was it? Aged sixteen, I sold myself very short.'[22]

This blunt assessment of Batty's character – made many years after they were involved with each other – suggests that Rayner had always longed to escape from the situation in which she grew up and start again. She may feel that she had every right to express herself in this way, though more than one source interviewed for this book has pointed out that Neil Batty has always maintained a diplomatic silence on the subject of their relationship. Speaking about her unplanned pregnancy to Paul Brand of ITV in 2020, Rayner also said: 'I felt really embarrassed about the situation because people just thought it was because I was "easy".'[23] With the benefit of hindsight, she concluded that she was quite simply naive. 'I was searching for that affection that I didn't have [at home],' she said. As we shall see, though, she has always believed that she soon became equal to the task of being a teenage mother and that, in many different ways, motherhood was the making of her.

CHAPTER 3

THE SAMARITAN

Rayner gave birth to her first son on 13 February 1997, six weeks before her seventeenth birthday. Like her, he was born at the Stepping Hill Hospital. She and Neil named him Ryan Stephen Batty. Although, as recorded in the previous chapter, Rayner has said that her father threw her out of the family home at 23 Baguley Crescent on the Bridgehall estate when she was sixteen and pregnant, she may not have been ejected immediately. Her parents' house was given as her 'usual address' on her child's birth certificate. So, too, was 77 Millbrook Towers, the council flat where her grandmother, Jean, lived. It is understood that as well as staying with Jean before Ryan's birth, Rayner and Batty lived for a short and unhappy time in Rayner's parents' house before taking on a council flat at 45 Handley Close, just a few streets away. Even after moving into their own property with their baby, however, there were problems involving Rayner's family. One friend of Rayner says that her father and her brother complicated what was an already delicate situation by interfering in her day-to-day life.

In her 2018 interview with Linda McDougall for the political profiles book *The Honourable Ladies*, Rayner said that she and Batty lived together in their flat only until she was old enough to have a tenancy in her name and that Batty 'left on her eighteenth birthday'.[1] This was a dramatic claim to make, and it has been repeated in at least one national newspaper since, but is it true? Not everybody who knew them then is sure that it is. Both Rayner and Batty were recorded on the 1998 and 1999 electoral rolls as living together at 45 Handley Close. The qualifying date for the latter was 10 October 1998 – more than six months after Rayner turned eighteen – and it was in force from February 1999 until February 2000. They did split up eventually, not least because Batty apparently found some members of Rayner's immediate family to be disagreeable. But as far as the council was concerned, they remained together in their flat with their son well beyond March 1998. After they went their separate ways, Batty continued to be a regular presence in his son's life, supporting him financially as and when he could. Members of the wider Batty family have apparently always been close to Ryan as well. Nevertheless, it is certainly true to say that within a few years of Ryan's birth, Rayner was a single mother.

Under John Major's Conservative government in the 1990s, single mothers were perceived by some voters to be a favourite target of high-ranking politicians. In October 1992, for example, Peter Lilley, the Secretary of State for Social Security, gave a speech at the Conservative Party Conference in which he declared war on welfare fraudsters, promising that 'I am closing down the something-for-nothing society'. Within his speech, part of which was delivered as a pastiche of the Gilbert and Sullivan opera *The Mikado*, Lilley indicated that those in his sights included 'young ladies who get pregnant just to jump the housing queue'. The following year Lilley's colleague John Redwood, the Secretary of State for Wales, went a step further, suggesting in a speech to Tory activists that single mothers should be denied welfare payments until absent fathers had been encouraged to support them. 'It must be right,' Redwood said, 'before granting state aid, to pursue the father and see whether it is possible for him to make a financial contribution, or even a fuller contribution by offering the normal love and support that fathers have offered down the ages to their family.'

As it happens, Lilley dismissed Redwood's idea, but the overall impression some detected at that time was that the governing party was not inclined to spend large sums of taxpayers' money helping every single woman who became pregnant if it did not have to do so. Because the circumstances of all individuals are different, it is impossible to know with total accuracy how much state provision Rayner would have had access to or how much she was willing or able to accept at the time of her son's birth. According to case studies that featured in national newspaper reports in November 1996, however, a single mother who did not work could expect the rent and council tax on her property to be covered by housing benefit. Income support of up to £49.50 per week, plus child benefit of £17.10 per week for the child of a lone parent, was also available. Other funds may have been accessible as well. These sums were in place when Rayner gave birth the following February.

Far from overwhelming her, Rayner has often said that experiencing motherhood at a young age was in many ways one of the best things that has ever happened to her, giving her a sense of purpose that she had been lacking.

My son was everything and [having him] changed my life ... and I think if I hadn't have had Ryan at sixteen, things might have been a lot different for me,

she told Paul Brand of ITV News in 2020.[2]

In 2018, she had explained to the *Sunday Times* that by the time she was eighteen, six of her friends had died in car accidents while joyriding, or as a result of overdosing on drugs.[3] Long-term residents of the Bridgehall estate who contributed to this book were surprised by this number. One said: 'There have been a couple of tragic deaths among the youngsters here. One lad drowned in a quarry and we have had some problems with drugs. But I can't think of who Angela might be referring to.' This would suggest that Rayner perhaps knew them from elsewhere. One former colleague, speaking on condition of anonymity, did say 'Angela once told me she knew some gangsters in Stockport during her childhood. She said she was friendly with them. But I do wonder whether she overegged stories about her childhood.' Whatever the truth, it may well be that the sad plights of her six late friends represent the 'different' path that she believed her life could have taken when she spoke to Paul Brand.

As for whether she ever took drugs herself, she steered the *Sunday Times* onto her father's brother, Lester, when asked about this, telling the newspaper that he was once a committed cannabis user. 'I might have had the odd toke of a joint,' she said. 'My Uncle Lester used to smoke a lot of it. You didn't even need to smoke. You could just sit in his caravan.' A different journalist from the same newspaper asked her in 2023 about her drug use and found her more forthcoming than she had been five years previously. 'She cheerfully owns up to trying cannabis and poppers in her early teens,' the *Sunday Times* reported.

Poppers made her 'laugh that hard that I annoyed the people around me, and therefore thought, well, this isn't fun. And weed made me sick, 'cos I smoked far too much of it and ended up throwing up all over the carpet, so I thought this isn't really for me.'4

Although the Conservatives were still in power when Rayner became a mother for the first time, they were voted out of office within three months – in May 1997 – and replaced by a Labour government under a new Prime Minister, Tony Blair. At the Labour conference in October 1996, shadow Social Security Secretary Harriet Harman had made it clear that a future Labour government would not be as hostile to single mothers as the Conservatives were thought to be. 'A welfare-to-work strategy must have at its heart a national childcare strategy,' Harman said.

> Particularly for single mothers, on their own, bringing up children, often on the breadline. The hopes and fears of single mothers are no different from anyone else. They want the best for their children. They don't want to depend on benefits. They want to work, but they can't. They need to work, but they can't … We will give a hand-up, not just a hand-out.

Labour was not prepared to give single mothers more generous welfare payments than the Conservatives had done, but Harman did pledge that the existing nursery voucher scheme would be scrapped and replaced with a system that created more nursery places. As Rayner was not politically engaged as a teenager, she may well have been unaware of the difference in tone between the two parties. As one of Neil Batty's relations said in 2021 when discussing what she was like a teenager: 'When we first knew her, she never showed any interest in politics. I don't think she could have even told you who was the Prime Minister at the time, or which political party was in power.'[5] Yet it is fair to say that not too many years would pass before Rayner's political antennae began to twitch.

In the meantime, she became restless. On the one hand she had her son to look after, and she liked nothing better than doing her best for him. 'I remember scouring the charity shops when I was a young mum,' she told Nick Robinson of the BBC in 2022.

> I'd get my income support and I'd walk for a couple of miles to the charity shops in Bramhall and it was like Christmas for me if I was able to get a nice outfit for Ryan in the charity shop. I thought like I'd done something, I'd been a good parent and I'd managed to achieve something.[6]

On the other hand, she began to explore new avenues, eager to fill her time constructively. It is at this point – when she was seventeen – that some aspects of her career become more difficult to discern, however. This is partly because she has never been totally explicit about the sequence of events following Ryan's birth. It is also a result of occasionally confusing statements she has made during interviews she has given in recent years.

According to Rayner's entry in *Who's Who*, she became a Samaritan in 1997, the year she turned seventeen, and she remained one until 2000, the year in which she marked her twentieth birthday. Indeed, in June 2023 when she was interviewed at the Global Institute for Women's Leadership by Julia Gillard, the former Prime Minister of Australia, she boasted 'I was the youngest Samaritan in the north-west.'[7] She did not tell Gillard exactly what sort of work she did for the Samaritans. It is conceivable that she helped with marketing, fundraising, organising events or assisting in a Samaritans shop, though in 2020 she indicated to Paul Brand of ITV News that for at least some of the time she was involved with the charity she served as an unpaid listening volunteer. This is one of the hardest roles that Samaritans perform, engaging with those who ring the organisation's telephone hotline in crisis feeling suicidal, despairing or in distress. 'I remember feeling incredibly privileged to help people and just be a listening ear for people when they [needed] it,' she told Brand.[8]

Not only would this position have required the utmost sensitivity and confidentiality, it would also have placed a fairly heavy demand on Rayner's time. As is the case now, in the 1990s Samaritans were expected to be available for at least one day shift of about three to four hours every week. They were also relied upon to undertake a regular night shift lasting four to six hours about six or eight times per year. A national spokesman for the Samaritans says that, at that time, listening volunteers had to be at least eighteen years old, but they could start their training at the age of seventeen. Before becoming a fully fledged listening volunteer, candidates had to provide references, attend an interview and take part in a series of weekly classroom-based training sessions before they were allowed into the duty room with a mentor. After spending several weeks in that environment, they would then have to return to the classroom for further training before entering a months-long probationary period. Clearing all these hurdles took a long time. In most cases it would be almost a year before a trainee could call themselves a qualified Samaritan.

It seems remarkable that Rayner devoted herself to this charity for up to three years at a point in her life when she was getting to grips with motherhood for the first time, having to help look after her mother, earning money in whatever way she could and, as we shall see, beginning her career as a Home Help. Samaritans are not encouraged to talk about their work and are instead advised to operate with discretion. In the 1990s, the Stockport branch of the Samaritans was run from Churchgate House near Stockport market. The only former volunteer who worked there in the 1990s and who could be traced for the purposes of this book could not remember Rayner. If nothing else, this makes it difficult to verify her admirable claim that she was once the youngest Samaritan in the north-west.

Early versions of Rayner's official website dating back to 2014, the year before she was elected as an MP for the first time, make no mention of her time in the Samaritans but do quote her as saying: 'I got a job as soon as I was old enough. Staying on in education wasn't something for people like me and I wanted to make sure my son had a better start in life than I did.' But in fact she did return to the class-room after leaving school, as her entry in *Who's Who* makes clear by referring to the fact that she entered Stockport College, a further education college open to those aged sixteen and above. And in November 2019, while serving as Labour's shadow Education Secretary, she even wrote an article for the *Huffington Post* under the headline 'Education Gave Me A Vital Second Chance That Too Many People Still Don't Get'. In it, she said that after her son was born in 1997 she realised that the two of them 'weren't going to get far if I didn't have a decent job'. She added: 'I needed to gain some qualifications, so I decided to enrol at Stockport College. It was there I learnt British Sign Language, and then I took a course on counselling.'[9] Oddly, in June 2023, when Rayner was interviewed by Julia Gillard, she told a slightly different story, saying: 'I only learned sign language for fun because I thought it'd be really interesting to do.'[10] Whatever her true motivation for learning sign language, though, she has said she achieved a Level 2 certificate in it.

Some mystery also surrounds the counselling course to which she referred in her 2019 *Huffington Post* article, for she has claimed that she was not allowed to see it through to its conclusion. In 2021, she told LBC's James O'Brien: 'I did counselling courses as well and they wouldn't let me do my diploma because they said nobody wants to be counselled by an eighteen-year-old. I was prevented from doing that.'[11] It is difficult to understand why Stockport College (or any college, come to that) would allow anybody to embark on a course to study counselling if a tutor or some other authority figure was then going to 'prevent' them from sitting the tests that would enable them to gain the qualification they had been working towards, solely on the basis of them being eighteen. O'Brien did not query this discrepancy, leaving Rayner's assertion unresolved. Since data protection and privacy laws were introduced in Britain, it has become all but impossible to ascertain independently any details of anybody's academic record. It is therefore unclear whether Rayner does have a certificate of any sort in counselling – which she might have gained when she was older than eighteen, for example – or whether her experience in the subject went no further than taking part in a course that she was not allowed to finish.

What is beyond doubt is that by 1998, when Rayner was eighteen, her desire for money and a career had grown. In 2012, she gave an interview to the website for the Manchester branch of UNISON in which she was asked to describe the worst job she had ever had: 'My worst job was cash in hand when I was 18 selling roses around pubs and clubs to make ends meet when I had a young baby to look after,' she said. 'It was long hours during the night for very little pay and I was exhausted all the time.'[12] Having realised that working as a flower seller was not for her, it could perhaps have been anticipated that an individual as spirited as Rayner soon decided she could get more out of life. Two chinks of light appeared that helped her to graduate towards a more stable future. The first came in the form of a job advertisement she saw seeking care workers; the second was Sure Start, the Labour government-backed project for parents of young children.

The advertisement Rayner saw opened the door to a career that, in many respects, was tailor-made for her, given her experience of looking after her mother. 'At the time I needed a job because I was going to prove that I wasn't going to be on benefits all my life and be the scumbag that everyone decided I was going to be,' she recalled to the BBC's Nick Robinson in 2018. She quickly established that somebody with no qualifications could work in domiciliary care and she began working for a private agency.[13] She was taken on straight away as a supply worker covering evening shifts. According to her entry in *Who's Who*, she began this job in 1998. Initially, Rayner has said, she was based in a care home in Stockport where she carried out basic domestic duties, including washing up. Then she became a Home Help, visiting elderly people in their own property to bring them their shopping, clean, prepare food and check on their welfare. Her grandmother, Jean, was instrumental in this endeavour. Because few others wanted to take on the evening and weekend shifts, Jean apparently agreed to look after Rayner's son once she had finished her own work commitments for the day, guaranteeing Rayner a steady income of between £3 and £5 per hour.

When discussing this early stage of her working life, Rayner has been honest about the fact that there was a darker side to it as well, in so far as some of those whom she and her colleagues were being paid to attend to did not always receive appropriate levels of support. 'When I did six months in the private sector I saw some of the horrifying things,' she told the BBC presenter Nick Robinson in 2018.

So for example we were told that eight-hour slots of care, we'd narrow it down to six, five-and-a-half hours, and how you do that is instead of someone getting a thirty-minute call, they get twenty-five or twenty minutes, and you rush out as quickly as you can. But at the time I just saw that as: 'Well, that's what you do, you just get round as quickly as you possibly can and leave.'[14]

Cutting corners in this way was, apparently, accepted as standard practice by those administering to the elderly. Rayner told James O'Brien a similar story in 2021. 'We'd have a twelve-hour shift that we'd do in six hours,' she said. 'Obviously we robbed people of care. I didn't see it that way. It's just the way it was organised. If someone had an hour call, you'd try and get it done in thirty-five minutes.'[15]

As an eighteen- or nineteen-year-old, newly placed in her first proper job and with a child to support, it is probably unsurprising that Rayner seems to have mimicked the habits of her colleagues without at the time questioning their professional conduct. Furthermore, it would be disingenuous not to acknowledge the potential practical pressures that can be associated with the type of work she was doing as a Home Help. And yet it is striking that she was apparently prepared to go along with what might have been considered to be the neglect of vulnerable people by others, some of whom were apparently dying. For, as already described, throughout this six-month period Rayner has also indicated that she gave up several hours each week to listen to the problems and worries of perfect strangers in her capacity as a Samaritan. The irony, of course, is that she undertook that important charitable work on a voluntary basis.

Rayner has said that after about six months of working in the private sector, she heard from a colleague that Stockport Metropolitan Borough Council was recruiting Home Helps. She has said she applied for a job, keen to work in a more structured environment. As she explained to Nick Robinson of the BBC in 2018, one of the driving factors in this decision was that she was told that they would pay for her travel time and that she would receive holiday pay.[16] Under Freedom of Information laws, Stockport Council has confirmed that Rayner was an employee from August 2000 and so, based on what she has said in interviews – and according to the council's employment records – it appears that having quit the private sector there was a gap of more than a year that is unaccounted for. However, when she did take up her full-time position with the council in August 2000, she found that it had other benefits as well. Notably, she was encouraged to return to Stockport College to study for a National Vocational Qualification Level 2 Diploma in Care. This course taught students how to improve their knowledge of matters such as welfare and safeguarding. What she could not have known at the time she secured this job was that it would, ultimately, put her on a path leading to Westminster.

The other source of positivity in Rayner's life in the early part of the twenty-first century came from the Sure Start programme. This nationwide scheme, which Rayner has spoken about frequently in interviews, was announced in July 1998, and the first centres opened in September 1999. It came to be seen as one of the flagship policies of the Blair government's first term in office. It was chiefly concerned with helping those living in disadvantaged areas to improve their parenting skills and their children's life chances through a variety of educational classes and playgroups. During its first three years in existence, £452 million was allocated to set up 250 Sure Start centres for children up to the age of three in districts with the highest levels of poverty. Representatives from statutory, voluntary and community bodies were invited to apply for funding and, once secured, each scheme would be developed locally. The idea was that every mother would be assigned an outreach worker who could guide them and their child in an effort to improve social mobility.

According to parliamentary records, Stockport was invited to apply in round three of the scheme, and its representatives had to confirm the town's interest by September 2000. Some sixty-four other districts around the country received an invitation at that time. A report titled 'Getting Sure Start Started: National Evaluation of Sure Start' published in July 2002 by the National Evaluation of Sure Start Team based at Birkbeck, University of London stated that round three participants were advised that each district applying for Sure Start funding 'should include between 400 and 800 children under four'.

The first programmes for round three districts began in March 2001, by which time Rayner's son was already four years old and therefore beyond the prescribed age. Nevertheless, she has said that they were able to use the service. Stockport Metropolitan Borough Council has confirmed under Freedom of Information laws that the first two Sure Start centres to open in Stockport were the Abacus Children's Centre at Garners Lane, Adswood; and Cuddington Crescent, Bridgehall. Perplexingly, having checked its records, it found that they both opened on 30 September 2005 – by when Rayner's son was eight years old. This makes it difficult to know exactly which services Rayner used and has been referring to when she has spoken of her personal Sure Start experiences.

While the strength of feeling that she had for her youngest son has never been in doubt, she has admitted that during the first few years of his life he could be hard to handle. She has said that engaging with the Sure Start programme brought into sharper focus her own shortcomings as a parent, teaching her the importance of reading to her son and showing him the affection that had been denied to her when she was young. 'I learnt that telling your child how much you love them is something that's so important,' she told Paul Brand of ITV News in 2020. 'If you're not nurtured in that way, you just assume children know they're loved.'[17]

As a young mother of one, Rayner has said she also studied the work of Dr Carolyn Webster-Stratton, an American clinical psychologist who has been active in the field of child behavioural therapy since the 1970s. Kathleen Potts, who as mentioned in Chapter 1 had been Rayner's Girl Guide leader, remembers how important Sure Start was to her. 'I only saw Angie once or twice after she left the Guides,' she says. 'She would pop in to the family ironmongery shop where I worked just to say: "Hello, Captain." I remember she sang the praises of the Sure Start scheme, which she said helped turn her life around.'

By 2001, then, Rayner was making the sort of parental and professional progress of which she would have been justly proud. She was certainly proving wrong anybody who had written her off a few years previously as somebody who would never amount to anything. Yet underneath the surface, sadness showed itself. Her grandmother, Jean, became ill and would die in October 2001, removing a much-needed support from Rayner's life and from her mother's life. This apparently led to her mother, who was by this point divorced from Rayner's father, needing a greater level of care herself.

In 2014, when she became a Labour prospective parliamentary candidate, Rayner paid tribute to her grandmother on her official website, noting the pivotal role she had played in her life over many years. Since 2014, Rayner has been more open about her grandmother's final years, even telling journalists how her poor health almost led to a tragedy involving her mother. In 2021, she said on Times Radio:

> And then when my nana got cancer, that's when I became a real carer. My nana was trying to convince my mum that she needed to give her loads of morphine because my nana was in all this pain. [I said:] 'Mum this is dangerous.' I ended up having to put my nan in nursing care because I had a one-year-old at the time and I was struggling with work and looking after my mum with her bipolar and looking after my nana and it just got all ... totally extreme for me.[18]

And in 2022, she gave an interview to Kate Mossman of the *New Statesman* in which she recounted a similar story. Mossman wrote:

> Rayner tells me when her eldest son was two she had to find her mother an assisted living place. Her mother was unable to cope after the death of Rayner's grandmother, a stable figure upon whom the Rayner children had relied for hot meals and baths. After being diagnosed with cancer Rayner's grandmother had asked her daughter to administer a fatal dose of morphine; she didn't, but it prompted a crisis.[19]

What is puzzling about these accounts is that when Rayner's grandmother died in October 2001, aged sixty-four, Rayner's son was not two years old but was in fact a few months shy of his fifth birthday. By then, her grandmother had become a resident of the Bryn Haven care home in Brinnington Road, Stockport. Sadly, it was not cancer that she succumbed to in the end but, according to her death certificate, a 'cerebrovascular accident' – in layman's terms a stroke – and malnutrition.

CHAPTER 4

UNIONISED

Whenever Angela Rayner has been asked about the origins of her political career, she has usually explained that they lie in her decision to quit her job as a private care agency Home Help and then take up the same post at Stockport Council. Within about twelve months of her arrival there in August 2000, Rayner has claimed, plans were put forward by the council's managers to outsource its Home Help service. Outraged by what she saw as the march towards privatisation, she joined a trade union, UNISON, to try to halt the scheme. Through her increasing involvement in UNISON's work over the next decade or so, she became a member of the Labour Party and then realised she wanted to seek a seat in the House of Commons. She told James O'Brien of LBC in 2021 that she was one of the last people to be hired as a Home Help before the council began to outsource the role. She went on: 'That's when I got political.'[1] In order to gain a fuller understanding of the context in which her political awakening began, and of the instincts and principles that have driven her, it is worth going back to the beginning of this timeline and charting her rise through the council and UNISON. It should be noted that UNISON itself was not able to help with every aspect of this task, because, as one of its staff admitted during the research of this book, record-keeping is not its strong point.

Rayner seems to have enjoyed her work as a Home Help, performing domestic tasks for her clients and keeping a close eye on their welfare, and she has been clear that this job not only put her on a surer financial footing but also benefited her personal development. For example, she has described how it brought her into contact with types of people she had not previously encountered. In this context she has frequently mentioned several retired professionals who were nearing the end of their life.

> When I became a home help, I started to look after a professor while he was critically ill and dying. I had never met a professor before then. I was his only contact throughout his last few months. He spoke to me as a human being, not as a scally off an estate,

she told *UNISON* magazine in 2020. 'I looked after judges who were very, very vulnerable. These big authority figures suddenly became people to me. They depended on me. And they treated me like I was on the same level with them, in a way that I'd never experienced.'[2] The job further proved to her that people whom she had previously dismissed as 'rich' because they lived in a large house were not necessarily so different to many others in society. She told Nick Robinson of the BBC in 2018 that her clients were both rich and poor and that this taught her a lot about class: 'When you're dying and you've got a terminal illness, it doesn't matter what background you're from, there are certain qualities people expect.'[3]

The lessons from these experiences were underscored by other realisations. For in between the appointments she had with clients in their homes, and when she wasn't looking after her young son or her mother, or volunteering as a Samaritan, the politics of her workplace reared its head as well. It seems that, quite quickly, she was swept up by the events around her and found that she gravitated naturally towards discussions about rights, laws and bargaining power.

In 2000, Labour may have been the biggest party in Westminster, but the situation in Stockport was different. After the elections in May that year, Stockport Council was under no overall control. The Liberal Democrats gained power in 2002 and it remained in that party's hands until 2011. Like most councils in Britain at the turn of the century, the social care budget at Stockport was kept under constant review, meaning that every job and service it offered was, to a greater or lesser extent, subject to potential change, including its 250 or so Home Helps.

In 2018, Rayner told Nick Robinson of the BBC that about a year after starting the job she heard the council were planning to privatise the Home Help service. She claimed to him that she didn't know what a trade union was at that stage, but at the urging of her colleagues she joined UNISON and became a shop steward almost immediately.

She added: 'I really honestly didn't know what a trade union was. I joined a trade union and became the shop steward within twenty-four hours.' Two years later, she gave an interview to *UNISON* magazine in which she covered the same ground. 'The managers wanted to outsource the homecare service and started discussions about how they were going to do it,' she said.[4]

I was completely mortified, because I'd only been there a few months. I'd just come from the private sector and I thought, 'Gosh, this is so much better here. You treat staff better, we get more time with our clients, we can look after them.' You know, it was really good. So I was like, 'Why would you want to outsource? This is crazy.' And I was explaining this to management. And the girls who I worked alongside said, 'You should be our union rep.' And I said, 'What's a trade union?' That's when I joined UNISON and, literally overnight, became the shop steward locally.[5]

Going further, she told James O'Brien during their 2021 interview that 'I became their union rep overnight. I joined the trade union that day and became their union rep. Basically, the girls elected me.'[6]

According to Rayner's memory of Stockport Council's outsourcing of its Home Help provision, therefore, there are two points to consider. First, she has said that after she initially heard about the proposed changes to the Home Help service some twelve months into her council employment, she joined UNISON and as a result of her advocacy during one meeting, she was immediately elected as a shop steward to represent her colleagues' interests. Secondly, she has – wittingly or otherwise – given the impression that the proposed overhaul of council services came as a complete surprise to her and, perhaps, to others. Considering the importance she has attached to this period of her professional life in terms of her political formation, and notwithstanding a sense of romanticism she may have about her union days, it seems important to test both assertions.

Although Stockport Council was not a closed shop – that is to say, a place of work where all employees must belong to an agreed trade union – UNISON dominated during Rayner's tenure there to the extent that it had its own designated office within Stockport

Town Hall. UNISON had been formed in 1993 after the merger of three other public services unions – the National Union of Public Employees; the Confederation of Health Service Employees; and the National and Local Government Officers' Association. Since 2000, it has always had about 1.3 million members and to this day it is one of the largest public sector trade unions in Britain, advising its members on pay and conditions and offering them legal advice.

In November 2012, Rayner gave an interview to the online magazine of UNISON's Manchester branch in which she said she joined UNISON in 2000. This would make sense on the basis that she became a council employee in August 2000. And in September 2016, she gave a speech to the Trades Union Congress (TUC) in which she declared: 'From my first day as a care worker when I joined my workplace union I have seen how that movement has fought for our shared values.' If this is taken as further proof that she had in fact joined UNISON on the day she joined Stockport Council in August 2000, it would also mean that the story she told the BBC about joining UNISON twelve months after becoming a council employee cannot be right. Moreover, UNISON's rules state that 'stewards are elected each year by the group of members that they represent'. So if she really was voted in as a shop steward 'overnight', as she has told the BBC, *UNISON* magazine and LBC, it was certainly a coincidence that she happened to join UNISON on the day it held its annual election – the same day, incidentally, that she discovered what a trade union was.

Interestingly, in 2012, three years before she became an MP, a different rendition of her history with UNISON featured in an interview she gave to *The Guardian* in which her elevation to shop steward took a lot longer than she has claimed more recently. Its reporter, Mark King, wrote:

By her own admission, Rayner at first 'didn't know what a trade union was', but as one of the youngest home helps to be recruited in Stockport, she was constantly questioning management. Someone said she would make a good union rep and within a year she was a senior steward.[7]

In her 2016 TUC speech she also said: 'Within a year, I was a UNISON rep.'[8] Of the various timelines she has offered in relation to her history in UNISON, it does seem most plausible that it was 2001 before she became a rep.

While there is no doubt that Rayner is remembered by some Stockport Council colleagues from the early 2000s for having been outspoken during at least one meeting with council managers about proposed changes to the Home Help service, the second question to explore concerns how surprising these plans were to anybody who worked for the council at the time.

On 18 January 1999 – more than eighteen months before Rayner became a council Home Help – the Stockport Social Services Committee produced an internal report titled 'Home Care Services'. Specifically, it outlined the impact of the NHS and Community Care Act. This piece of legislation was implemented in 1993 and was designed to keep people out of hospitals and care homes so that they could stay in their own home and receive help there instead. The effect of this was to place the council's finances under strain and to add to the duties of Home Helps.

One of Rayner's former colleagues explains:

What happened was that Home Helps had been recruited as Home Helps but were needed to take on additional responsibilities in terms of personal care, which some of the staff felt very

strongly was not their role. Originally they were just doing domestic tasks – shopping and cleaning. All local authorities in the
country were trying to create a new role which would include
personal care like washing, dressing and doing the laundry. It
wasn't a straightforward process.

This new, enhanced role meant that Home Helps would eventually
be known as 'Home Carers' or 'Home Supports'.

According to the 1999 report, changes to the job description of a
Home Help had been under discussion since at least 1997. Whereas staff on old contracts tended to work shorter hours over fewer
days, all newly recruited staff had to be available to work contracted
hours between 7 a.m. and 10 p.m. over seven days. These changes
were agreed with UNISON and came into force in March 1998 –
long before Rayner began working for the council – but it seems the
matter was revisited.

The report did not just set out the difficulties the council faced
in terms of its home care service, though. It carried warnings about
the expense of a publicly funded Home Help resource versus one
run by a private contractor hiring supply workers. 'It is self-evident
that a service which employs staff on permanent contracts at £4.71
per standard hour with enhancements for unsocial hours and pays
local authority sick and holiday rates is going to be more expen-
sive than most independently provided services,' it stated, adding:
'Members are asked to note that the whole service will be subject to
close evaluation as a result of the Best Value review.'

All this confirms that by the time Rayner joined Stockport Council as a Home Help in August 2000, change was already in the air,
and UNISON bosses were almost certainly braced for the various
challenges this would bring. From Stockport Council's point of

view, the worsening financial situation demanded action. In November 2000, it was revealed that it had overspent its social services budget during the previous year by £2 million. The following year was dominated by proposals to cut £3 million from the social services budget. In January 2001, Patsy Calton, the Liberal Democrat Social Services Committee chairwoman and council leader, was reported in the *Stockport Express* as saying that the council found itself 'having to take money from other areas like education' to make up this shortfall. In June 2001, the *Stockport Express* reported that if Home Help services, meals on wheels and residential care services were streamlined, £1.5 million could be saved. Of this sum, the council apparently believed that £628,000 was being spent on 900 'non-priority' service users who lived independently and received help with 'domestic cleaning, collecting pensions, personal hygiene, doing laundry and light shopping'. As a Home Help, these are the tasks that Rayner would almost certainly have been concerned with on a daily basis. By December 2001, UNISON bosses had told Home Helps not to agree to sign new contracts that could change their working hours. One of those quoted in the *Stockport Express* article publicising this row was UNISON's assistant branch secretary. His name was Mark Rayner, and he also happened to be Angela Rayner's future husband. Although he was seventeen years her senior, they are believed to have become close from 2004 or, possibly, earlier.

In 2012, Rayner claimed to *The Guardian* that 'I successfully fought the privatisation of the home care service'.[9] One individual who worked in the social services department at the time is certainly aware that Rayner raised objections to Home Helps being outsourced, and her stance was apparently noted by some managers at the time, but this person believes that Rayner's general interpretation of events is debatable. 'It wasn't as dramatic as she's saying,' they say. 'I am sure she's exaggerating. Outsourcing was a slow process.' Moreover, not all of the outsourcing that took place was of the strictly commercial variety. They add: 'A lot of the outsourcing was done to organisations that were not-for-profit or groups of Home Helps that got together and sorted stuff out between them and then started small businesses.'

Outsourcing was indeed a slow process. A report of a council meeting held on 11 July 2005 – six years after the 1999 report was published – declared the Home Help service was only then close to being phased out. 'Home Support Services continue to remodel to meet national priorities and continuing local demand,' it stated. 'Negotiations with UNISON and staff are concluding and will mean the deletion of the traditional role of Home Help.' According to employment records kept by Stockport Council, in March 2005 – four-and-a-half years after Rayner took up her post as a Home Help – she left officially. At that time, forty-seven Home Helps took voluntary redundancy. At this point she began working for UNISON on a full-time basis.

Strikingly, however, it seems that Rayner may have ceased to be a full-time Home Help long before 2005. According to UNISON's website, its shop stewards are allowed to take advantage of something called 'facility time'. This is defined as 'time off from an individual's job, granted by the employer, to enable a rep to carry out their trade union role. In some cases, this can mean that the rep is fully seconded from their regular job, enabling them to work full time on trade union tasks.' So, for example, a Home Help working on facility time would formally be allowed to continue calling themselves a Home

Help, and would be paid from the public purse as a Home Help, but would in fact be working full time for UNISON, representing the interests of its members.

One of Rayner's former colleagues believes that she was working for UNISON on facility time from as early as 2002. 'Angela quite quickly assimilated into the trade union,' remembers this person.

> So she was not only working through that transition period but she was an active trade union branch shop steward who was ne-gotiating with management over what they were doing, why they were doing it, how they were doing it, what benefit it was to her members, what their terms and conditions were. She was in it as an employee, but also in it as a young trade union representative, which she was very good at. The question I'd have to ask myself is, at what point did she retain her position but move to full-time trade union duties? She definitely did that – she retained her pay and conditions but actually moved to full-time trade union work on facility time. I believe it could have happened around 2002.

A spokesman for UNISON says that it believes Rayner became the young members' officer for her branch in Stockport in 2003 and an assistant branch secretary in 2004. When asked under Freedom of Information laws about Rayner having been on 'facility time', Stockport Council says it does not hold this information. Howev-er, her former colleague's memory of events may be accurate on the basis that, although in *Who's Who* Rayner describes herself as having been a 'Home help, private sector and local govt, 1998–2005', she also refers to herself in the same publication as having been a 'trade union lay activist from 2002–2015'. The term 'lay activist' is considered unusual by those with knowledge of the trade union movement. It may be that Rayner used this form of words as a way of acknowledging that she was on facility time from 2002. If true, this would call into question the claim she made on her official website in 2014 – when she was seeking election as an MP for the first time – that she had been a carer 'for almost a decade'. If her former colleague's memory is correct, it seems that she was a carer for a far shorter period of time than that. We can't know for certain, but from the available information and her other responsibilities it seems possible that Rayner was even a carer for just three years or so. But even if her ex-colleague is wrong, and she never worked on facility time at the council, her career performing the duties of a Home Help or carer appears to have lasted for, at the most, about five years, not, as she has claimed, almost ten.

• • •

If the tussle over the pay and conditions of Stockport's Home Helps was the vehicle on which Rayner travelled in the initial stages of her political journey, these things were not her sole focus as a young trade unionist. Having become a 'trade union lay activist', as she puts it, she also began to represent people employed in other areas of local government. Amusingly, her former headmaster at Avondale High School, Ian Tunnard, recalls meeting her in a professional context in the early 2000s, after he had been made headmaster of The Kingsway School in Stockport. Rayner was sent by UNISON to resolve a staffing matter there. In sharp contrast to the put-upon teenager to whom he had offered protection from bullies, he says he found himself dealing with a capable, confident, articulate woman who was, at the time, in her early twenties. He recalls:

Avondale might well have failed her, as she sees it, but I also like to think conversely it might have been the making of her. Clearly by the time she arrived at my next school, Kingsway, to help sort out a solution to the problem of a caretaker with long-term sickness, she was a very different person. As soon as she walked in the door I recognised her and she recognised me. She turned to her member and said words to the effect of: 'Don't worry. It's Mr Tunnard. We'll be all right. He's a good bloke.' And I am proud to say we did manage to sort the situation out amicably and to the satisfaction of everyone involved – for the caretaker, who agreed to settle for early retirement; for the union; for me as head; and for the school.

Yet although Rayner has perhaps portrayed herself as having been something of a trade union warrior within twelve months of arriving at Stockport Council, some with a close knowledge of its inner workings believe it was quite a few years before she was in any way prominent. 'We always saw her as the clerk in the office doing the admin,' remembers one.

When the council had disciplinary matters with employees, they were handled by HR and senior council officers. Councillors got involved when it came to appeals. If someone wanted to appeal a decision, the appeals panels were run by councillors, usually from one of each of the three main parties. Some of us knew who Angela Rayner was, but she never did any of the employment appeals, which is funny because the officer who handled the original disciplinary and employment issues would normally come to the appeals and represent at the appeal. I never saw Angela Rayner once on the appeals panel that I was on, and I did it for several years.

However productive Rayner's early years in UNISON were perceived to be by others, she went from strength to strength in the
union pretty quickly, becoming a young members' officer on the
National Executive Council in 2005, a national role open at that
time to those aged twenty-six and under. By July 2007, she had
been re-elected to the NEC and was a member of its twelve-strong
Labour Link Committee, giving her some authority over UNISON's
relationship with the Labour Party, notably when it came to funding. Having joined the Labour Party in 2006, she began attending
its conferences. There is even a photograph of her, accompanied
by her son Ryan, then ten years old, standing alongside the newly
installed Prime Minister, Gordon Brown, at the party's annual gathering in Bournemouth in September 2007. She had met Brown not
long before during a UNISON lobbying meeting in 10 Downing
Street. By the age of twenty-seven, therefore, Rayner was advancing
through UNISON very effectively, but her progress soon coincided
with a phase of enormous change in her personal circumstances.

A few years previously, Rayner had moved to 80 Vicarage Road, a
Victorian semi-detached house with two bedrooms and a garden in
the Cale Green area of Stockport that she rented from the council.
She liked the house so much that by 2006 she was actively exploring
acquiring it under the right-to-buy scheme. This measure, which
was introduced by Margaret Thatcher's government in 1980, allows
council tenants to purchase the property they rent for a generous
discount – in some cases 50 per cent – depending on how long they
have lived there. It was established to encourage home ownership
rather than as an investment vehicle. Anyone buying a right-to-buy
property must sign a form confirming, among other things, that it
is their only or principal home.

According to Land Registry records, Rayner bought 80 Vicarage Road from the council on 15 January 2007. At that point, its lease had 893 years left to run. She paid £79,000, securing the house with the aid of a residential mortgage taken out with the Cheltenham & Gloucester building society. The discount Rayner received from her local council was £26,000, or approximately 25 per cent. This was consistent with average right-to-buy discounts in the north-west at the time.

When Rayner bought the house, she was the 26-year-old single mother of a boy aged nine. Her status soon changed. By Christmas 2007, she was pregnant with Mark Rayner's child. In April 2008, she gave birth. The baby, another boy, who was given the name Charles Wilfred Rayner, was born prematurely at just twenty-three weeks and is said to have weighed only 1lb. She explained to the *Financial Times* during an interview in 2022: 'I was told he wouldn't be able to sleep, eat for himself, look after himself, he'd need 24-hour care. The doctors said switch the machine off. But we didn't and now he's walking and talking and going to mainstream school.'[10]

Happily, for Rayner, she and Mark Rayner soon tried for another baby. In June 2009, when Charles was a little over a year old, their second son, whom they called James Stuart Rayner, was born. In fact, Rayner has even said she left the maternity ward where she was waiting to give birth to James in order to vote Labour in that year's European Parliament elections, because she was so committed to keeping out the BNP, which was considered a threat. 'I couldn't have lived with myself if I didn't vote,' she later told *The Guardian*.[11] In any examination of Rayner's life and career, it is at this point that a riddle concerning her living arrangements presents itself.

When the Rayners were married in September 2010 at Bramall

Hall in Stockport, they were asked to record on their marriage certificate their 'residence at the time of marriage'. Mark Rayner gave his address as 126 Lowndes Lane, Stockport. This was a three-bedroom former council house that he and his father, Wilfred, had bought in 1991. Angela Rayner – using her maiden name, Bowen, of course – stated her address as 80 Vicarage Road, Stockport. Anybody reading this public document would have the impression that, despite having had two sons together in 2008 and 2009, Angela and Mark Rayner lived apart when they married in September 2010.

Oddly, other public documents would appear to confirm that they continued to occupy separate addresses for several more years. At the point at which they married, the Rayners were a family of five, including Rayner's first son, Ryan. Yet, according to that year's electoral roll, which had a qualifying date of October 2009, Angela Rayner – under her maiden name Angela Bowen – was the only adult registered at 80 Vicarage Road. At the same time, Mark Rayner lived at 126 Lowndes Lane – and according to the electoral roll, he shared the house with one other adult, Darren Bowen. This is the name of Angela's elder brother.

Subsequent editions of the electoral roll show that Angela Rayner – under her maiden name Angela Bowen – remained a resident of 80 Vicarage Road until the 2012 electoral roll was published. The 2013 edition of the roll also recorded her as living there, though for the first time since her marriage it had been updated so that she was listed under her married name, Angela Rayner. The 2014 edition – which at the time of going to print was the last roll available to view under ten-year privacy rules – also stated that Angela Rayner lived at 80 Vicarage Road. Over the same period, up to and including the publication of the 2014 electoral roll, Mark Rayner was listed as a resident of 126 Lowndes Lane, along with Darren Bowen. Joining them on the 2014 electoral roll was one other individual, Ryan Batty, Angela Rayner's eldest son. This would suggest that he was living with his stepfather and with Darren Bowen, but not with his mother. Whether or not the Darren Bowen living with Mark Rayner was Angela Rayner's brother, the question arises: what was the reason for this unorthodox set-up?

When visiting Vicarage Road to try to better understand the situation, a neighbour said they remember Angela Rayner well. They recalled that she had a housewarming party to which others in the street were invited as a friendly gesture. Mark Rayner was also at the party. But, they added, after the Rayners had children together, Angela moved out and Darren Bowen moved in. 'She [Angela] had tenants,' one said. 'Her brother, Darren, lived here.' This specific detail was recalled because, in their opinion, 'Darren wasn't particularly friendly'. Rayner has very rarely spoken of either of her siblings, though in 2018 she did briefly mention Darren while giving an interview to Nick Robinson of the BBC, in which she said: 'My brother, gosh, he went to Basra. He was in the Iraq War and he had some pretty Tory-type views.'

One former neighbour at Lowndes Lane said they remember Angela and Mark Rayner living at 126 Lowndes Lane from at least the summer of 2009, when James Rayner was born. They said Angela Rayner was 'very feisty', adding: 'I knew her to nod to and say hello, but it was probably Mark who we saw more of. We never met Darren,' and that so far as they were aware 'he did not live there. It was Angela and Mark and the two young boys throughout our whole time there. Ryan was there, too, but he was only just into his teens and we didn't see him very often either.' It is this person's belief that the Rayners lived together at 126 Lowndes Lane until Angela Rayner moved to Ashton-under-Lyne, after she was elected as an MP in 2015.

Confusingly, on 20 October 2010, six weeks after her marriage to Mark Rayner, Angela Rayner re-registered at Stockport Register Office the births of her two younger sons. She may well have done this in recognition of her sharing their surname from this point. One detail from each of the original certificates that appeared on the re-registered certificates was that 80 Vicarage Road was listed as her 'usual address' – that is to say, the address that she had given at the time of their births in 2008 and 2009 respectively. But a section of the updated certificate asked the now-Mrs Rayner, as the 'informant', to give her address at the point of the re-registration in October 2010. The address she gave, just above where her signature appears, was 126 Lowndes Lane.

Did Angela Rayner live in her two-bedroom house in Vicarage Road with – presumably – some, or all, of her children between 2007 and 2014, as the electoral roll states? And, if she did, was her boyfriend and eventual husband Mark Rayner living separately at his three-bedroom house in Lowndes Lane with Darren Bowen from 2009 to 2014? Or did the Rayners live together as husband and wife with their children at 126 Lowndes Lane? Moreover, why should this matter?

One reason that it may be of consequence relates to Rayner's right-to-buy purchase. Conditions are attached to any acquisition made under the right-to-buy scheme. One rule, under Section 156A of the Housing Act 1985, states that if the owner wants to sell their property within ten years of buying it, they are obliged to give the council first refusal in case the council wants to buy it back to ensure it is returned to social housing stock.

(There was certainly pressure on social housing in Stockport during that decade. Figures published in the *Manchester Evening News* in November 2005 stated that 6,683 families in Stockport were waiting for a council home, a rise of 11 per cent since 1997.)[12]

Another right-to-buy rule is that if an owner sells their property within five years of buying it, the council can claw back from the owner some, or all, of the discount they received. This five-year window is known as a 'pre-emption period'. Rayner faced a release fee to reimburse the council for the discount that could have run to thousands of pounds until the five years were up in January 2012. In fact she did not sell Vicarage Road until 2015, when the claw-back period had expired. A council has some discretion as to the level of reimbursement of the discount it seeks and might want to take into account the personal circumstances and needs of the owner.

If Rayner did, as alleged, move to 126 Lowndes Lane before January 2012, only she would know why she did not sell her own house, reimburse the council whatever money it felt was due and give the council the option of returning the property to its social housing stock so that those on low incomes could make use of it – or at any rate, why she did not inform the council of the change in her circumstances so that official records could be amended to reflect her residential status.

Right-to-buy owners are allowed to rent out their property during the five-year pre-emption period, but it is not without its complications. Someone with a mortgage who wants to grant a tenancy or licence of their property will normally need to get the written consent of the mortgage company. The mortgage company would then decide whether it required the existing residential mortgage to be converted into a 'consent to let' mortgage, allowing the borrower to rent out their home. The owner would also need to obtain the consent of the insurer of the property to any letting.

It is also advisable for a right-to-buy owner to notify the council if they sublet, given that there is a continuing relationship with the council for ten years from the original purchase under the relevant Housing Act legislation. The electoral roll should record who was living at the property, but there is some question as to whether the returns recording 80 Vicarage Road were accurate.

At the time of writing, in February 2024, Angela Rayner is the shadow Secretary of State for Levelling Up, Housing and Communities. In November 2023, she spoke of her desire, if in government, to reappraise the right-to-buy scheme. This reflected a feeling among many in the public housing sector that private landlords have muscled in to such a degree that housing stock rates have been driven down and rents in ex-council houses have been driven up. 'I think we need to review the way Right to Buy works,' she told *The i* newspaper. 'Not abolish it but make it fair and [make sure] we are replacing the [homes] lost.' She explained that she grew up in 'the same council house' and said her parents had also lived in the same one 'for thirty years' but said the system must be 'fair and equitable to the public purse, to taxpayers – and that we can then build more affordable housing off the back of it.' She said one area that needed to be looked at was 'how much of a discount' is on offer, with the clear inference being that she believes discounts to be too high.[13] Given her responsibilities and agenda, the history of her ownership and occupation of 80 Vicarage Road is a matter of legitimate interest. She was a UNISON official and, from March 2013, began attempting to become a Labour MP, no doubt involving some knowledge of right-to-buy and electoral laws.

Angela Rayner appears to have a series of questions to answer about her residence at 80 Vicarage Road, and why she acted as she did needs investigation, the more so given her position in public life. Issues arise as to whether she complied with the spirit and regulations of the pre-emption period, even though she qualified under the five-year ownership rules, and as to whether she observed the requirements of her mortgage lender. It also needs to be investigated whether there were any breaches of electoral law. Was it right that her name appeared on the electoral register at 80 Vicarage Road from the time she bought the house until at least 2014? And was it right that Darren Bowen's name was recorded on the register at 126 Lowndes Lane from 2009 until at least 2014? This register has been described by the government as being 'the key building block for our democracy'. The Electoral Commission states on its website: 'Residence has a particular meaning in electoral law and is not equivalent to residence for other purposes such as income tax or council tax. Normally a person is resident at an address for electoral purposes if it is their permanent home address.' Under the Representation of the People Act 1983, penalties can be applied for providing false information.

When detailed questions about this matter were put to Angela Rayner in February 2024 – including a specific request for her to state where she lived between 2007 and 2015; why she gave her address as 126 Lowndes Lane when re-registering her children's birth certificates in October 2010, even though this appeared to conflict with her declaration on the electoral register; and why Darren Bowen was listed as living with Mark Rayner for several years – the following statement was issued on her behalf by a Labour Party spokesman:

> While Belize-based Tory billionaire Lord Ashcroft kicks out at those who graft to get on in life, Labour supports the principle that if you live in a council house and work hard you should have the opportunity to own your own home. We have committed to reviewing the unfair discounts introduced by the Conservatives in 2012, but Angela's purchase long predates that and was done by the book. While the Tories have shattered the dream of home ownership, Labour will deliver the biggest boost to affordable, social and council housing for a generation. Angela, who had an older child from a previous relationship, and her husband maintained their existing residences before moving into their shared marital home. Their son was born just 23 weeks into her pregnancy and spent eight months in intensive care, requiring ongoing support from a wide network of friends and family, including Angela's brother. It's clear that Lord Ashcroft takes an unhealthy interest in Angela's family, but beyond the smears, there is no suggestion any rules have been broken.

Despite her political position, Angela Rayner failed to answer these straightforward questions concerning apparently conflicting pieces of information listed on public documents. It is striking that, instead of responding, a Labour spokesman acting on her behalf used a statement to launch a personal attack on me – while falsely accusing me of smearing her. Yet aside from this Labour spokesman knowing nothing about my background (my roots are in Burnley in a two-up two-down; the toilet was in the back yard and we used torn-up newspaper as toilet paper; my father was an enlisted infantryman and my mother a nurse) the Electoral Commission is clear. While not discussing Rayner's personal circumstances, a spokesman said its general position is: 'It is an offence to knowingly provide false information in the voter registration application form. If convicted, a person may be imprisoned for up to six months and/ or face an unlimited fine. This would be a matter for the police to investigate.'

Number 80 Vicarage Road was sold in March 2015 – seven weeks before the general election in which Rayner became an MP for the first time – for £127,500. As the house's owner, she would have been eligible to bank the increase in its value – potentially about £48,500 – minus any estate agent's fees. If Stockport Council were to review her case, would its representatives believe their residents had got a fair deal out of Rayner's ownership of the property? It seems only a full investigation of this matter will establish the facts.

•   •   •

As Angela Rayner has said, one consequence of the premature birth of her son in 2008 was that he had to spend a great deal of time in hospital – possibly as long as fourteen months, according to her account of the situation during an interview with Times Radio in 2021. She said: 'I spent eight months in the neonatal unit and six months in intensive care with him and nearly lost him many times and was told that he wouldn't even be able to feed himelf growing up because of the damage that was done to his ... brain.'[14]

Amid the stress and worry this must have caused to Rayner and her family over such a long period of time, it is impressive that she found room in her life for her work with UNISON. In January 2009, she was nominated for a Women's Seat representing the north-west region on its National Executive Council. The ensuing election was held in May 2009, and as far as the available evidence suggests Rayner went on to secure the seat that she desired. This two-year post gave her the power to help set UNISON's policy, to decide what issues it should focus on and how its subscriptions should be spent. Colleagues recall that she sat on the Policy Development and Campaigns Committee; the Staffing Committee; and the Welfare Board. Not only did the role elevate her profile, allowing her to speak in defence of public sector pensions at its national conference in Bournemouth in June 2010, for example, but it also brought her to the attention of some of UNISON's most influential figures. The Labour government under Gordon Brown had lost office in May 2010, and union bosses had already begun thinking about the future. Their links to the leadership of the Labour Party would eventually prove decisive for Rayner's political career.

In the meantime, as an assistant branch secretary and then as the branch secretary, she was often quoted in the north-west's regional press commenting on a range of local issues, such as cuts to youth budgets and the axing of lollipop ladies, as the coalition government led by David Cameron pursued its policy of austerity in order to restore the public finances after what it argued were unsustainable deficits left by the previous Labour government. In November 2011, Rayner appeared at a picket line outside Stockport Town Hall during a public sector strike over pensions that closed schools, libraries and courts in what was said to be the biggest national stoppage since the 1970s. She was quoted in the *Manchester Evening News* as saying: 'No one likes to go out on strike, but people are starting to understand. It is not the trade unions wanting a fight; it is the government using fighting talk.'

In February 2012, reflecting her burgeoning reputation, she was interviewed by *The Guardian*. The interviewer, Mark King, noticed several photographs dotted around her UNISON office, including a shot of her with Ed Miliband at an event during the Labour leadership contest in 2010, and another of her holding a placard at a Trades Union Congress rally in March 2011. There was also a picture of Emmeline Pankhurst, the suffragette, which apparently prompted Rayner to announce:

> People underestimate me, too. I'm a pretty young woman, lots of red hair, and everyone expects me to be stupid when I walk into a meeting for the first time. I'm not stupid and most people know that now, but I still like to be underestimated because it gives me an edge. It gives me a bit of stealth.[15]

King spent a day with her and watched her at work, observing how she 'challenges and cajoles council leaders at every opportunity, quick to pounce on an issue, which might have negative fallout for the workers she represents.' Stockport Council was at this point halfway through a four-year round of budget cuts that was estimated to total £50 million. King admitted that he found the meetings he was allowed to sit in on mundane, but he was impressed by Rayner's enthusiasm for her job as she settled disputes and defended the interests of public sector workers. She even revealed to him that she was paid 'twenty grand a year' as UNISON's branch secretary. King wrote:

> In meeting after meeting, if Rayner is not frantically taking notes she is asking probing questions about new reporting lines, staff changes and budgets. In one afternoon meeting, a senior member

of the council answers query after query, before rolling his eyes and telling me: 'She's a force of nature.' A smile betrays his respect for the battling unionist sitting opposite.[16]

In view of how pivotal to Angela Rayner's union career her husband, Mark, had been – and given that he was himself a UNISON representative in Stockport – it is perhaps surprising that he was not mentioned in the article. Having become UNISON's branch secretary in Stockport, Angela Rayner was the main point of contact with the wider union. She was also in charge of administration and, along with the branch chair, all other matters including, if necessary, negotiations. She represented the interests of about 4,000 members. Those who know Mark Rayner have said he and Angela were always considered an unusual pairing yet, thanks to his own long association with UNISON, there can be no doubting his influence on her position in Stockport up until the time she decided she wanted to graduate to national politics. One Labour Party stalwart says:

> Mark clearly had a hand in stewarding her in that industrial journey. The bit of the union he was in was no way near the politics of the union. So he wasn't a senior union official or a well-networked union official, but he was able to give her the benefit of his experience.

Another adds: 'Mark was so important to her career. He has been the key influence on her life. He certainly shaped her politics. His guidance, and the framework that the union offered to Angela, got her to where she is today. There is no doubt about that.'

In fact, Mark Rayner might have been thought of by some in UNISON as a thorn in its side. He was well known, certainly in the north-west, for having put his forensic skills to use pursuing the length of time and the cost of building UNISON's new headquarters in London. It opened in 2011 almost twelve months late and £8.5 million over budget. Without his guidance, however, it is an open question as to whether Angela Rayner's progress through UNISON would have been as smooth or as well targeted as it undoubtedly was. (In 2012, she was also UNISON's north-west regional treasurer.) Yet by the time she was in her early thirties, there was a tangible sense that she was becoming a big fish in a small pond. One former colleague says: 'She was going places and she knew it, and all credit to her. Why shouldn't she?'

A Labour source says:

Angela's union career is the most convincing part of her backstory. Sometimes the union movement can give purpose and meaning to people who've failed in education. There's an intergenerational network of people who gave her a vocational training, which in turn gave her an education, albeit an unusual one, that allowed her to think she could make more of herself. That's the essence of her. The trade union movement does that a thousand times over. It's just that those who benefit from it don't end up very often becoming deputy leader of the Labour Party.

CHAPTER 5

'IN MY OWN LITTLE NORTHERN WAY'

As the embers of the Tony Blair and Gordon Brown era died in the late spring of 2010, some on the political left of the trade union movement were adamant that changes needed to be made. The wrong candidates were being fielded in national polls and the House of Commons did not reflect the country at large, they felt. Plans were hatched by union bosses to actively encourage their members to consider standing for Parliament in time for the next election. Not just anybody would do, however. These individuals had to meet certain criteria. Most importantly, they had to be recognisably working class. 'There was a big drive after 2010 and before 2015, especially by UNITE, but also in other unions, to promote working-class candidates, because the proportion of MPs from working-class backgrounds had sunk to an unbelievably low level,' explains one Labour Party source. 'And then there was also the left/right issue in the Parliamentary Labour Party. So the aim was to get more working-class and left-leaning candidates into winnable seats. Some progress was made on that in time for the 2015 election. Angela was one of those people who benefitted from that drive.'

Indeed, by 2013, Rayner was seen by some union figures as having all the qualities of a star in the making. She was married with three children; she had an interesting life story; she had proved her worth to UNISON both in Stockport and on the NEC; and she had a good working relationship with several of its senior members. Chief among them were Frank Hont, who was UNISON's north-west regional secretary until 2012, and his successor Kevan Nelson, who is now the international secretary of the Communist Party of Britain. 'Angela was a protegee of Kevan's,' adds this source. 'She was highly regarded.''

Yet it wasn't just UNISON and Nelson who got behind Rayner's bid for Westminster. Unite, the major Labour donor whose general secretary at the time was the influential left-wing trade unionist Len McCluskey, drew up a list of forty-one approved individuals who it wanted in Parliament. Rayner was among them. Ironically, it later came to light that a significant percentage of the forty-one were not what most people would perceive as 'working class'. In a further twist, not every one of them was a Unite member either (Rayner wasn't, for example). Nor did they necessarily share Unite's politics. Nonetheless, Rayner was grateful for Unite's endorsement, which she considered to be highly valuable to her prospects.

Influential figures at the top of the Labour Party, which had been led since September 2010 by Ed Miliband, were duly briefed about Rayner by UNISON representatives. They were asked to give her the benefit of their wisdom when it came to winning a parliamentary selection contest. One who was approached for this task recalls:

> UNISON was pretty good at trying to get working-class candidates in, and they'd obviously seen something in her. She was being pushed. They needed very strongly to put not just professional

negotiators in but shop stewards, branch officers, NEC members and ordinary union members as well. In the way that the trade union movement works, they were pushing Angela without a lot of expectation that she would be selected straight away, but they wanted to be seen to be doing the right thing.

Rayner would have been aware that finding a parliamentary con-stituency to represent is among the most unforgiving elements of the business of politics. It is full of false starts, dashed dreams and unwelcome expenditure. It can also take years to achieve. Yet she was serious about becoming an MP from the word go. In March 2013, just shy of her thirty-third birthday, she attended a parliamen-tary training school in London organised by the Trade Union and Labour Party Liaison Organisation (TULO). This two-day course was mostly aimed at those with union links who were merely thinking about trying to become a Labour MP. Unlike most other attendees, Rayner had already set her eyes upon a constituency – Manchester Withington – and had just launched a campaign to be adopted as its candidate. It had been held by the Liberal Democrat John Leech since 2005, having previously been a Labour stronghold since 1987, and regaining it was considered essential if the party was to have any hope of returning to power.

Rayner created a website featuring the slogan 'Because Change is Worth Fighting For', which first appeared online that month. She also posted a promotional video on YouTube in which she told a brief story of her life, complete with photographs from her child-hood and pictures of her with her two youngest sons. Whereas just a generation ago there would not have been many – perhaps any – aspiring women MPs who would have been advised to be so open about becoming a mother at a young age, Rayner did not hide her own experience, though in what may have been a slip of the tongue she did say: 'I became a single mother aged seventeen' rather than sixteen. Her husband, Mark Rayner, is said to have managed her campaign.

Manchester Withington was considered a prize well worth fighting for, and Rayner was not alone in wanting to be its next MP. Jeff Smith, a Manchester City councillor, threw his hat into the ring shortly before her, as did his council colleague Andrew Simcock. Having been born in Withington and served on Manchester City Council in several roles since 1997, Smith was considered the man to beat. Rayner seldom talks about her effort to become the Labour candidate for Manchester Withington, presumably because her attempted nomination did not get off the ground. By June 2013, she knew that Smith had clinched it and, in the event, she came second out of three. 'At Withington she ran a tough campaign, but she didn't run the right campaign for that area, and it was quite bitter, really,' remembers one Labour Party figure with knowledge of it. 'She didn't handle herself very well. She was rude about her opponent, Jeff Smith. You never really prosper if you do that in a Labour Party selection, because the members don't like it. I think it showed a little bit of her character.' In this person's opinion, it also showed a degree of naivety that was perhaps not altogether unexpected in someone as politically immature as Rayner undoubtedly was. Her entire life up until this point had been based in and around Stockport, working mostly for a trade union.

Undeterred, Rayner continued her search while carrying on with her day job representing UNISON members who worked for Stockport Council. Although by now UNISON's north-west convenor, technically putting her in charge of some 200,000 members in the region, others saw in Rayner somebody who lacked the *savoir faire* that might have been expected of an aspiring MP. One former council colleague says:

> I remember when Barry Khan, the council solicitor and monitoring officer, left the council to be deputy chief executive of North Yorkshire County Council. We had a party for him to say goodbye. Angela was there wearing a T-shirt with the slogan 'Never Kissed a Tory'. During the party she tried to hand Barry a brown envelope with the word 'Bribe' on it. She kept trying to do this. I remember Barry was incredibly embarrassed about it. Considering she was UNISON's most senior elected official in the north-west, and was trying for Westminster, I just thought she seemed incredibly juvenile.

In the spring of 2014, news came through that David Heyes would be standing down as the MP for the Greater Manchester constituency of Ashton-under-Lyne at the 2015 general election. Heyes had remained on the backbenches since arriving in the Commons in 2001 and was quitting for health reasons. His constituency, which Labour had held continuously since 1935, represented a perfect second opportunity for Rayner given its close proximity to Stockport, which is less than ten miles away. At the 2010 election, Heyes had achieved a majority of just over 9,000 votes. As many MPs will grimly admit, there is no such thing as a 'safe' seat in Parliament, but in 2014 Ashton-under-Lyne would certainly have been viewed as tantalisingly secure by any budding Labour candidate. Better still for Rayner, rumours were circulating that, in order to boost female representation in Parliament, party bosses in London were going to insist on imposing an all-woman shortlist when it came to the selection battle. Local party members immediately held a meeting at which they voted unanimously to have an 'open' list, allowing both women and men. By June, however, it was clear that their wishes had been ignored. David Heyes, the outgoing MP, voiced his dismay at this decision. He told the *Manchester Evening News* he was 'disappointed' and emphasised that even the women's section of the constituency party had voted against the idea.

It is worth noting that Rayner addressed this episode in 2019 by explaining that she had not been in favour of an all-woman shortlist either. Recalling the situation while talking to students at Oldham Sixth Form College, she said:

When I was going to be a Member of Parliament, I didn't want to stand in an all-women shortlist. I wanted to stand on an open list. I'm as good as any bloke, and I've proved that since … I should have been selected years before I was selected. I had to get selected on an all-women shortlist. I'm more successful than a majority of the men that are in Parliament, but I had to prove I was even better than them, like miles ahead of them. That's not fair. That's not equality.

The website she had used at Withington in 2013 was reactivated and on it Rayner explained why she wanted to represent Ashton-under-Lyne, emphasising her commitment to being a local MP. By late July, the *Manchester Evening News* reported that internal campaigning had begun. It named Rayner as the frontrunner and stated that she had secured the backing of 'all the major trade unions'. The paper noted: 'Although brought up in Stockport, she, like other candidates, is stressing her local connections and working-class roots.'[1] Rayner was quoted as saying 'I am a local girl who grew up round the area and am putting my name forward because people are sceptical about politics and politicians.' On 7 August, the paper named her five rivals as Julie Reid, a Manchester councillor; Jean Stretton, an Oldham councillor; Catherine Hynes, a Trafford councillor; Ann Courtney, who had helped to run the Labour MP Andy Burnham's unsuccessful leadership campaign against Ed Miliband in 2010; and Victoria Desmond, a 25-year-old civil servant who had recently graduated from the London School of Economics. It also recorded that Rayner had already gained the most votes from rank-and-file party members.[2]

Rayner may have led the field from the start of the race, but the campaign was not without incident. At one stage, what appeared to be a genuine Angela Rayner campaign leaflet was posted through letterboxes in the constituency. On closer inspection, it soon became clear that it was in fact a comically themed smear, featuring a picture of her seemingly drinking alcohol through her nose with the aid of a breathing tube. This photograph, together with several others of her socialising with other young women, had almost certainly been culled from Rayner's Facebook page, and it appears to have been genuine. Under the heading 'Setting the record straight', the leaflet stated: 'Dear Member, Some people have been saying I'm not fit to be an MP. Well I say, they're just a bunch of miseries who don't know how to have a good time like me.' It went on:

> Some people have been saying I have a drink problem. Well I say, someone who can snort sambuca up their nose through a hospital breathing tube has proved she can handle her drink. And if I'm going to be an MP I need all the boozing practice I can get.

It added: 'Some people say I put silly pictures on my Facebook page. I say, what's to be ashamed of if you know how to have a good time with your mates. Best wishes, Angie.'

More damagingly, perhaps, the mocked-up leaflet also implied that the contest had been rigged in Rayner's favour, and that her campaign may even have broken the law. Under the heading 'How to run a contest to be an MP' it listed the following sarcastically written points, some of which were so specific that they were taken seriously by other candidates:

- Be part of a deal between union bosses to force through an all woman shortlist against the unanimous wishes of members.
- Make sure that union bosses nominate you for the job without asking their members for their views.
- Get big money backing from the union to pay for a glossy campaign.
- Get hold of an illegal copy of the membership list and start lobbying members weeks in advance of start date.
- Make sure union bosses bully and threaten competitors to withdraw from the contest.
- Bend the rules to send out emails in other people's names.
- Turn up on doorsteps with a professional photographer and cajole reluctant members to become 'endorsers'.
- Promise lots of jobs in the MP's office to secure support from members who are looking for work.[3]

The identity of the culprit responsible for producing and distributing this leaflet is unknown. The Guido Fawkes website claimed that 'Unison heavies, with the help of senior Labour MPs like Andrew Gwynne' – whose constituency is also in Greater Manchester – had played a significant role in Rayner's campaign, angering elements of the local Labour Party. It further stated that it was a 'Red on Red' revenge attack for this perceived interference. Ultimately, this attempted sabotage had no tangible effect on the outcome. On 6 September, it was announced that Rayner had secured the nomination with ease.

Up to this point, Rayner's political beliefs had not been tested particularly robustly, and it became apparent that she would need to develop a credo if she was truly to succeed. As one former colleague who worked closely with her explains:

> She's described as soft-left sometimes. That is fairly meaningless. I would say she didn't have an ideological history herself – she hadn't been an activist in left organisations of any kind as far as I'm aware – but she was backed by and closely allied with the left in UNISON in the north-west. So she had strong class politics and a broad left orientation

Class politics was indeed an area that she would soon focus on, but when she spoke to reporters about her victory, she said that her prematurely born son Charles's experience of the NHS six years before had shaped her views. 'There was no way I would have been able to afford his treatment,' she told the *Manchester Evening News*. 'In most countries he probably would not have survived. If it wasn't for the NHS he wouldn't be here today.' The newspaper stated that Rayner still lived in the Cale Green area of Stockport – which is where, as discussed in Chapter 4, her right-to-buy property at 80 Vicarage Road is located – but also emphasised that she had pledged to move to the constituency if she was voted in as its MP. Further evidence of what had motivated her to get into national politics was to be found in the other comments she made that day. 'I've spent most of my working life as a care worker, sometimes on pretty low pay,' she said.

I know exactly what people in Ashton, Droylsden and Failsworth are facing under this government, that's why I'm standing to be our MP. Times are too tough for too many and we need real people, with real life experience to bring a bit of common sense to policy-making in Westminster. The Tories – with their millionaire cabinet – are completely out of touch with what folk here need. I hope I'll bring something a bit different to the House of Commons.[4]

As discussed in the previous chapter, there are good reasons to conclude that, by 2014, she had in fact spent far more of her working life on UNISON's payroll and far less time as a care worker.

She wasted no time in capitalising on her new standing as a prospective parliamentary candidate. Two weeks later, she was to be seen making a speech at the Labour Party conference, which was held that year in Manchester. During a debate on education and children chaired by the shadow Education Secretary Tristram Hunt, she issued the sort of rallying cry that would have made her UNISON colleagues proud, saying:

Support staff in education, who make up half of the school workforce, have been overlooked these last four years. The government cuts have disproportionately affected support staff and our members have been largely ignored and their pay held down, their funding for training cut and their national training resources hidden. That's why we warmly welcome the announcement from Tristram Hunt that the next Labour government will reintroduce the school support staff negotiating body. This will give huge hope to this forgotten and important group of staff. But we also ask that the next Labour government protects support staff from reckless outsourcing and privatisation.

From that time onwards, it was a steady run into the 2015 general election. Rayner campaigned in the constituency regularly, sometimes with a large party of volunteers, at other times with just a few activists, and often with her husband. In January 2015 she also found time to visit Auschwitz, filing a report for the *Morning Star* to coincide with the seventieth anniversary of the death camp's liberation. She had been invited there as part of a 'study tour' organised by UNISON in her capacity as regional convenor of UNISON's northwest region. Commemorating the slaughter of six million Jews was obviously a profoundly sobering subject on which to reflect, and Rayner's article was accordingly dignified. But that is not to say that she was prepared to squander the chance to make a party-political point. Referring to a forthcoming international event taking place at Auschwitz on Holocaust Remembrance Day – 27 January – Rayner observed that countries such as France and Germany were to be represented by their highest-ranking politicians. 'Britain,' she wrote,

> will be represented by Eric Pickles, Secretary of State for Communities and Local Government. Pickles will be seen by some as a questionable choice of representative, given his comparatively low status and the controversies of recent days – notably the High Court ruling that he had unlawfully discriminated against Travellers when determining planning appeals.[5]

Further insights into her brand of politics could be found a few weeks later, on 18 February 2015, when she put out a message on her Facebook account that said: 'Today is the 10th anniversary of the end of hunting with dogs. I support the campaign to #keeptheban.'[6] Next to it was a photograph of a fox running past 10 Downing Street with a speech bubble coming out of its mouth, which read:

'Cull the Tories!' And on the same day she posted another message on Facebook: 'Really fresh this morning out on the doorstep in St Peters with the local Labour team. Lots of positive responses from residents wanting to see the back of the Tories and their nasty policies against the working class.'[7] There is no mistaking the fact that Rayner believed campaigning along these lines would aid her cause.

One of the volunteers who worked with her at this time recalls:

Part of her campaign was to ensure that she had the party on board in Ashton. She needed quite a bit of advice – how to position and present herself, her website, what was the public face of Angela Rayner and so on. I remember she needed help with writing statements, letters, press releases etc. because writing is definitely not her strong point. She just couldn't do it. She couldn't string two sentences together in writing, but of course she excelled verbally. But I liked her and the working-class shtick that she did ad nauseam, and I thought she was a promising potential politician. Her husband really managed her campaign, in as far as anyone can manage Angela. He had the UNISON connections. There was a Unison official in Liverpool called Frank Hont who was advising her as well, I think, but mainly it was Mark and her.

Under the Fixed-term Parliaments Act, which was a key part of the coalition deal between the Conservatives and Liberal Democrats when they formed a government in 2010, it had been decided well in advance that the general election would take place on 7 May. Rayner was pitted against Tracy Sutton for the Conservative Party; Charlotte Hughes for the Green Party; and Carly Hicks for the Liberal Democrats. Maurice Jackson, UKIP's candidate, was the sole man standing. Although there were five candidates, it was soon evident that only three of them had anything approaching a chance of winning. Rayner topped the poll with 19,366 votes; Tracy Sutton for the Tories came second with 8,610 votes; and – representing a dramatic seventeen-point increase on UKIP's 2010 result – Maurice Jackson was just 142 votes behind Sutton, with 8,468. Rayner's majority was 10,756, leading to a swing to Labour of 1.4 per cent and a very solid success for Rayner's campaign.

Nationally, the situation was very different. After five years of leading a coalition government whose watchword was 'austerity', the Conservatives under David Cameron pulled off a surprise victory, giving them a total of 330 MPs in the Commons. This translated into an overall majority of eleven seats. Labour lost forty-eight seats and was pushed back to having 232 MPs in Parliament. The party's leader, Ed Miliband, and his deputy, Harriet Harman, both resigned immediately, meaning that one of Rayner's first major acts as a new MP would be to help choose their successors. First, however, she had to deliver her maiden speech, which she did on 2 June.

It was a well-received effort in which she expressed her pride at being Ashton-under-Lyne's first ever woman MP, spoke about her time as a care worker and her support for the NHS and wasted no time in telling MPs a little more about her life experiences and character. 'I promise that I will do all in my power to live up to the examples shown by my predecessors,' she said. 'Of course, I could never fill their shoes – mine tend to have three-inch heels and to be rather more colourful – but I walk in their footsteps.' She went on:

I lay claim to being the only Member of Parliament ever to have worked as a home carer. I have known the insecurity of zero-hours contracts myself, as a worker, and also the insecurity of the people who depend on our care … A care worker becoming a Member of

Parliament: that is real aspiration for you. Perhaps I am also the only Member who, at the age of sixteen and pregnant, was told in no uncertain terms that I would never amount to anything. If only those people could see me now!

She added:

Many Members on both sides of this House will have cause to be thankful for the care the NHS has provided. One of my sons owes his life to our NHS. He was born at just twenty-three weeks' gestation. He clung to life for months in an intensive care unit in Manchester's St Mary's hospital. He finally pulled through thanks to the care of our NHS staff. Members may therefore understand that I will be watching intently how this Government treat our NHS over the next five years both as an MP and as a mother, and let me give a warning – an angry mother is someone you just don't want to tangle with.

Summing up she said 'I will always tell it how it is – my constituents deserve no less – and I will do so in my own little northern way. I also have a message from my constituents to the Treasury Bench: stop privatising and selling off our NHS.'

A week later, nominations opened for those wishing to stand to be the next Labour leader. Rayner was one of sixty-eight Labour MPs who backed Andy Burnham, the 45-year-old Manchester MP who had served in the governments of Tony Blair and Gordon Brown. Burnham had stood to be Labour leader in 2010, coming fourth out of five candidates on that occasion. In the 2015 contest, each candidate needed the support of at least thirty-five MPs to make it to the members' vote. With the party in the political doldrums, Burnham was expected to be pitched against just two others: Yvette Cooper and Liz Kendall. He was widely considered to be the favourite. Yet at 11.58 a.m. on 15 June, two minutes before the poll closed and to the surprise of many commentators, Jeremy Corbyn joined the trio on the ballot having secured the nominations of thirty-six MPs.

It was reported at the time that Corbyn, a hard-left backbench MP of thirty-two years' standing who had a contentious relationship with the IRA and Hamas, had only scrambled onto the final list. Twelve MPs who did not actually support him had agreed to 'lend' him their vote in order to broaden the debate that they felt needed to be had by the Labour Party if it was to return to power as a unified force. One of the twelve was the veteran MP Margaret Beckett. By 22 July, when Corbyn had become a major contender thanks to Len McCluskey and the Unite union having switched their support to his campaign, Beckett admitted to the BBC that she was a 'moron' for having backed him.[8] As will become clear, however, it could be argued that Angela Rayner owes her subsequent career to Beckett and the eleven others who endorsed Corbyn that June. On 12 September, it was announced that Corbyn had won the leadership election by a landslide, achieving 59.5 per cent of the available vote. Burnham came a distant second with just 19 per cent. This result marked the beginning of four years of upheaval for the Labour Party – a period through which Rayner would be given the opportunity to shine. Had Burnham or one of the other more moderate candidates become leader, however, it is not at all clear that she would have risen as quickly up Labour's ranks as she was about to do.

•   •   •

After being elected as an MP for the first time in May 2015, Rayner was quick to try to make her name, speaking on nine occasions in the Commons Chamber during her first full month in Parliament. One intervention – a Point of Order – concerned a visit that the Health Secretary, Jeremy Hunt, had made to Tameside General Hospital in her constituency without notifying her first. She took umbrage at this and wrote to David Cameron about it. She believed that Hunt was in breach of the ministerial code, and she was backed by the Commons Speaker, John Bercow. The Department of Health denied the allegation and the row, such as it was, soon fizzled out. Yet her very public objection to Hunt's presence without her knowledge certainly showed that she was serious about the promise she had made in her maiden speech to 'always tell it how it is'.

She also took positions that some felt were rather more contradictory. In July, she abstained, along with 183 other Labour MPs, on the second reading of the government's Welfare Reform and Work Bill. The main changes proposed by this Bill were reducing the household welfare cap from £26,000 to £23,000, abolishing child poverty targets, cuts to child tax credits, cuts to Employment and Support Allowance and cuts to housing benefit for young people. A few days before the vote, however, the recommendation of the Independent Parliamentary Standards Authority (IPSA) that MPs' salaries should increase from £67,000 to £74,000 – a rise of 10 per cent – had been endorsed by David Cameron among others. Although some new Labour MPs spoke out against this pay rise, including Tulip Siddiq and Catherine West, Rayner does not appear to have done so publicly.

Inevitably, the main political story that summer revolved around Labour's leadership contest. As a new backbench MP with a lot to learn, Rayner's views on Jeremy Corbyn were neither widely sought nor well known. But one former colleague is adamant that she quickly hedged her bets.

It's known she backed Andy Burnham in the leadership election, but this sounds maybe more significant than perhaps it was, because there were quite a few people on the left who initially did that – especially because in the beginning Corbyn wasn't a candidate in the campaign. I suppose it does indicate how she was positioning herself.

Once Corbyn had received a sufficient number of nominations to stand, and when it became obvious that he would win, Rayner's class politics and connections to the unions stood her in good stead. The fact that she had also become close to Rebecca Long-Bailey, a solicitor who was about Rayner's age and also represented a constituency in the north-west, was not a hindrance either. Long-Bailey was one of Corbyn's thirty-six original backers. She and Rayner would go on to share a flat in London together during the week.

When Corbyn emerged victorious on 12 September 2015, it was announced that his deputy was to be Tom Watson, who had served in both Tony Blair's and Gordon Brown's governments. Watson's and Corbyn's different political views would become a source of friction at the top of the Labour Party over the next few years, but the fact that Rayner had not backed Watson to be deputy leader and had instead supported Angela Eagle – who came third – was undoubtedly an advantage, for it freed her from any tie she might have had to Watson and gave her greater credibility with the new leadership team. Rayner was immediately appointed a junior whip – her first frontbench post. There was nothing unique about this promotion. Indeed, she was one of several north-west MPs to be made a shadow minister or shadow whip that month, at least one of whom – Jeff Smith – was also new to the Commons. Moreover, Corbyn's first shadow Cabinet was something of a coalition in that it was populated by those from both wings of the party. But Rayner's elevation was obviously a vote of confidence in her, allowing her to get a foot on the ladder. And, because a whip is in many ways a manager who helps to organise parliamentary business, especially in relation to votes, the job was not without significance; the government had a thin majority.

Rayner's stock was rising and, in Corbyn's eyes, it was not harmed in any way when, straight after being made a whip, she used a Westminster Hall debate to speak out against the defence industry. As the chairman of the Stop the War Coalition until September 2015, Corbyn's opposition to the arms trade was well known. A couple of months later, she continued with this pacifist theme by voting against air strikes against ISIL in Syria, having given the House of Commons Chamber her opinion on this international issue. 'I do not believe that David Cameron has offered either a credible, or comprehensive, strategy for war,' she told MPs. 'It is based more on hope than experience. And after Iraq, we cannot make the same mistake in Syria.' Sixty-six Labour MPs voted in favour of the air strikes after Corbyn allowed them a free vote on the issue.

Rayner's closeness to Corbyn and the socialist project that he wished to pursue was evident to his inner circle straight away. After his election, one supportive parliamentary aide ranked Labour MPs' perceived loyalty to him on a scale they had devised. The Core Group were those who were closest to the new Labour leader; next came Core Group Plus; then Neutral But Not Hostile; followed by Core Group Negative; and then Hostile. A former colleague of Rayner's explains:

By the time Jeremy was leader, Angela backed his leadership and was part of the Core Group in Parliament. Jeremy was nominated by thirty-six MPs, the number needed to get on the ballot paper, but the Socialist Campaign Group – who made up his natural support base in Parliament – only had about twenty MPs. But others had backed him in order to have a debate within the party or because they wanted to secure themselves a job and wanted to ingratiate themselves with the membership. Someone like Emily Thornberry – who was a self-proclaimed Brownite – was part of the Core Group. There was a group of about thirty MPs who met regularly at the beginning of Jeremy's leadership and Angela was part of that. She was explicitly supportive of Jeremy as soon as he was elected.

As Rayner's first months in national politics drew to a close, she could certainly feel pleased with her progress. In one nimble leap she had gone from Stockport trade unionist to junior opposition whip in Westminster; she had successfully forged links to the Labour leadership; and she had begun the process of developing a personal brand. Even if she was a beneficiary of the peculiar circumstances that had rocketed Jeremy Corbyn into the Leader of the Opposition's office, she was close to the centre of power on the left in Britain, despite having been based for all thirty-five years of her life in the same few square miles of the north-west. With that said, when her biography appeared in *The Politicos Guide to the New House of Commons 2015*, which profiled all 177 new MPs, it did note the previously unknown achievement that she 'volunteered as a campaign worker for John Kerry at the 2004 presidential campaign.'[9] The profile was compiled by Tim Carr using open-source material. Rayner has never mentioned her time working for Kerry since, yet if Carr was mistaken, it does not appear that she has ever asked him to correct it.

It was not all plain sailing, however. In early November 2015, Rayner's reputation was dented thanks to one dubious decision she made in relation to her self-declared obsession with footwear. It was reported that she had used House of Commons-headed paper to complain to the manager of a shoe shop about his 'poor customer service' in relation to her attempt to buy a pair of £195 novelty Star Wars shoes with four-inch heels. She said she had ordered a pair of these shoes in advance and been told on the day they were released that the shop, called Irregular Choice, had sold out of them. This prompted her to write an angry (and error-strewn) letter on headed paper to the head of retail of the Brighton-based store, Daniel Theophanides. Her letter stated:

> I have been a customer of yours for several years and have bought many thousands of pounds worth of shoes ... This is not the sort of service I expect. I have only ever brought [sic] your shoes and I am loathed [sic] to do so again, or recommend your shoes to others. I am writing to let you know that treating customers in that way will only cost you more in the long term.[10]

A copy of the letter was also sent to the firm's head office, together with invoices for some of her previous purchases including a £100 pair of silver shoes with a pink and white lamb for a heel; and £115 Squeezy shoes with a gold teddy bear for a heel.

The Sun reported that Mr Theophanides was so 'shaken' by the letter's tone that he spent some time locating a pair of the Star Wars shoes in Rayner's size. When he telephoned her to let her know he had found some, she apparently 'ranted' at him before terminating the call. Mr Theophanides told the newspaper:

> I was personally very shocked. It was the wording of her letter on House of Commons headed paper. I wouldn't dream of writing a letter of complaint on company notepaper. The customer believed she was on a pre-order list but we had a strict rule that the shoes went to customers who came through the doors. But I decided I would put a call in and see what I could do. I found a pair in a shop in China. But when she returned my call, she didn't give me a chance to tell her. She said 'It's clear you're not going to listen to me' and hung up.

It may have seemed like a relatively trivial incident, but Mr Theophanides's instincts were in fact correct. Parliament has strict rules about MPs' use of headed notepaper being for official business only. It should not generally be used for personal correspondence. For a few days it seemed possible that the Commons authorities might inquire into the matter, but, luckily for Rayner, they chose not to do so. One former colleague says that some of those who worked for her soon began to expect this sort of conduct from their boss. 'Angela can be wild at times,' comments this person.

> Her judgement goes completely. The story about the Star Wars shoes is a classic example of what she could do. It was literally a case of 'Do you know who I am?' She became so jumped-up and entitled. It says it all. I was appalled at her behaviour, her treatment of people. She was like an unguided missile with no thought for anyone or for her own position as an elected representative.

She didn't think about the consequences. She was always the big 'I am'. She was already becoming too big for her boots at this point. What's remarkable is that she didn't learn the lesson from that.

The reference in her maiden speech to colourful shoes with three-inch heels took on a new significance. So, too, did her assurance that she would always 'tell it how it is … in my own little northern way'. Some who were close to Rayner were to find out eventually that this 'little northern way' was not necessarily as amusing or as mischievous as she had suggested. In the meantime, her rapid rise continued.

CHAPTER 6

THE DIVA

The year 2016 got off to a bumpy start for Jeremy Corbyn. Three of his shadow junior ministers – Jonathan Reynolds, Stephen Doughty and Kevan Jones – resigned abruptly in protest at two senior colleagues, Pat McFadden and Maria Eagle, being removed from their jobs covering Europe and Defence respectively. Labour sources tried to play down the row, but there was no mistaking that an ideological battle was being fought in the open – not least after the shadow Chancellor, John McDonnell, described the trio of quitters as 'a right-wing clique'. Corbyn had to replace every departee, and this in turn prompted a wider reorganisation of his shadow team that took far longer to complete than anybody had anticipated. One newspaper calculated that the reshuffle dragged on for sixty-five hours and fifty-eight minutes. Corbyn reportedly claimed that his 'great failing in life is to listen to everybody at whatever great length they wish to speak'.[1] Not that Angela Rayner had cause to complain about the protracted discussions. She was a beneficiary of them, being promoted on 7 January to the post of shadow Work and Pensions Minister.

The reality was that Corbyn and his lieutenants regarded this minor crisis as an opportunity to reshape the Labour front bench after what had been a shotgun shadow Cabinet construction the previous September. 'There was an attempt to bring on members of the Core Group, which comprised members of the Socialist Campaign Group plus actively supportive left-of-centre MPs in the PLP,' recalls one figure with a ringside seat. 'Angela was one of those and that's how she got the shadow pensions brief.' Although Corbyn and his allies had been in a fairly small minority when his first shadow team was assembled, particularly in terms of policy making and policy development, he was urged by those closest to him to turn sharply leftwards at this fork in the road in order to honour the mandate he had been given by the 250,000 Labour members who had voted for him. The ensuing sense of the different wings of the party being in competition with each other inevitably led to disenchantment among some in the shadow Cabinet, though. By late January, Corbyn's head of policy, Neale Coleman, had resigned. Having previously worked for Boris Johnson when he was Mayor of London, Coleman was seen by moderate Labour MPs as a significant loss. Yet even after it, Corbyn still wasn't able to behave in an entirely unconstrained fashion. 'Until this point those on Jeremy's side had found it very hard to make any real policy advances apart from over some very basic things like austerity and rail nationalisation,' says one senior Labour source. 'Then there was a kind of interregnum when Neale Coleman left soon after the reshuffle. Jeremy was blocked by the bureaucracy at what was then Labour HQ in Southside from appointing a new policy chief. So there was little real change or development in policy at that time.'

Throughout this period of struggle, Rayner faced a similarly challenging task in getting to grips with her new job. The shadow Work and Pensions Secretary – and her immediate boss – was

Owen Smith, a Welshman who had previously worked as a BBC producer and lobbyist for the pharmaceutical firm Pfizer. Although Smith had only been in the Commons since 2010, he was known to have designs on becoming Labour leader himself and he was protective of his turf. This would have made it difficult for Rayner to make any headway, even in more benign times. 'She was a new MP and it's rare to be on the front bench so quickly,' observes one former colleague.

> Her being on the front bench reflected the fact that the PLP was very out of kilter politically with Jeremy and the mass of the membership in terms of what had been voted for at the conference and among the membership. Angela's promotion was part of an attempt by Jeremy to move up the actively supportive MPs who'd been elected in 2015 – especially working-class MPs, all of whom joined the Socialist Campaign Group. She was very supportive and co-operative from the start. Her joining the front bench was an attempt to better reflect Jeremy's leadership and his support within the party.

It appears that Rayner tried her best to familiarise herself with the fiendishly complicated world of annuities, retirement funds and fiscal consolidation and even asked to be left alone to master this task over the long term for the good of the party. In June 2016, *Corporate World* magazine published an interview with her in which she said:

> One of the conversations I had with Jeremy when I took on the role was 'Do not move me again. If I am going to learn all this stuff, work with the individuals and get us to a position where we

can establish half a page in the manifesto, I want some commitment that I'm going to be here for a while.' And Jeremy said 'You will be here as long as I am.'

And yet, despite her best efforts, those who worked around her at the time say it was not her natural forte. 'She gave the impression of being across her brief, but it was all skin deep,' says another former colleague.

> She didn't have any affinity for the subject at all. But she made a decent fist of it, because she's good at that – she's good at presenting an image of competence. Quite a lot of the time she was bullshitting like crazy. Someone would say something technical and complicated at a meeting, and a few minutes later she would regurgitate it as if it was her idea. She was very quick and good at that. But you could almost see her frantically pedalling under the desk because she was trying to keep up with stuff. Some of the meetings she sat in on were turgid, really, and arcane and full of jargon that no sane person would understand anyway. She worked hard to give the impression she knew what she was talking about but it was all an act, really, albeit quite a convincing one.

She found other ways to make a contribution, however, for example using one Commons debate on education, skills and training to share with MPs further details about her background. She explained that she felt 'an obligation' to expand upon what she had said about herself during her maiden speech a year previously in order that the lives of others might be improved. As she admitted:

> I was a NEET – not in education, employment or training – and

I had no GCSEs at grade A to C; and, as I said, I had a baby at 16. School, for me, was not a place where you went to be educated, but a place where you got away from your parents for a couple of hours while they got some respite from you, and where you were able to see your mates. Rather tragically, it was also the place where I got a hot dinner. I often did not have a hot meal when I went home, and I often went to school without having had breakfast, so getting to lunchtime was quite tricky for me.[2]

If anything, her words strongly suggested that her principal interest lay not in work and pensions, but in the field of education.

Although she has spoken with pride about the support she was able to show for the Women Against State Pension Inequality (WASPI) campaign, which fights for women born in the 1950s who are affected by the changes to the state pension age, Rayner's short tenure covering work and pensions was in any case overshadowed by the Brexit referendum. She played no major role for the Labour Party as it wrestled with this national debate and in fact in late April 2016 was more concerned with joining junior doctors on a picket line outside St Thomas's Hospital in London. She posed for pictures alongside shadow Cabinet colleagues including her flatmate, Rebecca Long-Bailey; Richard Burgon; and Clive Lewis while patients arriving for appointments realised they had been cancelled. Rayner had also been busy house hunting in her constituency that spring, eventually settling on a four-bedroom detached property that has what one friend says is a 'massive' garden. Land Registry records show that the house was bought three days after she was on the picket line – and on the same day that Mark Rayner sold 126 Lowndes Lane in Stockport for £145,250. The price paid for the new house was £375,000 plus stamp duty. Only Angela Rayner's name featured on the deeds, though in October 2022 'notice of home rights' was granted in favour of Mark Rayner under the Family Law Act 1996 following the breakdown of the couple's marriage.

When it came to the Brexit vote, Rayner chose to back Remain. This was an interesting decision given the strength of anti-EU feeling in the north-west, where a clear majority of voters backed Leave. In Ashton-under-Lyne, of course, UKIP's support in 2015 had soared by 17 per cent to 8,500 votes, a number that could not be ignored by Rayner. This may explain why she put out a message on Twitter a few days after it was announced that the Leave side had won, saying: 'Democratic vote to leave EU taken by voters in the UK, Jeremy Corbyn worked as hard as anybody to get a Remain vote, now is the time to unite.'

Her words were carefully chosen. At this time, there was dismay among some of Corbyn's senior Labour Party colleagues that his stance on Brexit had been far less robust than they would have liked. Most, if not all, members of his shadow Cabinet had voted for Remain, and they believed that he had done almost nothing to promote their view around the country. Some of them felt a genuine sense of anguish over the result. Others even suspected that in the privacy of the voting booth, he had backed Leave. As Corbyn's Euroscepticism stretched all the way back to the 1975 referendum on Britain's EEC membership, which he had voted against, his shadow Cabinet cannot have been surprised by his half-heartedness. Of even greater concern to them, though, was their belief that David Cameron's resignation as Prime Minister on the morning of 24 June might trigger a snap general election. They had concluded long before that Corbyn becoming Labour leader had been a disaster for the party. His truculence during the Brexit campaign had merely reinforced the idea in their minds that he was so weighed down by ideological baggage he wouldn't have a hope of being able to fight – and win – at the ballot box. For these reasons, as well as his perceived tolerance of extremist groups such as the IRA and Hamas, they harboured an urgent desire to dislodge him.

On 26 June, three days after the plebiscite, Hilary Benn, the shadow Foreign Secretary with whom Corbyn had always had a very uneasy working relationship, was sacked for telling him he had lost confidence in his leadership. Benn's departure inspired a further eleven of his shadow Cabinet colleagues to resign that day. As Corbyn was lining up their replacements, the plotting against him continued. On 27 June, a further eight shadow Cabinet members quit. But that was not the end of the rebellion. That afternoon, as Corbyn was putting the finishing touches to his new shadow team, Labour MPs in a different part of the parliamentary estate were organising a no-confidence motion in his leadership. When Corbyn released his list to the press early that evening, Rayner's name was on it. She had received a promotion to become shadow Minister for Women and Equalities.

As the list reached reporters, Rayner was to be found addressing a hastily arranged pro-Corbyn rally taking place in Parliament Square. A senior colleague remembers the event well:

Jeremy should really have resigned that night, but a stage had been put up and the next I know, Angela's on this stage defending Jeremy with a fist in the air like a hard-left comrade. I remember thinking: 'What on earth is going on here?' She was a moderately sensible, UNISON-backed official, and she'd just gone all rancid and then she ended up in the shadow Cabinet.

Another former Labour MP adds:

There's footage of her with a clenched fist and they're all chanting: 'Corbyn, Corbyn.' Seventy per cent of the PLP wanted rid of Corbyn. The whole thing was terrible. Women MPs were very unhappy about Angela's support of Corbyn on the platform. The chief whip, Rosie Winterton, told me: 'Angela Rayner's been in here in tears.' Somebody had spoken to Rayner and told her it was outrageous that she was at the rally. I don't know who spoke to her. But she was in tears because people were upset with her for going on it.

This story is backed up by another source, who says:

In certain parliamentary circles, they were absolutely livid with her. Some MPs have never forgiven her. On the night of that event in Parliament Square, there were all these Labour MPs who'd given up their frontbench roles, who were being fired at by Twitter trolls and Len McCluskey, and this colleague of theirs who'd only just been elected was on stage. And then it was like she [pretended] she didn't know what she was doing. She went to see the chief whip in tears, saying: 'Some Labour MPs are being horrible to me.' And it was the first time she'd ever been challenged. All of a sudden there was a reaction to something she'd done. She wasn't aware that that would be the reaction.

Perhaps her tears were not so surprising. Others have said they sensed that Rayner had not made many friends within the parliamentary party by this point and was even regarded as 'a bit of a loner' by some.

However thin-skinned she showed herself to be on that occasion, she was not upset for long. On 28 June, the no-confidence motion against Corbyn passed by 172 votes to forty. Other leaders might have thrown in the towel at that point, but Corbyn refused to do so, pointing out that the ballot had 'no constitutional legitimacy' because MPs do not choose the Labour leader, the party's members do. He said that to resign would be to 'betray' the 250,000 people who voted for him. Only a formal leadership contest in line with the party's rules would put his future to the test. The Labour-supporting *Daily Mirror* joined the many calls for him to step down that day, with an editorial comment insisting that filling dozens of vacancies with 'inexperienced lightweights' was like 'using a toothpick to prop up a collapsing skyscraper'.[3] The newspaper said Corbyn's attempt at 'clinging to power increasingly looks like an act of vanity'. On 29 June, the last member of the shadow Cabinet to resign was the shadow Education Secretary, Pat Glass. Remarkably, Glass had been appointed to this post only two days earlier having been brought in to replace Lucy Powell. Glass's sudden exit caused a new headache for Corbyn, but Rayner cured it when she agreed to succeed Glass, becoming the third MP to hold the post in the space of a week. In doing so, she had secured her second shadow brief in forty-eight hours.

In 2018, Rayner explained to Nick Robinson of the BBC why she stuck by Corbyn at this time. 'I thought it was an injustice not to back him,' she said. 'I wasn't a Corbynista, but I thought: "This is the right thing to do." I felt he hadn't been given time or the opportunity to do what he'd been elected to do. He was elected with a good mandate and I thought: "Come on, give him a chance."'[4]

Quite apart from the political pressure Corbyn faced, to say nothing of the growing expectation that he would be forced to resign eventually, he also had to confront the very practical problem of staffing the front bench so that basic parliamentary duties and functions could continue. Alongside the twenty-one shadow Cabinet resignations, dozens of shadow ministers and parliamentary private secretaries had also quit, meaning that some sixty MPs stood down in the space of a few days. Some who were close to Corbyn at the time freely admit now that, even if Rayner had had three A-Levels and a degree, it is highly improbable that she would ever have found herself being given this brief at any other time, simply because she had so few political miles on the clock. They accept that she profited from the mutiny.

'It was an emergency,' says one senior Labour figure who had a hand in reacting to it.

Angela was one of several MPs who had supported Jeremy and hadn't resigned and because the shadow Cabinet had to be filled ASAP, a whole raft of people were promoted, including her and Rebecca Long-Bailey and Richard Burgon, in a way that wouldn't have happened in the normal run of things. Usually, MPs gain experience over a period of years. The party didn't have that luxury, so it happened fast. People either sank or swam. The pressure on Angela was great. This is no reflection on her abilities, but to be able to do a job like that a year after becoming an MP – and with no experience – is a big ask. She wasn't the only one. Others were in the same boat. Others sank, but Angela swam. It was a steep learning curve. But she is very determined, ambitious and competent, so she had the ability to succeed.

The shadow education brief is considered one of the most important for any opposition party, but, given that surveys show those who work in schools and universities to be more sympathetic to the left, it is of particular significance in the Labour Party. Previous holders of the post in recent decades include Neil Kinnock, Jack Straw, David Blunkett and Ed Balls. A former colleague of Rayner recalls that she felt no fear in accepting the job and that, ironically, her own lack of achievement in the field of public exams was felt by her to be a card she could play to her advantage. 'Education was much better for Angela than the work and pensions job was,' remembers this person. 'There was less detail, less specialist knowledge needed. She was hard-working and she was driven, and she could just shoot from the hip.'

Within a week, she began doing exactly that, attacking the government over teachers' pay and conditions and refusing to condemn strike action called by the National Union of Teachers. Instead, she advocated talks to 'thrash out a better deal for the next generation, which is what every parent wants', and said: 'This Tory government is letting down parents, pupils and teachers. On their watch, class sizes have soared and the number of unqualified teachers in our classrooms is up.'[5] When she obtained some figures that summer showing that two out of five trainee maths teachers did not study the subject beyond GCSE level, and called this a 'Tory teaching crisis', some sniped that it was ironic for a shadow Education Secretary who had no GCSEs above a D grade to be making political capital in this way. Such jibes were, seemingly, brushed aside by Rayner.

On 11 July, Angela Eagle, whom Rayner had backed to be deputy leader in 2015, decided to formally challenge Corbyn in a leadership election. Two days later, Eagle was joined on the ballot by Owen Smith, Rayner's former boss. By 19 July, Eagle had withdrawn from the contest, turning it into a head-to-head scrap. Two months later, Corbyn emerged from it in a stronger position than when he had won the leadership race the previous September, securing the votes of 313,209 Labour Party members and increasing his share of the vote from 59.5 per cent to 61.8 per cent. Thanks to this result, Rayner's own position was safe, even if she had recently generated anger in sections of the press after a 2014 video surfaced of her colleague, the shadow Chancellor John McDonnell, telling an audience of trade unionists of his desire that Margaret Thatcher should have been assassinated. Rayner was seen in the video laughing as McDonnell spoke about this.

Just as Labour was embroiled in an internal struggle of its own making, the repercussions of David Cameron's resignation the morning after the referendum result had been troubling the Conservative Party. After a leadership contest that was ultimately abandoned before party members had an opportunity to vote, Theresa May was crowned Tory leader and automatically became Prime Minister on 13 July. A few weeks later, it was reported that May wanted to open a series of new grammar schools, thereby expanding selection at secondary school level. For many in the Labour Party, academic selection is considered immoral. A belief exists that it creates what amounts to a publicly funded elite and that grammar schools help to reinforce social divisions – though, ironically, forty-nine serving Labour MPs, including Corbyn, had attended a grammar school themselves at this point. This marked another early test for Rayner as shadow Education Secretary. She was considered to have passed it easily enough: 'Selection belongs in the dustbin of history and has no place in modern society,' Rayner said in response to May's putative plan. 'There must be no going back.'[6] One former colleague remembers that she was particularly motivated to take on this battle because of a communications adviser she had recruited, Matt Finnegan. 'She did a lot of work in particular on grammar schools,' they say.

She got hold of the grammar schools issue and she and Matt Finnegan milked it for all it was worth. It played perfectly to her base in the party. So it was more grist to her mill. She could tackle it because she didn't need to know much detail or any of the technicalities. She could safely rely on an ideological attack. Of course, because of her lack of ability with the written word, the plethora of by-lined articles and press statements that issued from her office at this time contained very little direct involvement from her.

That September, Rayner addressed the Trades Union Conference in Brighton. Her speech centred on education, as she again hit out at Theresa May's grammar school policy. 'Not so much education, education, education as segregation, segregation, segregation!' she told delegates.[7] Soon after, the Labour Party Conference was held in Liverpool. The announcement on its first day that Corbyn had defeated Owen Smith and been re-elected as leader ensured that his cohort was able to bask in his reflected glory, and Rayner was no exception. She gave two speeches. During the first, to the Labour Women's Conference in her capacity as the shadow Secretary of State for Women and Equalities, she spoke of her own troubled childhood and that of her mother, who was in attendance, also using the occasion to turn her attention to the veteran MP Margaret Beckett. Noting that Beckett was born in her constituency of Ashton-under-Lyne and had cut her political teeth there, Rayner announced the launch of the Dame Margaret Beckett Prize for Public Speaking for teenage girls. Looked at one way, this was certainly paradoxical. As mentioned in the previous chapter, the year before, Beckett had called herself a 'moron' for having backed Jeremy Corbyn's leadership bid. Yet it was only because of Corbyn's leadership that

Rayner had risen so quickly up Labour's ranks and was addressing the Labour Women's Conference in the first place. Incidentally, the week after Labour's conference, and just three months after taking up the post, Rayner ceased to hold the women and equalities brief.

After her speech, Rayner organised a dinner attended by her staff, her mother and some constituency activists. Some felt it shone a light on an aspect of her character that they found unappealing.

We were all told we had to go. We had no choice in the matter. It was part of the job. At the end of the night the bill arrived and it was split, so we had to pay for our own dinner. Under any other circumstances, I don't think any of us really wanted to be there. That just showed how tight she could be. Eyebrows were raised. She didn't buy drinks for staff either. It was noticeable. At the very least, one could say she's careful with money.

During her first formal speech to the main Labour conference as the shadow Education Secretary the next day, she again attacked the notion of academic selection and then she claimed to have been mocked for the way she speaks. 'Some Tories look down their noses at me because, as you can hear, I wasn't born with a plum in my mouth,' she said.

I get snobbery too from some pundits and commentators, from the hate-filled trolls on social media. Some of the Tories say: 'She left school at sixteen, she doesn't have a university degree, what does she know about education?' I say, I may not have a degree – but I have a Masters in real life.

As already discussed, some Tory MPs may have considered her appointment as shadow Education Secretary to be incongruous, given her educational background. (Similar remarks emanated when the Conservative MP Gavin Williamson, a graduate of the University of Bradford, was appointed Education Secretary in 2019.) There is also a strong sense that certain MPs, and perhaps civil servants, wrote off her chances of succeeding in this post. Yet those who are close to Rayner say this underdog status spurred her on. As one former colleague says: 'At every point she has been underestimated or patronised, and that puts her in such a position of power. She thrives off it.'

With that said, even if the list of naysayers that she reeled off in her speech was accurate, what she perhaps did not realise was that, even at this early stage of her political career, there were others in her own party who were also inclined to look down on her for a range of reasons. Some objected to the fact that she had been elevated despite not appearing to have a coherent political philosophy. Others thought she would be out of her depth. A waspish observation circulated in Labour Party circles that 'the only test she's ever passed is a pregnancy test.' A political colleague says: 'It shows they don't quite know what the back story is. They feel it's overplayed. They respect her, but they cannot respect the way she's prospered. They've almost got more respect for the Corbynistas, who at least have some ideological belief.'

Others who worked with Rayner say that, especially after the Star Wars shoes episode, they also began to detect further signs of what they took to be self-importance. One former colleague recalls:

There was a pomposity about her. At the conference in Liverpool we were walking across to a meeting and she suddenly stopped in the middle of the forecourt and exclaimed: 'Where are all my staff?' I explained that everyone was busy with work for the conference, and she said: 'Well they should be here with me.' And I said: 'They've got stuff to do.' And she said: 'But I look like I haven't got any staff. I'm Billy No-Mates. It's just me and you and it doesn't look good.' She wanted people with her wherever she went – a sort of entourage – to big her up so that people would take notice of her. That was the ego going mad. Staff started to take the mickey behind her back and began calling her 'The Diva'. We'd say: 'What's The Diva up to today?' or 'You'll never guess what The Diva's doing now'.

This alleged desire to present herself to the outside world as a woman of influence and power was not restricted to the parameters of that year's Labour Party conference, where Jo Cox, the Labour MP who had been murdered a few months before by Thomas Mair, a far right extremist, was remembered. This source continues:

She was doing this in the constituency as well. She wouldn't want to be on her own at any public appearance. She wanted an entourage with her wherever she went, even when it wasn't necessary, because she thought it looked better to people in the party or in the community. She wanted to make a splash. Staff complained that it was taking them away from the work they had to do – dealing with casework, the media, answering the phone and emails and so on – because they had to nursemaid Angela constantly. I said to her: 'This can't carry on, you need to drive yourself or ask [your husband] Mark to drive you,' and she went absolutely spare. Then she mentioned Jo Cox's murder as the excuse for her to be accompanied all the time. Of course it was very difficult to argue with her once Jo Cox's name had been mentioned. It was very clever of her, manipulative and controlling.

Corbyn's successful second leadership campaign in the summer of 2016 had been built around a ten-point platform that was seen by his team as an attempt to create the core of what would become the next Labour Party manifesto. After it was announced at the 2016 conference that he had been re-elected by the Labour membership, the plan was adopted by the party's ruling body, the National Executive Committee, and then the conference. Covering employment, workers' rights, the environment, housing, tax, the NHS and foreign policy, it was a socialist blueprint for Britain's future. 'The advantage of it was that it gave the basis for the shadow Cabinet to fill that policy framework and do all the things Jeremy hadn't been able to do before the coup,' explains a source. One of its principal ideas was the creation of what Corbyn called a National Education Service. Very much in the tradition of the National Health Service, it advocated universal public childcare; the restoration of free education for all; and a guarantee of quality apprenticeships and adult skills training. 'Jeremy had talked about a National Education Service and Angela built on that effectively in the run up to the 2017 election,' says this source.

In fact Corbyn used his own party conference speech in 2016 to set out how his new education scheme might be funded, as he explained that he wanted the National Education Service to become as important as the NHS. 'To help pay for a National Education Service, we will ask you pay a little more in tax,' he said.

We've already started to set out some of this, pledging to raise corporation tax by less than 1.5 per cent to give an Education Maintenance Allowance to college students and grants to university students so that every young learner can afford to support themselves as they develop skills and get qualifications.[8]

Rayner personally was singled out for praise by Corbyn in his speech, as he declared 'What a great job Angela Rayner is doing in opposing [the Tories].' This drew loud applause. Not only did his support for her appear to be rock solid, but this public acknowledgement also helped to guarantee that there would be more interest in Rayner generally. She was still capable of asserting her independence, however. At one point during Corbyn's speech, he explained why he felt he had been right in making his recent apology for the Iraq War. Although many MPs around him stood to applaud this sentiment, Rayner, along with Andy Burnham (who resigned as shadow Home Secretary that day) and the party's General Secretary, Iain McNicol, stayed seated.

Nevertheless, as 2016 drew to a close it seemed that under Jeremy Corbyn, Rayner had a bright future. Former colleagues say she met regularly every Monday night in Westminster with members of Corbyn's circle but tried to keep it secret from her colleagues. What Corbyn probably didn't realise was that she was not always as supportive of him behind the scenes as he might have assumed. Fascinatingly, one former colleague remembers Rayner mocking his brand of 21st-century socialism. 'She did say to me at various times: "These people are Trots,"' reveals this person.

But then she'd serve alongside them anyway. Ambition is the key to Angela. That was where the power was at that time in the Labour Party so she played the game with Corbyn. She would do anything to further her own career and position. She's really driven by that thirst for position and power.

Corbyn is even said to have begun to think of her from this stage as leadership material. Rayner's own thoughts on her prospects were not quite so lofty, but the same source says that she did believe that she could become deputy leader of the Labour Party within a few years and was already working towards achieving that goal.

CHAPTER 7

RISING STAR OF THE YEAR

According to one of Angela Rayner's former colleagues, she developed something of a fascination with the media after becoming an MP. Like many politicians, she was well aware of its potential as a marketing tool to help further her career but, more than that, this person says it fed her ego. She even thought she might be able to make money out of it on top of her MP's salary. 'If the BBC wanted her to do something, they'd have to send a car,' this source remembers. 'She'd insist on that. She had ideas well above her station. She did ask me once at the start of her career as an MP if she was going to get paid for an interview. I said: "No" and she said: "Why not? It's my time."'

In January 2017, she was invited by the *Huffington Post* to give one of her first lengthy interviews on camera. She turned up alone and over a period of half an hour spoke about her background in more detail than she had done previously. She was also able to set out certain strands of her political philosophy that strongly suggested she did not want to be labelled a Corbynite. 'Ideology never put food on my table,' she said in one evidently heartfelt passage.

I talk about Tony Blair's tenure, because it changed my life, it gave
my children a life that I could never have dreamt of having and I
want us to get back to that. There was a council house waiting for
me when I had Ryan, there was a welfare state. I never put into
the system before I took out – I was on income support before I'd
even paid a penny of tax. Thank you to the taxpayers of the UK
because instead of taking my child off me like they used to in the
'50s and '60s to single parents at that age, you let me be a mum to
my son and my son is at college, he's working, he's a great young
person, you'd be proud of him, I'm proud of him and I pay taxes
now, and continue to pay taxes now because of what you did for
me. It was a tremendous thing and that's what Labour stands for,
that's what you do when you're in power.[1]

She remained relatively unknown to the general public at this stage,
but the idea of any MP acknowledging taxpayers in such a personal
manner was certainly unusual. That Rayner, who had already been
labelled a hard-left socialist by some journalists, also praised Blair
allowed some Tories to wonder privately if she might have more
in common with them than with Jeremy Corbyn's Labour Party.
This interview also strongly suggested that she was happiest talking about herself and her background and that if the conversation
moved onto hard politics, she was prone to personalising her answers rather than discussing bigger ideas or theories. This did not
worry her, though, and her decision to talk to the *Huffington Post*
was almost certainly not coincidental. Rumours about Corbyn's
leadership persisted at this point, and succession planning was
thought to be underway. Rayner's flatmate in London, fellow north-
west MP Rebecca Long-Bailey, had already established herself as
one of his potential successors, and there can be little doubt that

her ambitions rubbed off on Rayner. Quite quickly they were being spoken of as the representatives of the Labour Party's future.

This idea was reinforced in early February 2017 when Clive Lewis, the shadow Business Secretary, quit his post after defying Corbyn to vote against the triggering of Article 50, which began the Brexit process. Long-Bailey was asked to replace Lewis. This was a significant promotion, confirming her status as a kindred spirit of the shadow Chancellor, John McDonnell, and of Corbyn. And what of Rayner? Soon afterwards, Corbyn visited Greater Manchester, where he was asked by reporters whether Long-Bailey or Rayner might take over as leader. He spoke effusively, saying he felt that either of them could do so. 'They're absolutely brilliant,' he said. 'I came on the train last night from London with Becky. She's a great friend, she's an absolutely brilliant person. She's done a superb job in the Treasury. Angela came in to do education and I think she's made such a mark and such a difference … Angela is brilliant.'[2]

Not everybody seemed to agree. That weekend, the *Sunday Times* concentrated its attention on the claims that Corbyn's time as leader was coming to an end and that his allies were plotting to line up his replacement. The newspaper obtained a leaked copy of a focus group report organised by Labour's pollster BMG Research, in which Manchester-based voters were asked for their views about the two young frontbenchers. The responses to Rayner were said to be 'overwhelmingly negative'. She was considered 'not likeable', a 'bit charity shop-looking' and 'weird', with one participant suggesting voters would not take her seriously. The group was far better disposed to Long-Bailey, describing her as 'passionate', 'genuine', 'sincere' and 'very smart', although some saw her as 'aggressive' and 'rough'.[3]

Who leaked this information? One former colleague believes it came from Corbyn's office. 'It was deliberately leaked by the leader's office to discredit Angela and bolster Long-Bailey,' says this person.

> They never really trusted Angela. I think they always had a sus-picion about her. I don't think it was a political thing. I think it was more a question of: 'Who is she? What does she believe in?' When this story dropped on the Saturday night, all hell broke loose. Angela went bonkers. She was ranting and raving to me. The next day I had to pretty much comfort her and persuade her not to resign, which she was threatening to do. She was distraught. Lying in her dressing gown, it looked as though she hadn't slept all night. She looked awful. She was adamant that she was going to resign. She was saying: 'I've played the game with these bastards and this is what they've done to me. I'm giving up now.' It was a huge over-reaction, really. She was terribly hurt – particularly by the charity shop description. She repeated it endlessly to me over the next few days. She was adamant that she was going to quit and then a couple of days later she said she'd had a word with Corbyn's office and then it suddenly blew over as quickly as it had blown up.

If the contrasting feedback publicised to great effect by the *Sunday Times* generated any tension between the flatmates, they did a good job of disguising it. A month later, on the afternoon of 22 March, a Muslim terrorist called Khalid Masood drove a car into pedestrians on Westminster Bridge, injuring fifty people, four of whom later died. He then ran into New Palace Yard on the parliamentary estate where he was confronted by PC Keith Palmer, who was unarmed. He confronted Masood and stalled him before being fatally stabbed. Masood was then shot dead by police. One Labour insider recalls:

Becky and Angie were always together. On the day of the West-minster attack, Parliament went into lockdown and the police made everyone go to their offices. There were forty or more members of staff plus Jeremy in one room for several hours with the lights off. It was packed to the gills. But Becky and Angela were in a different office, on their own. They were close.

The following month, on 18 April, Theresa May put an end to long-standing speculation by calling a general election. The next day, a vote was held in the House of Commons in which 522 MPs backed this course of action, with just thirteen MPs voting against it. Under the terms of the Fixed-term Parliaments Act, the threshold of two-thirds of MPs voting to dissolve Parliament had been met. Two weeks later the campaign began, with the poll scheduled to take place on 8 June. Entering the election, May had a working majority of seventeen seats. She told the BBC she hoped to achieve a larger majority to strengthen her hand in the Brexit negotiations.[4] With Labour, under Corbyn, having nosedived in the opinion polls, especially after losing Copeland to the Conservatives in a recent by-election – the first time since 1982 that the governing party had snatched a seat from the opposition – a large Tory majority was considered by many political pundits to be a forgone conclusion. As both main parties promised in their manifestos to honour the referendum result, the 2017 election was billed as the 'Brexit election'. It turned out to be rather different.

For Rayner personally, this was the first time as a sitting MP that she was seeking re-election, and she is said to have felt nervous about the prospect. 'In the run-up to the 2017 election everything was about Article 50,' says one former colleague.

Ashton-under-Lyne voted for Leave. Angela was fine with Labour's position, which was to respect the result and negotiate a jobs-first Brexit. She made clear in shadow Cabinet meetings that she was happy with this position. More than policy issues, the problem she had was media confidence. We went into the election twenty-four points behind and MPs were worried about retaining their seats and wanted to focus on their constituencies. But we needed frontbenchers who could be message carriers beyond Corbyn and John McDonnell. Angela was seen as a developing media performer and her voice was needed. She agreed to be a voice, but getting her to do it in practice was hard work.

Even for an experienced politician, facing the media can be difficult. Having to field questions on any topic, having to be on top of every issue at all times and having to know the party line on all policies is challenging. In a general election campaign, the pressure is even greater – and MPs are required to give interviews that are quite different from the type she had given to the *Huffington Post* in January. Indeed, in November 2016, Rayner's shaky grasp of economics had been exposed by Andrew Neil when she appeared on the BBC's *Daily Politics* programme. Under persistent questioning about raising corporation tax and capital gains tax structures, she gave such a poor account of herself that Neil gave up live on air, saying with barely concealed exasperation: 'You don't know, do you? You just don't know, do you? I'm lost.' Years later, this interview is still often posted on the internet by some of Labour's opponents to illustrate what they see as Rayner's incompetence.

During the 2017 election campaign, there were occasions when she performed perfectly competently, such as when she was sent onto the BBC Breakfast programme to pledge that Labour would

fund its £5.6 billion National Education Service by raising corporation tax from 19 per cent to 26 per cent. Yet according to one Labour
source, on those occasions when Rayner did not cry off, she did not
always cope as well as had been hoped.

> Sometimes there were genuine reasons for her absence, but trying
> to get her to do media in 2017, and even afterwards could be quite
> difficult. It was a lack of confidence and experience. She was very
> new to the job, she hadn't done much national TV. She wouldn't
> have been asked if people didn't think she could do it. She would
> worry she hadn't got the line on a particular topic – the briefing
> given to every MP. Because of the precarious position Jeremy
> was in before 2017 and the internal opposition to his leadership,
> there were problems about getting agreed briefings that actually
> reflected the positions the party held. Angela was anxious about
> that and there was a general lack of confidence. Sometimes she
> would agree to do media and then duck out of an interview. And
> sometimes it was to do with fear of losing her seat. MPs are given
> to bouts of anxiety about their seats.

Evidence of her losing her way was not hard to find. On one occasion during the campaign she was interviewed by Nick Ferrari
of LBC to announce a key education policy concerning class sizes.
Rayner said that under Labour, no child aged five to seven would
be in a class with more than thirty pupils. When Ferrari asked her
repeatedly how many children this would affect, she was unable to
answer. After a series of embarrassing exchanges in which Ferrari
had to remind Rayner that she was the shadow Education Secretary, he eventually answered his own question on her behalf – about
520,000 primary school pupils in England. 'Do you not think you

should have had that number?' Ferrari asked. Rayner replied: 'I'm not going to play that numbers game.' Later that day, she worsened the situation when questioned by other journalists about the interview by consistently calling Ferrari 'Nick Farage' and then blaming him for making an error with the figures.

All was not entirely smooth between Rayner and John McDonnell, either. While her focus was on schoolchildren, his seemed to be on those in higher education, especially after he pledged to scrap university tuition fees, a policy that some thought could cost as much as £11 billion.

'There were tensions between her and McDonnell and the shadow Treasury team over the amount of money allocated to the spending package for the 2017 manifesto between further education, schools, and non-university apprenticeships and the commitment to scrap tuition fees,' reflects one observer.

> Angela wanted greater commitment to spending on working-class kids when it came to education and training. She backed the abolition of tuition fees commitment, which was an important part of Labour's platform in 2017, but there was a class tension around it. That was an issue to some extent. I think it's quite revealing about her own priorities and about tensions in trying to stitch together an electoral and political coalition between the different parts of Labour's middle-class and working-class constituency.

Despite these bumps in the road, Labour's election campaign generally proved itself to be far more robust than most people had expected. At the beginning of the contest, the party's polling numbers were stuck at about 25 per cent. Matters were not helped when officials at the party's Southside HQ – most of whom were staunchly opposed to Corbyn's leadership – gave a briefing to the party saying that manifestos don't count and the best the party could hope for was a 2 per cent lift between then and polling day. As the weeks passed, however, a body of opinion formed that Theresa May had overestimated her personal popularity and that of her party.

The Tory campaign began to unravel when one of the proposals in the party's manifesto – that any elderly person with assets worth more than £100,000 would have to fund their own care if they became dependent but could defer payment until after death – was torn apart. It was swiftly labelled a 'dementia tax' and was widely denounced. Within a few days, May was forced into a humiliating U-turn, an almost unimaginable position for a governing party to find itself in. By comparison, Corbyn showed himself to be made of much sterner stuff. His campaign slogan 'For the Many Not the Few' was centred on increased public spending and it resonated, particularly with younger voters. His pledge to scrap university tuition fees was particularly popular. And he surprised many by showing himself to be an effective campaigner. Thousands attended his rallies. For the first time since the days of New Labour, there seemed to be considerable excitement around the country for the Labour Party. And because this so-called 'snap' election effectively lasted for almost eight weeks, Corbyn was given the time he needed to gain momentum. Day by day, the race tightened markedly.

The 2017 election has gone down in history as a disaster for the Conservatives. They lost thirteen seats while Labour gained thirty seats, ending up with 40 per cent of the vote on a swing of 9.6 per cent. The Tories' share of the vote had increased compared with 2015, but that was the only consolation in an otherwise bleak picture. Theresa May lost the majority she had inherited and found herself in charge of a minority government reliant upon the Democratic

Unionist Party for support. For Labour, all the received wisdom propagated by its officials at the start of the campaign was shown to be untrue. In Ashton-under-Lyne, Rayner secured 24,005 votes, increasing her majority by 539. Her nearest rival, the Conservative candidate Jack Rankin, managed to garner barely half as much support. The net result of the campaign was that Jeremy Corbyn's hand had been strengthened significantly. For the first time since becoming leader almost two years previously, he controlled the Labour Party machine.

The result seemed to put a spring in Rayner's step as well. Afterwards, she continued to be put forward as one of Labour's most prominent spokeswomen, appearing on most of the major television news programmes of the day. At that year's party conference in Brighton, her platform speech in front of a packed audience received rapturous applause as she pledged £500 million to reverse years of cuts to the Sure Start scheme. Yet some of her colleagues noticed that, as had been the case a year previously, she had relied to some degree on her own life experiences, as she spoke of her upbringing and of being a single mother. 'At sixteen I was out of school and looking for work but without qualifications to offer,' she said.

> I supported myself and my son as a care worker, looking after the elderly and disabled in their homes. Low qualifications meant low wages. No skills meant no security. As a trade unionist with UNISON, I could change that. Not just for myself, but for the carers I worked with, and the people we cared for. Workplace education meant we had the chance to learn more and earn more. Other people need that chance. So, our National Education Service will be life-long, providing for people at every stage of their life.[5]

One former colleague says her advisers tried to persuade her to 'change the record' and find new things to talk about, but she refused.

> We did say to her: 'Angela, we've got to move on from this stuff and focus on the future. You need to give them some idea of where you want to take people.' But she would always hark back to her hard-luck history because it was the failsafe method she used to disarm journalists or critics and for building up her reputation within the Labour Party. I always thought it was more underclass than working class. But when she told her back story at Labour meetings they would always lap it up, and she would say: 'It's catnip to them.' Those were her words. She was privately very dismissive of their response, but publicly she'd accept all the hugs and embraces people would give her as a self-proclaimed working-class heroine. She knew it played so well in the Labour Party.

Other colleagues noticed a growing confidence in her and a renewed interest in the possibilities of the media. In early November 2017, she was named the *Spectator* Rising Star of the Year. When accepting her award at the Rosewood Hotel in London, she apparently joked that she wasn't used to opulent dinners and hadn't seen so many knives on a table since a recent Stockport police amnesty. It was an amusing line, but it did suggest that she still felt like an outsider – or wanted to be thought of as such – despite having been in the shadow Cabinet for the past eighteen months. A few weeks later, she became a grandmother aged thirty-seven after her son, Ryan, and his partner became parents to their daughter, Lilith. In a move that was guaranteed to attract attention, Rayner announced the news in an early-morning tweet an hour after the baby was born, using the opportunity to let the public know that she had also decided to give herself the new portmanteau nickname 'Grangela'. She ended 2017 with an appearance on the BBC comedy panel programme *Have I Got News for You*, for which she was paid £1,500. One former MP says:

> From then on in, she was a bit of nightmare. She started talking about herself in the third person. She kept talking to people about 'Project Angela'. She had begun to believe the hype. Even her friends were saying: 'This is ridiculous, she thinks she's going to be a Labour leader.'

Another former colleague recalls:

> Overall, it's how she changed. Her ego expanded. It was always fairly substantial in the first place, but she became really high and mighty. The irony was not lost on us. She morphed into being someone who you wouldn't really have recognised. She became much more autocratic and arrogant. Staff members would tell stories about her. One memorable incident was when Angela was being driven in her constituency one Friday, going about constituency business. They came to a junction and another driver waved the car through and according to Rosie, her office manager, Angela said: 'Oh, they obviously recognise me.' Rosie just giggled about it. It showed Angela was deluded – she had delusions of grandeur. She just got carried away with herself and thought everyone knew who she was. She'd suddenly become quite formal with people who she'd previously been informal with, and you could see them thinking: 'What's going on here? Why has she suddenly changed?'

Rayner's final act of the year was to give an interview to the editor of *The Spectator*, Fraser Nelson, which was revealing in its way. The interview was published in the early days of 2018. While her life story once again formed the crux of the piece, she did give the impression of being more thoughtful than perhaps she had perhaps been given credit for. She disclosed that she had a photo of Theresa May hanging over her desk. 'That picture motivates me, in a strange way,' she said. She also made clear that, as well as trying to shift Labour's education policy by aiming her attention at primary rather than tertiary education, she had deliberately tried to put some distance between herself and Corbyn by 'refusing to sign a loyalty pledge demanded by Momentum, his personal campaign group'. Perhaps most strikingly, she spoke of how the state had failed white working-class children. Nelson wrote: 'Focusing on ethnic minorities and women's agendas, she says, has had a "negative impact" for white working-class boys.' Rayner was quoted as saying:

They have not been able to adapt. Culturally, we are not telling them that they need to learn and they need to aspire. They are under the impression that they don't need to push themselves, in the way that disadvantaged groups had to before. I think that is why there is a bit of a lag there. I think we need to do much more about the culture of white working class in this country.'[6]

This sentiment was probably closer to the views expressed by members of right-of-centre think tanks than it was to the thoughts of many prominent Labour MPs. It certainly set her apart from Corbyn's clique, most of whom not only lived in north London but were felt to be wedded to an intellectualised view of left-wing politics that some say is synonymous with that area. Coming a year after she had said it was important to have immigration controls, Rayner's politics were becoming increasingly difficult to categorise.[7] A feeling grew that, if anything, her opinions accorded with what could be called Old Labour, which is often deeply socially conservative in outlook. In the interview she did defend Labour's spending and borrowing plans, however, albeit bluntly. 'We are in different times, radical times where we need to have a real investment in Britain's future,' she said.

> Genuinely. I don't mean that as a slogan, I mean it as an economic strategy. It is a bit of a shit-or-bust strategy, I get that. It's a high-risk strategy. But all of Britain's great advancements in the past have been because we've had the gumption to take a risk.

Was she as freethinking and as trenchant as this in shadow Cabinet meetings? Two people who attended them at the time have differing memories of her behaviour in that setting. 'She ended up in the shadow Cabinet and basically didn't do the work,' says one.

> She didn't go to many meetings and it was a problem. Jeremy's office didn't get on particularly well with her, because she was erratic and she kept her own time. Her policy development was all reactive stuff. Around the shadow Cabinet table she never dived too deeply. She barely said a thing. Sometimes it's a strategic decision not to take part in a meeting. With her, I just don't think she thought it was worth her while.

On the other hand, another source says she could sometimes be a prominent performer. 'She would be there, sitting around that square table in the new shadow Cabinet room in the Norman Shaw North building each Tuesday at 10 a.m.,' says this person.

She could be outspoken. Not over the top, but she could speak strongly and be quite emotional in a controlled way. Not regularly, but I do remember that over Brexit a few times. She wasn't afraid to make critical comments about issues involving the leadership, but she was loyal to Jeremy generally. And she was on top of her brief. She felt passionately about issues like the educational maintenance allowance, investments in schools, her own background. She made the National Education Service her own project even though it came from Jeremy originally. She's got quite a stormy personality. She took umbrage at times. My relationship with her was good, but she did fall out with others.

Among those she had had a disagreement with by the end of 2017 was her long-time chief adviser, Matt Finnegan. He left her operation abruptly in circumstances that the Labour Party has been careful to ensure have never been made public. What Rayner probably didn't anticipate at the time, though, was that Finnegan would soon be plotting his revenge.

CHAPTER 8

BETRAYAL

The year 2018 began with the publication of an interview about Rayner's life and career that she had given to the *Sunday Times Magazine*. The journalist who was sent to Ashton-under-Lyne to speak to her used the opening paragraph of the article to tell readers she had felt worried when watching her subject posing for photographs outside in the freezing cold wearing only a short-sleeved dress. 'I'm fine,' Rayner is said to have replied when it was pointed out to her that the temperature was so low her skin might turn blue. 'Of course I'm fine, I'm northern, I'm hard.'[1] Behind the bravado, however, Rayner had a problem.

The acrimony between her and her recently departed special adviser, Matt Finnegan, was palpable. He and Rayner had worked closely together for several years, and he was a key member of her team. Before being hired by her he had spent fifteen years as a senior journalist on the *Manchester Evening News*, moved across to Tony Blair's press operation in Millbank during the 1997 general election campaign, been a Labour Party candidate and served as the communications director for Liverpool City Council and then the Mayor of Salford. His experience was seen as a vital piston in the Rayner engine. He wrote her speeches, crafted policy and attack lines and helped to steer her responses to key issues on a daily basis. But after an intense few years, he was forced to take a period of sick leave after falling ill with Type 1 diabetes. During his absence, he was dismissed.

Labour sources say that Finnegan was deeply hurt by this unexpected parting of ways. He believed he had been treated shabbily and he soon launched an action for 'unfair dismissal and disability discrimination'. The dispute dragged on for several months, but it reached a crescendo early in 2018. One Labour figure with knowledge of the affair says:

> Matt was a member of the National Union of Journalists. Michelle Stanistreet, the NUJ's general secretary, was aware of his situation and she had to explain to John McDonnell that Matt had a very clear case and was willing to make public, in an industrial tribunal, written communications from Angela, including texts and emails. They were considered to be explosive and immensely damaging to her. McDonnell used his influence to knock some sense into Angela's head and things were then resolved.

Government records show that Finnegan withdrew his claim on 16 February 2018 before it reached a full employment tribunal hearing. But there were strings attached to this deal. Although Finnegan's salary was paid via Parliament, the Labour Party offered to give him £20,000 out of its own pocket on condition that he signed a non-disclosure agreement. This meant that the matter was covered up. It did not stay entirely hidden for long, though. Finnegan found an artful way to make his feelings about Rayner known, setting to work on a political thriller that he called *Betrayal*.[2] This novel makes for fascinating reading.

The plot, which unfolds over the week of a Labour Party confer-ence, centres on a ruthless Labour MP called Abigail Jeffers, who is caught making a bogus parliamentary expenses claim to cover a hotel bill she paid after a drunken one-night stand with a fellow member of the shadow Cabinet. After the shadow Chancellor finds out about her behaviour, he tells her to resign. When he falls into a diabetic coma, she gives him a fatal overdose of insulin to conceal her misdeed. Her crime is eventually discovered by a *Daily Mail* journalist.

While this story is clearly far-fetched and invented, some of the descriptions of its unsympathetic protagonist appear to be rooted in fact, whether consciously on the author's part or otherwise. In her *Sunday Times Magazine* interview of January 2018, Rayner had re-ferred to herself as 'a gobby northern ginger lass, from a trade union background'. Perhaps these words sparked a creative urge in Finne-gan, for Abigail Jeffers – known as Abi – is, like Rayner, a young MP with a northern seat. She is 'gobby but bright' having 'never had a proper education' and has a child 'who she gave birth to at the age of sixteen and who figured in many of her speeches'. The mischie-vous parallels do not end there. In the book, Abi speaks of how the Sure Start scheme 'rescued' her and her baby daughter, at one point saying: 'I remember when I was a young, unmarried mum, and every day I had to count the pennies to see what I could afford, to feed my baby daughter.' She becomes a UNISON shop steward. Soon after her election as an MP she is promoted to become the Labour Party's education spokesperson.

Abi has long hair and a penchant for colourful clothes and shoes. In one scene she orders an aide to bring a different pair to be worn on each day of the week-long event. Even the Star Wars episode re-ferred to in Chapter 5 of this book is alluded to, as Abi breaks House of Commons rules by using official notepaper to book a table at the Ivy restaurant in London. Another coincidence concerns Abi's computer password, 'VomitBreath69'. A friend of Rayner's who has read the book says that Rayner is known to have used this password as well. 'Angela used to tell a story that when she and Mark went on a first date together they had a bad Indian meal and in the hotel room afterwards they were both sick, so "vomit breath" became her Commons password,' says this person. 'It's disgusting, isn't it? It says a lot about her. But it was her Commons password.'

Finnegan, who is believed to have left Britain several years ago, has only spoken about *Betrayal* once, and that was to the *Daily Mail* in 2020. He told the newspaper: 'The book draws on my experience in the Labour Party over thirty years. But it is a work of fiction.' When asked if he based Abigail Jeffers on Rayner, he said, cryptically: 'People who read the book will draw their own conclusions about the characters in it and what happens when politicians pursue power ruthlessly.'[3] Since the book's publication in 2019, Rayner has never commented on it publicly.

As an aside, it is noteworthy that in July 2018 she claimed for and received £2,000 from the Independent Parliamentary Standards Authority, which is responsible for the regulation and payment of MPs' expenses, for what was described as 'policy excess to an employment practices liability claim'. Unless Rayner was involved in any other disputes with former staff at that time – and she is not believed to have been – it appears that she charged this sum to taxpayers as a result of Finnegan's departure. Whether this was a reasonable use of public money is a question to which only she knows the answer.

● ● ●

During the early months of 2018, Rayner turned her own hand to writing, filing a column for the *Sunday People*; criticising the soaring salaries of university vice chancellors in an article for the *Sunday Times*; and showing her progressive side by detailing her support for transgender schoolchildren in *The Independent*. She also busied herself trying to repeal an amendment to the government's Universal Credit Bill concerning changes to the allocation of free school dinners (Labour lost the vote by 312 votes to 254 after Tory MPs accused her of 'scaremongering' over the plan) and continued to lobby hard on school funding. Another notable endeavour was her unearthing of figures claiming that more than 35,000 teachers who had qualified since the Tories entered Downing Street in 2010 had left the profession.

All this was meat and drink to a shadow Education Secretary who made no secret of her desire to exert as much pressure on the government as possible, and it was clear that she took her work seriously. In the spring of 2018, she gave an interview to Nick Robinson of the BBC in which she discussed her ongoing plans for developing a National Education Service. By admitting that 'I don't consider myself to be an expert in education or a person that has all the answers', she earned respect for her candour while lessening the weight of expectation on her shoulders, but overall the message was clear.[4] She said that she believed the education system was 'not fit for purpose', but she did not think that abolishing private schools would solve the problems she had identified. She also gave an insight into her political leanings by declaring: 'I can honestly say I'm not a Corbynista' and explaining that she and her leader often exchanged views energetically. Switching to the third person, she said: 'Anyone who knows me knows you don't put Ange in a corner and tell her she can't say something, because I'll just say it.' It was the kind of spirited performance that seemed to have become second nature to her.[5]

Yet colleagues were surprised to find that when the beady eye of the media was not trained upon her, she could behave somewhat recklessly. One former Labour MP reports:

Rachel Reeves told me that when Rayner was shadow Education Secretary, she visited a school which was, I think, in Reeves' constituency. Obviously if an MP visits a school, they've got to say to the kids: 'You must work hard every day, have big ambitions, do your best, and if you work hard, you can achieve anything you want' etc. That's the normal spiel. Angela Rayner apparently went in and said: 'Well, you know, I left school at sixteen with no qualifications and look at me now, I'm an MP and the shadow Education Secretary.' I wasn't there, but I was told that was the message. And apparently the headteacher said to Rayner afterwards: 'We're trying to give these kids high aspirations and ambitions. Please don't ever go into another school and say that.'

She also managed to upset some Labour members in early September 2018. At that point, the party had been wrestling with one of the periodic bouts of antisemitism allegations that dogged it during the Corbyn years. Rayner put out a tweet quoting party membership figures as compiled by the House of Commons library. Labour was said to have 540,000 members – at least 100,000 more than every other major political party combined. Below these numbers was a photograph from the film *Jaws* and the self-created caption: 'We're going to need a bigger smear.' This was a reference to one of the most quoted lines from the film: 'You're going to need a bigger boat,' which is uttered when one of the lead characters, Chief Martin

Brody, sees the great white shark at close range for the first time. Rayner deleted the post when other Twitter users asked her which 'smear' she was talking about. She claimed to have been referring to anti-Labour smears in general. Not everybody was convinced. One Twitter user wrote:

> The problem is that the most commonly referred to 'smear' especially over the past few months has been on antisemitism. So by mentioning smear without any reference people will see it as such. Genuine question as I am baffled but what smear by the MSM [mainstream media] are you referring to?

Others piled in to ask the same question. Rayner went quiet. One former Labour MP comments:

> When she said: 'You're going to need a bigger smear,' she basically said the antisemitism allegations were a smear. It was outrageous. A load of people – Pat McFadden, Hilary Benn – served in Corbyn's shadow Cabinet because they thought it'd be better to be in there trying to influence things than be on the outside. That didn't last long. They all left. Most people didn't go back. Some people like Keir Starmer did. And Angela Rayner joined the shadow Cabinet and stayed. She obviously didn't feel as strongly about the antisemitism as others did.

Later that month, wearing her shadow Education Secretary's hat, she used rather more careful language when she told *The Guardian* she rejected the idea that attending a university is desirable or essential.[6] In 1999, Tony Blair declared that half of all young people ought to enrol in some form of higher education. Successive governments had adopted this target with gusto. Yet Rayner's remarks suggested that she felt it was just as vital to focus on the 50 per cent of people who did *not* go to university, arguably presenting herself as a champion of the working class in the process. 'I don't see an out of work brickie at the moment, and the sparkies are doing really well,' she said.

> I think technical education and vocational skills and having a trade mean something. It's not grubby manual people, it's like really valuable skills and yet there's too much snobbery around it still. People are still programmed to think that if your child doesn't get straight As, get A-levels and go to a Russell Group university, that somehow they are not going to achieve in life. I think that's sad.

Two years later, the Conservative Education Secretary, Gavin Williamson, reached the same conclusion. He announced the abandonment of Blair's 50 per cent pledge, calling it an 'absurd mantra'.

It was a leaner-looking Rayner who took to the platform at the Labour Party conference in Liverpool the following week. One aide explained to the *Sunday Times* she had been on a strict diet during which she had shown 'phenomenal willpower'. Rayner herself was characteristically blunter about the reason behind her health kick. She was later reported as explaining that she had lost weight because 'fat birds don't win elections'.[7]

In her conference speech, she announced that a Labour government would call time on the free schools programme and on the academy system. The second of these two policies was significant because academies, which are in effect independently run state schools that operate outside of local authority control, were another product of the Blair era. Rayner said they were 'not fit for purpose' as she lashed out at the 'fat cat' salaries paid to the executives of some academy chains. A few weeks later, Labour announced more plans, endorsed by Rayner, to bring schools back under council control. A 'common rulebook' would be launched to guarantee uniformity of teaching and rules instead of allowing headteachers to exercise their own judgement. Again, the liberalisation of the education sector that had dominated since the 1990s did not sit well with her. She, or her advisers, appeared to believe in state control.

Yet her criticisms at this time were not aimed solely at the government. The tensions that had existed between her and John McDonnell during the 2017 general election campaign resurfaced in the autumn of 2018, after he said he would not oppose almost £10 billion of income tax cuts announced by the chancellor, Philip Hammond. This move was felt by many on the left to benefit the middle class, rather than anybody else. Rayner was among a range of Labour figures, including the Manchester Mayor, Andy Burnham, and the shadow Foreign Secretary, Emily Thornberry, whose outrage prompted them to speak out against McDonnell. She said it was 'the wrong priority'.[8]

Education was not the only subject over which she was prepared to lock horns with those on her own side. Throughout 2018, Parliament had collapsed into what amounted to a collective spasm over Brexit. In shadow Cabinet meetings, Rayner made clear that she was on the side of those who didn't want to deviate from the Labour's policy during the 2017 general election. She would tell colleagues that she wanted to respect the referendum result and negotiate a deal with the EU. At the 2018 party conference, however, a motion had been hammered out after lengthy debate involving activists, unions and Sir Keir Starmer, the shadow Brexit secretary, that concluded:

'If we cannot get a general election Labour must support all options remaining on the table, including campaigning for a public vote.'[9] Starmer was determined to stick to this commitment. He had then surprised colleagues – and angered Jeremy Corbyn – by using his own speech to go further. Adding a line to his text which had not been cleared by the leadership, he declared: 'And nobody is ruling out Remain as an option.' The positive reaction in the conference hall to his words confirmed his status among Labour's anti-Brexit members as the man of the hour. It also sent a clear signal to many people within the Labour Party that Starmer was intent on succeeding Corbyn as Labour leader. Rayner was not happy.

One source comments: 'Like all MPs in Leave seats, Angela was resistant to the pressure to ratchet towards a second referendum in which we would back Remain. When it became a controversy – especially internally – she spoke out. Especially when it came to having a second referendum, which Keir wanted.' Indeed, things became increasingly tense and divisive from the summer of 2018 until the summer of 2019. 'Angela was among the more outspoken in the shadow Cabinet against that trend,' this source adds.

> At each point in the evolution of the policy, she was accepting of where we got to, for example over the support for a customs union that would be negotiated with protections and having a voice in a future trade deal and so on. She didn't oppose that. But from the 2018 conference until 2019, when the position started to shift, she began to speak out and was part of that bloc in shadow Cabinet meetings who warned against that. So she was lined up against Keir.

Indeed, she made no attempt to hide her opposition to Starmer's point of view. In December 2018, she was accorded the honour of appearing as a panellist on the last edition of *Question Time* to be hosted by David Dimbleby, who was retiring from full-time BBC work after a career spanning almost sixty years. During the programme, she made clear her belief that a second Brexit referendum could undermine 'democracy in itself'. Even though Labour's policy was, officially at least, to keep open the option of a second referendum if there was to be no general election, Rayner went against the party line. 'Saying that we'll just have a second referendum and everything will be fine, I think, is a very serious position and it undermines democracy in itself,' she said. 'People made the decision and you can't keep going back saying: "Would you like to answer it a different way?"'[10] Whether by accident or by design, her stance mirrored that of Len McCluskey, the general secretary of Unite, who had told Labour MPs recently that if they backed a second referendum, it could be seen as a 'betrayal'.[11]

In January 2019, rumours began to circulate that Rayner was weighing up her own chances of filling a senior leadership role in the Labour Party after she was seen lunching in the House of Lords with Lord Levy. As Tony Blair's one-time fixer who had raised more than £100 million for the Labour Party between 1994 and 2007, earning himself the nickname 'Lord Cashpoint' in the process, they were not seen as natural allies. At the same time, Corbyn was said to have made little secret of the fact that he had revised the view he had held two years previously. He no longer looked upon Rayner as his first choice – or even second choice – as successor. This cooling in relations cut both ways. As Rayner had carved out her own identity pretty successfully, not least via the growing number of interviews she had given to a range of publications and broadcasters, it appeared that she no longer felt she needed his endorsement in order to progress in politics.

A few weeks later, while watching Blair give an interview on television, she took to Twitter to heap praise upon him and, in what some took as a thinly veiled dig at Corbyn's more ardent supporters, to remark that 'all shades of red' should be welcome in the Labour Party. Corbyn's inner circle was aware of this. 'She made positive remarks about Blair and New Labour. It was definitely noticed,' remembers one colleague. 'She was making a point I think, making clear she wasn't any kind of left sectarian and wanted to be seen as broader than Jeremy Corbyn politically.' Her positive acknowledgement of Blair prompted a backlash, with other Twitter users posting insulting or threatening messages about her. Rayner then took to Facebook to disclose the repercussions they had caused. Explaining that the abuse she had received 'proves we have a problem with some on the left that cannot disagree respectfully', she added:

> It was only a couple of weeks ago someone claiming to be a Jeremy Corbyn supporter was arrested for making threats to rape and murder me on social media. My house has panic buttons fitted. My colleague [Jo Cox] was assassinated doing her job that I do week in week out. Jeremy was attacked this weekend. We have to stop the personal attacks and be kinder to each other.[12]

She agreed to give a talk to pupils at Oldham Sixth Form College a few weeks later and, perhaps in keeping with this sentiment of being kind, during a discussion about feminism she again came out in support of transgender people. 'My thing this year has been about transgender women, because transgender women have had hell,' she said.

And I've had women on the left accusing me of not being a feminist because I believe transgender women have a right to be women. I don't even understand why we're having the debate. To me it's simple. You're a woman. Why are you even debating it? But we still have that debate to have, which is absolutely heartbreaking. But I don't want to be fighting my sisters – who call themselves feminists – over this. I want us to fight the discrimination that we all face. Every woman.

By this point, the Brexit debate in Westminster was reaching fever pitch. No consensus could be reached among MPs about the terms of Britain's break from the EU and its future relationship with the bloc. Originally, Theresa May had declared that Britain would leave on 29 March 2019, but the process was repeatedly delayed, as MPs voted against her proposed withdrawal agreement three times in the first ten weeks of the year. Both the Conservative and Labour parties were riven over the issue. The difference was that the argument that raged within the Labour Party concerned whether there ought to be a second referendum. A series of 'indicative' votes were held in Parliament on what amounted to an increasingly complicated menu of Brexit propositions, including membership of a customs union, membership of the European Economic Area, a confirmatory public vote and revocation of Article 50 in the event of no deal being reached.

No majority agreement could be settled on. The 29 March deadline came and went. On 2 April, a desperate Theresa May invited Labour to enter talks with her in an attempt to find a way to break the spell. Ultimately, these came to nothing, and because Britain remained a member of the EU, the country was forced to participate in the EU elections that took place on 23 May. The Brexit Party, a new operation run by Nigel Farage, topped the poll, gaining twenty-nine seats. Labour's MEP tally was halved as it was pushed into third place with ten seats. The Tories collapsed into fifth place with just four seats. May was forced to resign and Boris Johnson replaced her as Tory leader and Prime Minister in July 2019.

Rayner's was not a prominent voice in the Brexit debate. Whether that was because she did not feel particularly strongly about the issue, or because she represented a Leave constituency, or because she lacked the confidence to wade into a discussion that had tested the minds of some of the brightest people working in British politics, or because her brief as shadow Education Secretary did not require her to become actively involved, is an open question. Amid the sound and fury, perhaps the more interesting line of inquiry to contemplate relates to the state of her working relationship with the men who were responsible for driving Labour's Brexit policy, Sir Keir Starmer and John McDonnell.

One of Labour's principal players who worked closely with all three of them says:

She and Keir did not appear to get on well, particularly because of Brexit. Keir pushed relentlessly to move towards a Remain position, which we didn't get to, and he pushed for a second referendum. Angela was on the other side in that argument to the extent she was involved – which she was only to a limited extent, it was Rebecca Long-Bailey who took part in the negotiations with the government as the shadow Business Secretary. Angela had strong views, though, and felt we were going in the wrong direction. She didn't want there to be EU elections at all. She wanted the government to crash and burn and if possible to get Brexit through without Labour fingerprints being anywhere near it. She would express that view in shadow Cabinet meetings. She was sometimes quite outspoken and angry. Keir's not a very chummy sort of guy. He dealt with his team, negotiated what he wanted with Jeremy Corbyn, he's a process guy. I doubt they had much of a relationship. There was a group including Richard Burgon who were influenced very much by John McDonnell, who was moving towards a kind of pro-second referendum position, and Angela didn't go along with that. She wasn't one of McDonnell's protégés in the way that Rebecca Long-Bailey was. Rebecca was close to McDonnell. She worked closely with him as shadow Chancellor. She was more in his orbit, whereas Angela and McDonnell had a more tense relationship.

If McDonnell was not much of a friend to Rayner among the Parliamentary Labour Party, then to whom, apart from her flatmate Rebecca Long-Bailey, was she considered close? Some of those who have contributed to this book have mulled over this question themselves. Each has been consistent in saying that they believe Rayner was not overburdened by friendships during her first years in the Commons and, independently of each other, they offered the same handful of names unprompted. 'I always thought her friends on the centre-left and the left were Jonathan Ashworth, Louise Haigh and Lisa Nandy,' says one Labour source. Another says:

She doesn't really belong to a political faction. And she doesn't have many MPs you could call close friends. She does have a close group near her. There's Nick Parrott, who's worked for her as her chief of staff for a long time. His partner is Lisa Johnson, who was a political officer in the GMB union. If any two people have helped Angela brand herself, it's those two. Jonathan Ashworth is part of her social circle. Louise Haigh is also in that network.

But she's definitely not a team player. She'd probably acknowledge that herself.

A third says: 'I asked her once who she's close to in Westminster. I assumed she'd name a few MPs, and she said Nick Parrott. I thought it was revealing that she didn't name any MPs who were friends.'

If these views reflect the truth, and Rayner is not somebody who finds it easy or necessary to form close friendships, at least with her fellow MPs, then the notion that she can be seen as a 'loner', as one source advanced in Chapter 6, cannot be disregarded easily either. One Labour veteran comments: 'Ultimately, I think she is a loner and I'm not quite sure where her project is going to go. It's a bit like Boris Johnson. Anyone who's ever worked with Boris will tell you he's a loner.' This parallel has been put to Rayner before. During an interview she gave to the *Financial Times* in November 2022, a journalist pointed out to her that she and Johnson may be more alike than they think in so far as they 'share unconventional child-hoods, charismatic personalities and complicated private lives'.[13] Apparently, she did not entirely shrug off the comparison, but she launched into a tirade about Johnson's morality before it could be developed and a possible examination of this side of her character was dropped.

Even though Brexit dominated British politics between 2016 and 2019, Rayner had a brief to fulfil as shadow Education Secretary and she did so diligently. One idea, announced in late May 2019, was that under a Labour government children aged five and above would be taught about the ecological and social impact of climate change and the school curriculum would be designed to prepare them to work in the renewable energy and green technology in-dustries. Soon afterwards, she spoke in favour of achieving gender

LEFT ABOVE Rayner and Starmer arrive at the 2023 Labour Party conference in Liverpool. Her formal dress was in contrast to his more casual approach, emphasising, for some, a difference in personality that extends beyond fashion. 'It's not a close relationship,' says one of their former colleagues.
© Leon Neal via Getty Images

LEFT MIDDLE Rayner insists she is not a Corbynite, but would she have reached the top of the Labour Party so quickly without Jeremy Corbyn's backing? After a 2020 EHRC report into antisemitism found that, under his leadership, Labour had been responsible for 'unlawful' acts of discrimination, Rayner told the BBC he is 'a thoroughly decent man'.
© Jack Taylor/Stringer via Getty Images

BELOW Many have compared Rayner with one of her predecessors, John Prescott – including her. 'I'm John Prescott in a skirt, me,' she told the *Daily Record* in December 2021. 'I do consider myself to be like him. I wear my heart on my sleeve. I think that is a very northern thing.'
© Anthony Devlin/Stringer via Getty Images

ANGELA RAYNER 🌹

Real *People*, Real *Politics*, Real *Change*

Dear member,

Setting the record straight

Some people have been saying I'm not fit to be an MP. Well I say, they're just a bunch of miseries who don't know how to have a good time like me.

Some people have been saying I have a drink problem. Well I say, someone who can snort sambuca up their nose through a hospital breathing tube has proved she can handle her drink. And if I'm going to be an MP I need all the boozing practice I can get.

Some people say I put silly pictures on my facebook page. I say, what's to be ashamed of if you know how to have a good time with your mates.

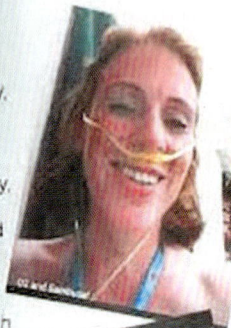

Best wishes, Angie

Email: angela@angelarayner.com

Twitter: @AngelaRayner

Phone: 07977 517585

How to win a contest to be an MP

* Be part of a deal between union bosses to force through an all woman shortlist against the unanimous wishes of members.

* Make sure that union bosses nominate you for the job without asking their members for their views.

* Get big money backing from the union to pay for a glossy campaign.

* Get hold of an illegal copy of the membership list and start lobbying members weeks in advance of start date.

✔ Make sure union bosses bully and threaten competitors to withdraw from the contest.

✔ Bend the rules to send out emails in other people's names.

✔ Turn up on doorsteps with a professional photographer and cajole reluctant members to become 'endorsers'.

✔ Promise lots of jobs in the MP's office to secure support from members who are looking for work.

The leaflet that was circulated in Ashton-under-Lyne in the summer of 2014 alleging Rayner's bid to become the constituency's Labour Party candidate was rigged. The author has never been unmasked. Rayner secured the nomination with ease.

ABOVE Rayner at the Labour Party conference in Brighton in 2021 after being criticised for a fringe speech in which she called Conservatives 'homophobic, racist, misogynistic … vile, nasty, Etonian … scum.' Her colleague Emily Thornberry observed that 'there may have been drink partaken' before the broadside.
© Joel Goodman via London News Pictures

LEFT Rebecca Long-Bailey has been one of Rayner's staunchest allies in the Parliamentary Labour Party. They were flatmates for several years and in 2020 agreed that Rayner would stand for the deputy leadership when Long-Bailey went for the top job. Yet there are reasons to believe they are no longer as friendly as they once were.
© Yui Mok via PA Images/Alamy Stock Photo

ABOVE 80 Vicarage Road in Stockport, which Rayner acquired aged twenty-six for £79,000. She received a £26,000 discount under the right-to-buy scheme. The electoral roll states she lived there for at least a decade, but did she? The property was sold in 2015 for £127,500.

LEFT Rayner is more popular among Tory politicians than she may care to admit. Her closest Tory friend is Nicholas Soames, Winston Churchill's grandson. 'She sometimes sends me these wonderful texts,' says Soames. 'She sent me one at New Year from Churchill's nightclub in Manchester, where she was dancing with some friends.'

© WBA Pool/Pool via Getty Images

Rayner protesting alongside fellow UNISON members in 2012. She has been a UNISON member for more than twenty years and calls herself a socialist, but many say her politics are hard to place. Oddly, only £3,820 of the £286,500 raised for her deputy Labour leadership bid came from UNISON. © Pete Maclaine via Alamy Stock Photo

Rayner and Sir Keir Starmer 'taking a knee' in June 2020 in solidarity with the organisation Black Lives Matter. Rayner is also a strong advocate of transgender rights and gender self-identification.

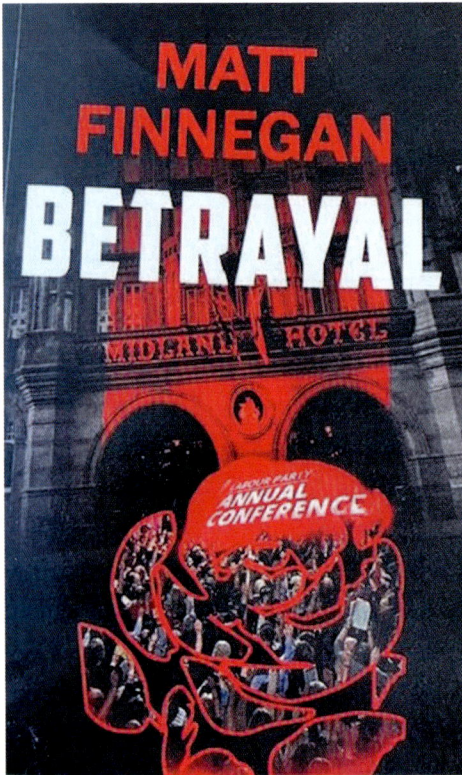

Betrayal, the thriller written by Rayner's former adviser Matt Finnegan after the Labour Party paid him off with £20,000. Its plot is invented, but many believe its protagonist was inspired by Rayner, who was nicknamed 'The Diva' by her staff.

Angela Rayner
Candidate for Manchester Withington Selection

Rayner first tried to become an MP in 2013 when she sought the nomination for Manchester Withington. One Labour figure says her campaign was 'quite bitter', adding: 'She didn't handle herself very well. She was rude about her opponent, Jeff Smith. It showed a little bit of her character.'

Stone the crows! Tories accuse Rayner of Basic Instinct ploy to distract Boris

DENIES CLAIM: Labour's Angela Rayner and, top, at PMQs

By Glen Owen
POLITICAL EDITOR

ALL is fair in love, war and Commons duels with Boris Johnson, it seems, if the claims of Tory MPs are to be believed.

Conservatives have claimed that Labour Deputy Leader Angela Rayner likes to put Mr Johnson 'off his stride' in the chamber by crossing and uncrossing her legs when they clash at Prime Minister's Questions.

The exchanges between Ms Rayner and Mr Johnson – which take place when leader Sir Keir Starmer is absent – have become a highlight of the Commons calendar, pitching the comprehensive school-educated Labour MP against the Old Etonian.

But Tory MPs have mischievously suggested that Ms Rayner likes to distract the PM when he is in the dispatch box by deploying a fully clothed Parliamentary equivalent of Sharon Stone's infamous scene in the 1992 film Basic Instinct.

It is suggested that Ms Rayner also employs the tactic when sitting next to Sir Keir when he faces Mr Johnson at PMQs.

One MP said: 'She knows she can't compete with Boris's Oxford Union debating training, but she has other skills which he lacks. She has admit-

ted as much when enjoying drinks with us on the [Commons] terrace.'

Last night, a spokesman for Ms Rayner described the allegation as 'categorically untrue'. Ms Rayner, 41, a socialist grandmother who left school at 16 while pregnant and with

'They have a problem with women in public'

no qualifications before becoming a care worker, has frequently landed blows on the Prime Minister during sparky – some say flirty – exchanges.

During one encounter in January, Mr Johnson raised claims that she was agitating to succeed Sir Keir by saying: 'We all know what job she wants.'

Ms Rayner hit back: 'I've heard on the grapevine there might be a vacancy for Prime Minister soon, so maybe I should show aspiration.'

In Basic Instinct, Ms Stone played Catherine Tramell, an enigmatic writer involved in a relationship with a police detective played by Michael Douglas. Ms Stone claimed the scene in which she uncrossed her legs was filmed without her knowledge.

Last week, Ms Rayner accused Mr Johnson of having 'mocked [the] sacrifice' of Britons during the coronavirus pandemic. She said: 'As a care worker, I know the sacrifices they made in the pandemic on the front line, putting themselves at risk to care for others. It is the least that they deserve for the Prime Minister to be held to account for his own conduct.

'While the Prime Minister was partying, they were unable to be with their loved ones in their dying moments, or unable to attend miserable funerals with only a handful of people because they were following his rules.'

A Labour source said: 'Just when you think the Conservative party can't get any lower they outdo themselves. The Conservatives clearly have a problem with women in public life.

A spokesman for Ms Rayner said last night: 'I'm telling you categorically it's untrue.'

FAMOUS SCENE: Sharon Stone in the 1992 movie Basic Instinct

The April 2022 *Mail on Sunday* report likening Rayner's behaviour to that of a character in the film *Basic Instinct*. Four Tory MPs say they heard Rayner tell a lewd joke about herself. This inspired the story, but it almost cost Glen Owen, the reporter who wrote it, his career.
© DMG Media Licensing

In what was her first big promotion, Jeremy Corbyn made Rayner his shadow Work and Pensions Minister in January 2016, just eight months after she became an MP. One former colleague says she was ill-suited to the brief. 'She didn't have any affinity for the subject at all,' says this person. 'You could almost see her frantically pedalling under the desk because she was trying to keep up with stuff. But she made a decent fist of it because she's good at that – she's good at presenting an image of competence.'
© Nicola Tree via Getty Images

Rayner and her then-boyfriend, the Labour MP Sam Tarry, leaving her taxpayer-funded London flat in January 2022. Their affair ended in 2023, by when Tarry had been deselected by his local party.

© The Sun / News Licensing

Rayner and Ian Hislop in 2017 after her appearance on the BBC's *Have I Got News for You*. One former MP says: 'From then on in, she was a bit of a nightmare. She started talking about herself in the third person.'

equality among construction workers. And in a third intervention, she said she believed there was 'a moral imperative to ensure that all young children receive LGBT-inclusive education'.[14] In fact, she felt so strongly about this last issue that in early June, she even reported fellow Labour MP Roger Godsiff to the party's chief whip, Nick Brown, after she found out that Godsiff had told the parents of primary school children in Birmingham who were protesting against gay equality lessons that they had taken on a 'just cause' and were 'right' to have done so. Rayner publicly called Godsiff's remarks 'discriminatory and irresponsible'.[15] Her intervention had career-ending consequences for Godsiff. Within months, Labour's ruling body, the NEC, blocked him from standing as a Labour candidate in the forthcoming general election. He stood as an independent instead, but he lost. And when Tory MP Esther McVey advocated parents having the right to take primary school-aged children out of lessons on same-sex relationships if they wanted to, Rayner called the idea 'illegal, immoral and deeply dangerous' and said McVey was 'not fit to be an MP'. She added: 'We cannot and will not fail LGBT young people. Not only do we have a moral duty to ensure that all young people receive LGBT-inclusive education, there is a legal requirement too under the Equalities Act.'[16]

By the middle of 2019, as Boris Johnson's campaign to succeed Theresa May as Tory leader gathered steam, fresh questions about Corbyn's leadership were forced into the open. Having turned seventy, stories appeared suggesting that his health was in doubt. Labour's Brexit policy was also unclear to most voters and remained the subject of a protracted row between the party and the Unite union, led by Len McCluskey, who was fiercely opposed to a second referendum. Another bone of contention that had dogged Labour ever since Corbyn became leader in 2015 was a long-standing perception that some hard-left elements of the party harboured antisemitic instincts. Rayner felt moved to comment on this last point while addressing a Fabian Society conference, saying she was 'totally exasperated by the failure of our movement to be able to deal with this issue'.[17] For a perceived-Corbyn loyalist to speak in such terms was considered a very bad omen as far as his prospects were concerned. As the summer wore on, some in the Labour Party looked with envy at how swiftly the Conservatives had managed to replace Theresa May. Hopes about whether there might be a way to replace Corbyn did not diminish.

Once Johnson had been installed as the new Prime Minister, and it was clear that his intention to complete Brexit was going to highlight Labour's dithering over the issue, Labour quickly cast around for what it considered to be legitimate criticisms that could be levelled against him. The fact that Johnson was the 20th premier to have attended Eton College was one line of attack that was deployed. Another was the calculation that 64 per cent of the members of Johnson's first Cabinet were privately educated. One left-wing group backed by John McDonnell, Labour Against Private Schools, even said it wanted to 'abolish Eton'.[18] Rayner took to the airwaves to argue that 'it is now clear that Boris Johnson is running a government of the few, by the few, for the few'. When it was pointed out that both Jeremy Corbyn and John McDonnell had also been the beneficiaries of a private education during their childhoods, Labour appeared to deny that its position was in any way hypocritical.

In late August, Johnson authorised £14bn of extra funding for schools over the following three years. There was little Rayner could say about this positive piece of news other than to accuse him of offering a cash injection that was 'clearly designed as an election bribe'. Johnson was of the view that only the public could determine how Brexit should be resolved. It was apparent he felt that a general election had to be called as soon as possible. This would put Rayner's assumed leadership aspirations in the spotlight. She would be under pressure to make a strong impression at that year's party conference in Brighton. In an interview with *The Observer* as the conference began, she emphasised that she wanted to change the education system so that working-class children could excel. The newspaper pointed out the paradox that she in fact embodies social mobility 'in a system she believes is designed to choke it off'. Rayner brushed this aside, saying that her own success in life had been down to good fortune.[19]

Her mission to equalise educational opportunities was prominent in her conference speech. She vowed to make 'the whole education system fairer through the integration of private schools' into the state system. She added: 'I can say today that our very first budget will immediately close the tax loopholes used by the elite private schools and use that money to improve the lives of all children.'[20] This would be achieved via the introduction of VAT on school fees. At that conference it was also agreed by the Labour Party that a cap should exist limiting to 7 per cent the number of privately educated pupils who could attend a university. Another announcement was that the schools' inspectorate, Ofsted, would be scrapped. These were hardline policies that she knew would generate headlines and appeal both to Labour's left-wing members and to the teaching unions – both crucial constituencies to secure if she ever wanted to attain an elected position in the Labour Party. By explaining in her speech that she and John McDonnell would work together on developing these initiatives, she left anybody who had listened to the speech with the impression that she wanted to be thought of as a radical thinker. Afterwards, Labour delegates went even further, voting to abolish private schools altogether and to move their endowments, investments and properties into the state sector. These ideas went beyond Rayner's own views and she could not be held responsible for them. But when a movement calling itself Shut Down the Tories staged a rally in Manchester the following weekend, as the Conservative Party gathered in the city for its annual conference, Rayner was prominent among the marchers. Once again, her politics were hard to pigeonhole. She had begun the year by praising Tony Blair, who had attended Fettes; and being seen in public with his millionaire fixer, Lord Levy. Now she had apparently taken on John McDonnell's belief that those who choose to spend their taxed income on private school fees should be penalised financially, while at the same time rubbing shoulders with people who thought the Tory Party had no right to exist.

When Boris Johnson had to acknowledge that no consensus over Brexit could be reached by MPs, he also had to admit that he would not be able to honour the recent promise he had made that he would achieve Brexit by 31 October. For this reason, he decided to call a general election. After extensive parliamentary wrangling, Parliament was eventually dissolved on 6 November after the Commons voted for an election to be held on 12 December. In the days leading up to this point Rayner, in common with her colleagues, would have known that Jeremy Corbyn would be unlikely to survive as leader if Labour went down to a major defeat. She would have also realised that she was going to have to defend her party's confused Brexit policy in her Leave-voting constituency, perhaps placing her own position as an MP in peril. This would have given her plenty to think about. But when Labour's deputy leader, Tom Watson, announced on 6 November that he was standing down as an MP, the stakes rose higher still and the election gained a new dynamic as far as Rayner was concerned. Come what may, Watson's post would have to be filled.

Rayner's associates say there is no question that she recognised immediately that this was an opportunity that could not be wasted. The general election campaign would fulfil the very useful function for her of being an unofficial testing ground for her ambitions of becoming one of the two highest-ranking politicians in the Labour Party. In contrast to 2017, when she had to be persuaded to promote Labour on television and radio and sometimes mysteriously ducked out of interviews, she was far more readily available in 2019 to the extent that she even seemed put out when she wasn't offered more media slots. One party figure recalls: 'During the 2019 election, she felt she was being sidelined by the Labour press office. But it wasn't true.'

Among her more prominent appearances was a five-way Channel 4 debate involving Philippa Whitford of the SNP; Adam Price of Plaid Cymru; Jonathan Bartley of the Green Party; and Jo Swinson, of the Lib Dems. She also took part in a seven-way BBC *Question Time* debate for the under-thirties in which she said that in the event of another Brexit referendum, she would vote to leave the EU if 'we get a deal that protects jobs and the economy'.[21] As the programme continued, she clashed with fellow panellist Nigel Farage, who was sitting beside her, talking over him and telling him to 'stop peddling hate in our country' as he tried to answer a question about immigration. It was widely considered the most exciting moment of the evening.

As the polls closed at 10 o'clock on election night, the scale of Labour's drubbing became clear. The BBC exit poll estimated that the Conservatives had won with a majority of eighty-six seats. In fact, the true total was eighty seats. Under Boris Johnson, they had gained forty-eight seats and ended up with 365 MPs in the House of Commons, while Labour had lost sixty seats and been reduced to 202 MPs, its worst result since 1935. In the early hours of Friday 13 December, Jeremy Corbyn was forced to admit that his time as Labour leader was over. He said he would not resign immediately, but he would not lead the party into another election.

In Ashton-under-Lyne, Rayner was run much closer than she had perhaps expected. She lost more than 12 per cent of the votes she had secured in 2017, polling 18,544. The Conservative candidate, Dan Costello, was in second place, increasing his share by over 5 per cent to reach a total of 14,281. The Brexit Party candidate, David Brock-lehurst, trailed in third with 3,151. Rayner's majority was cut by just over 7,000 votes, from 11,295 to 4,263. Even though the combined total of the Tory vote and the Brexit Party vote would not have been sufficient to defenestrate her, local sources say she became concerned about her future over the last few days of the campaign. 'When the postal votes came in, councillors were invited by the council to watch them arrive, so you could see roughly how many votes each candidate got,' remembers one Conservative activist.

> You're not meant to take the result out of room with you. But it was clear that she was losing the postal vote. We were amazed. We were ahead by a few hundred. When she heard about it, it spooked her. She was meant to be doing some big education launch in London, but they had to move it to Tameside College in the constituency instead. She knew she had to be in her seat to try to shore up her local vote.

Having been returned as Ashton-under-Lyne's MP for the third time in four-and-a-half years, Rayner now had an even more volatile constituency of voters to consider: the 500,000 members of the Labour Party. Before the general election, she and Rebecca Long-Bailey had agreed that in the event of Corbyn resigning the leadership, they would each stand for one of the available leadership positions and then endorse the other. It sounded like an amicable arrangement, but was it really?

CHAPTER 9

THE PROGRAMME

Just as Jeremy Corbyn's elevation to Labour leader in September 2015 opened up possibilities for Angela Rayner's prospects as a new member of the House of Commons, so his exit four years later provided an opportunity for her to scale higher still up the political ladder. As Labour MPs picked over the wreckage of their disastrous 2019 general election campaign, Rayner's allies were able to confirm to *The Guardian* that she had already discussed with them making a bid for the party's vacant deputy leadership. These were not idle words. She was deadly serious and her plans were well advanced. Remarkably, after less than five years in Parliament, she was going to put herself forward as a contender to hold the post previously occupied by some of the leading figures in Labour politics of the previous 100 years, including J. R. Clynes, Clement Attlee, Aneurin Bevan, Roy Jenkins, Michael Foot, Denis Healey and John Prescott.

It is perhaps too easily forgotten by those who do not belong to the Labour Party that its second-in-command is directly elected by Labour members and can be a force in their own right. Even though their precise powers are not set out in the party's constitution, they have their own mandate and power base and can – with the leader's blessing – pursue their own agenda to some degree. How had Rayner, who was still only thirty-nine and with relatively little frontline political experience, gained the status of contender so quickly? Insiders have pointed to several reasons. For one thing, the circumstances were favourable. Having lost sixty seats overnight, Labour's talent pool was far shallower than it had been, and competition for the deputy's job was not exactly intense. Furthermore, she had played her hand well over the previous four years, becoming a prominent figure by ensuring that she was noticed. Some politicians of the past had used a prop that somehow came to reflect their personalities – Margaret Thatcher's handbag; Winston Churchill's cigar; and Harold Wilson's pipe and mac – and Rayner had done the same via her many pairs of brightly coloured shoes, whether she was conscious of this or not. On top of this, she had given so many interviews and speeches in which she discussed her background that nobody who had heard the stories she told could forget them. Rayner had already acknowledged how valuable her past could be to her in advancing her political career. In an interview with *Prospect* magazine in September 2017 she remarked:

> I remember colleagues saying to me, 'It's great you say so much about your backstory, but I wouldn't do it too much, because it can prevent you from being a leader.' Or, 'It's really good that she's got a good backstory, but it doesn't really qualify her to be Education Secretary.' So it does cloud people's judgement. But it can also help you – and you can use it to your advantage.

Crowning all of these points, however, is the fact that she had actively wanted to be the deputy Labour leader for a long time and had already put her back into making it happen. 'I remember her talking about becoming deputy leader of the Labour Party from as far back as 2016,' says a former colleague.

> I talked to her directly about it. I remember saying: 'Who with? Who'd be the leader?' And she would throw out various names. She definitely had it in her sights. She was always focussed on it, so it wasn't a big surprise to me when she went for it. Over the previous few years she'd toured the constituencies. She'd got Rosie, her office manager, to set up a programme of constituency visits. So the two things came together – her ambition and the circumstances. And of course being a woman when only one woman, Harriet Harman, had held the job on a full-time basis before, that was all part of it. She had a programme. It was all worked out.

If she truly believed that her life story gave her an upper hand, she also knew that she could rely on the support of some of Britain's biggest trades unions, both for votes and for financial backing. Even before she formally launched her bid on 6 January, it seems she was convinced that her chances were stronger than most – perhaps all – of her rivals.

Before the end of 2019, Rayner and her flatmate Rebecca Long-Bailey had agreed that the former would stand for the deputy leadership and the latter for the leadership. Exactly how this pact was worked out has never been revealed publicly, though Labour figures have always been at pains to stress that the arrangement lacked the intrigue of similar plans hatched by two of their predecessors, Tony Blair and Gordon Brown. They are said to have met in a restaurant in Islington called Granita in 1994 and decided that Blair would stand to be Labour leader, would appoint Brown as his

Chancellor if and when he became Prime Minister and would serve no more than two terms in Number 10. 'It wasn't a Granita-style deal, I know that,' jokes a friend of Rayner. A second party insider stresses that because Labour was in a state of demoralisation and disarray immediately after the 2019 election and was preparing for another term in opposition – as opposed to 1994 when it was beginning to ready itself for government – there was some tension. 'Rebecca wasn't gagging to become leader,' says this person. 'Both she and Angela wanted to inherit some of Jeremy's support from the members. Angela wanted to be seen as the inheritor of Corbynism, and so did Rebecca, and there was a difficult set-up between them.'

Rayner and Long-Bailey have very different personalities, and their socialism is not fully aligned either. Whereas Long-Bailey is reserved and ideological, Rayner is outspoken and pragmatic – somebody who sees politics through the prism of her personal experiences. In one sense, they were plausible running mates in so far as they were longstanding allies who complemented each other. On the other hand, their different approach to politics arguably made their pact rather unlikely. The outcome of the leadership contest would ultimately determine whether Labour was to remain a hard-left party in the mould of Jeremy Corbyn or whether it might tack back to somewhere approaching the centre ground under a new leader like Lisa Nandy. Rayner had already made clear publicly that she was not a Corbynite, even if she was keen to pick up the support of as many Corbynites as she could, and yet she had decided to form a partnership with a candidate who represented that extreme – if popular – wing of her party. Was Long-Bailey merely useful to Rayner's ambitions? One hypothesis is that Rayner toyed with the idea of running for the leadership herself. She only abandoned that idea when she realised she did not have sufficient backing among

Labour MPs to win the top job and was advised that she had a much better chance of becoming the deputy. Having established this, she was therefore happy for Long-Bailey to try for the leadership herself and backed her for it knowing that, after the failure of the Corbyn project, Long-Bailey was unlikely to be Labour's next leader anyway.

For her part, Long-Bailey has said she saw things differently. In 2021, she told the BBC:

> Because we love each other, neither of us wanted to stand against the other and we both wanted to make sure that we were in the strongest possible position to win and to help the party. And that's why we agreed to run together. I'd support Angela, she'd support me, and there was a hope there that we'd win.

Notably absent from this polite explanation, however, was any sense of *how* they had reached their agreement. Needless to say, if anybody was advising Rayner about this crucial matter, they did their job well.

In order to stand, those hoping to become the deputy leader needed the nominations of at least 10 per cent of Labour's MP and MEPs combined – that number being twenty-two – by 13 January. They would then need to secure the backing of at least 5 per cent of the Constituency Labour Parties or other affiliated groups, including at least two trade unions, by 14 February. Those who cleared these hurdles to make it onto the final ballot paper would face a vote by full party members, union affiliates and registered supporters. Alongside Rayner, the other candidates who made it to the final stage to contest the deputy leadership were Dawn Butler, Richard Burgon, Ian Murray and Rosena Allin-Khan.

Rayner returned to the Bridgehall estate in Stockport to launch her bid on the morning of 6 January 2020. Joining her at the community centre where she spoke were fellow north-west Labour MPs Navendu Mishra, Lucy Powell, Jonathan Reynolds and Afzal Khan. Also in the audience was the newly elected MP for Ilford South, Sam Tarry, whom Rayner had picked to run her campaign. Like Rayner, Tarry had strong trades union links. He had also worked on Jeremy Corbyn's two leadership election campaigns in 2015 and 2016 and he had enjoyed a good working relationship with John McDonnell.

She opened by saying:

> I wanted to make this speech here, on the estate where I grew up and lived for most of my life. I talk about my background because for too long I felt I wasn't good enough; I felt ashamed of who I was. It took me time for that shame to turn into pride. I want children growing up here now to know they are worth as much as anyone else. And I want the world of Westminster politics to hear that too. Because I remember when I first spoke from the front bench in the House of Commons, a parliamentary sketch writer said I must have got lost from the set of *Little Britain*. It was another way of saying I didn't know my place. Maybe I don't. But I know the place I came from. It's here. Not *Little Britain*. Real Britain. And people here deserve the very best our country has to offer. But they will only get it from a Labour government.[1]

It was a strong start and it certainly captured the applause that she sought. Some who were watching even tutted in dismay at the barb she said she had faced from this unnamed journalist, who was quickly identified as Quentin Letts of the *Daily Mail*. What the audience perhaps did not realise, however, was that her statement was factually incorrect. It is true that Letts once wrote of her: 'Mrs Rayner, a loss to the cast of TV's *Little Britain*, would be entrusted with our schools should Jeremy Corbyn form a Government. A terrifying thought.' He had added: 'But the teaching unions would be happy because Catherine Tate-lookalike Mrs Rayner is keen on more public spending.' But the article in which he wrote these words had been published in July 2017, more than a year after Rayner joined Labour's front bench and by which time she had spoken in the Commons in her capacity as shadow Education Secretary many times.[2] Did Letts really mean to imply that Rayner should never have been on Labour's front bench and 'didn't know her place', as she had alleged? Or was Rayner merely the latest in a long line of MPs from all parties whose personal style and political views Letts – who has been writing parliamentary sketches since 1997 – had studied and then lampooned for satirical purposes?

Rayner went on to warn those gathered that Labour had to 'win or die'. Of the election, she said: 'We can't afford to hide from the scale of this defeat or its lessons. We have now lost four elections in a row.' Labour's campaign strategy came in for criticism, as she argued that 'we tried to fight target seats where we'd effectively already lost' and decreed this 'cannot happen again'. She also acknowledged that the left was in decline. 'Across Europe, social democratic parties are collapsing,' she said. 'Either we face up to these new times, or we become irrelevant.' Boris Johnson and Donald Trump were mentioned disparagingly as she spoke of the 'dark forces' of the Tory government. Noting that 'I owe so much of my life to Labour', she called for 'a united party that starts winning elections for all' and emphasised the need to stamp out antisemitism in her party. She concluded her speech with the bold statement: 'As a party, we face a choice: win or die. And I fight to win.' It's not clear whether she or anybody else linked to her campaign realised 'I fight to win' was the same phrase uttered by Margaret Thatcher when she was challenged for the Tory leadership in November 1990, but 'Fighting to Win' became Rayner's slogan.

After the speech, Long-Bailey confirmed that she would back Rayner, though Labour's former deputy leader, Tom Watson, was quick to voice his concern that Long-Bailey would be a Corbyn 'continuity candidate'. While giving an interview to Sky News, Rayner defended her flatmate, saying:

> Well, to be honest, as a northern working-class lass, I've been un-derestimated, and told my place, ever since I was born. And two northern women, I can tell you, will not be being told that we are continuity anything from any man ... I won't be told what Angela Rayner should be either. I'm there to support my electorate.

Rayner then made clear that she would happily deputise for who-ever was voted in as Labour leader. When asked who she wanted to lead the party, she replied:

> Well, I would take any of [the candidates] as my boss ... I will obviously support my flatmate and friend, Rebecca Long-Bailey, because I think she's another fantastic northern woman who will really be able to give it to Boris Johnson and the Tories, and hold them to account, but I'll happily work under any of our leadership contenders. It is not for me to say who our membership should vote for.[3]

Some felt it was as though her backing for Long-Bailey was quali-fied, or that she was already hedging her bets.

She was, arguably, just as noncommittal when fielding questions about her own politics. 'I don't consider myself to be of one political persuasion or another,' she told *The Guardian* after her launch.

I'm not a Blairite, I'm not a Corbynite, I'm not a Brownite. I'm an Angela Rayner – a member of the Labour Party who has various different opinions on lots of different things just in the same way MPs and other party activists would. I hate it when people try and pigeonhole me.[4]

On the surface this may have sounded like a reasonable show of independence, but some felt that the advantage to Rayner of refusing to be categorised was that she did not have to have, and did not even have to pretend to have, a deep understanding of the political beliefs of any of those she had mentioned – Blair, Corbyn or Brown. By presenting herself as an instinctive politician, she could pick and choose her political beliefs as she went along, much like many voters are inclined to do. This certainly rings a bell with one former colleague who had worked with her over the previous four years. 'She's ambitious, she's politically opportunist and she doesn't have deeply embedded ideological politics; some would say that's a good thing,' they say. When pressed to detail her own politics, Rayner added:

I am definitely a socialist and I'm proud to be one. I am actually proud that you can actually say that because I think at one time saying that you're a socialist meant you were some sort of loony left which is a term that I don't like. In fact that was levelled at me during the general election by a Conservative MP, which I think is quite offensive to people in our movement.

Two weeks later, it was reported that some of Corbyn's most trusted
allies had decided to shun Rayner, unconvinced that she had always
been sufficiently loyal during his leadership. John McDonnell and
Diane Abbott were among those who instead opted to back Richard Burgon, a prominent member of the Socialist Campaign Group
of Labour MPs. This left Long-Bailey as the only key Corbynite to
nominate Rayner. It is impossible to know what her endorsement
was worth to Rayner in terms of votes, but Rayner's own efforts
in attracting support over the previous few years appeared to have
paid off. By the end of the contest, she had secured eighty-eight
out of a possible 212 nominations from MPs and MEPs and was
far ahead of her four rivals. Indeed, she led at every stage of the
race, with the opinion polls suggesting that she was always the clear
favourite. The numbers spoke for themselves. She managed to nail
down the backing of 365 out of 647 possible CLPs; and twelve out of
a possible thirty-two affiliates. She had also been able to call upon
the support of Momentum, the radical socialist grassroots organisation founded by Corbyn's associate Jon Lansman.

One person who observed Rayner as she worked her way around
the country during the previous few years making friends within
the Labour movement had expected as much. 'The party styled her
as a good campaigner,' says this person.

I'm not sure what that means other than that she excited the
activists. She had always gone down well in the constituencies,
so the Labour Party was happy to facilitate her visits. She was
building her base from a very early stage – several years before
2020. She was doing what any sensible politician would do. And
that was partly because she saw the response she got from Labour
members to her back story, and she liked that. And that made her

think 'They love me in the constituencies, so who knows how far I can go?' She worked it very well.

In between the various deputy leadership hustings that took place, she was similarly adept at choosing her media appearances, though she did so with a discerning eye, giving fewer interviews than she might have done. One significant publicity exercise to which she did agree involved Paul Brand of ITV News. It was arranged that he would interview her and her mother, Lynn Bowen, at Mrs Bowen's home in order to discuss Rayner's childhood and background. During their conversation, Mrs Bowen spoke frankly about her illness and the crucial role her daughter had played in seeing her through it. 'I was really depressed and suicidal,' she said. 'When I was in a very dark place she [Rayner] used to bath me, look after me, feed me. If it wasn't for her, I don't think I'd be here today.' At the end of the interview, she also said of her daughter: 'Watch this space. She'll be the Prime Minister soon. Watch out, Boris, you won't be there for long!'⁵ Such an open discussion told viewers – and Labour voters – even more about Rayner's personal life, and it would not have been out of place in the arena of American politics. Some Labour figures were concerned that Rayner had overstepped the mark in allowing her mother to talk on camera about her personal struggles in the context of the deputy leadership election. 'Perhaps it came across as a bit "misery memoir",' says one. Rayner is said to have thought nothing of it, however.

A company called Angela Rayner Ltd was set up and run by her longstanding aide, Nick Parrott, for the duration of the campaign to handle finances. It claims to have had fourteen employees. During the three months of the contest, Rayner accepted donations and gifts in kind worth a total of £286,500. Yet this generous sum did not come from the sources some had presumed. UNISON, with which Rayner had such a long history, gave goods and services worth only £3,820. It therefore fell to other unions to step in and provide the financial muscle required to help her to victory. The GMB union, with which Parrott had strong links, gave Rayner £83,000 in goods and services. The CWU union donated £25,000. And USDAW, another union, pledged £10,000. Furthermore, 45 per cent of her campaign's income came courtesy of individual donors and businesses. The Labour-supporting businessman Lord Alli led the pack with a cheque for £50,000. Rajesh Agrawal, the Deputy Mayor of London for business, made a private donation of £10,000. It did not go unnoticed that Rayner also accepted £25,000 from a hedge fund tycoon, Martin Taylor; and a further £25,000 from the privately educated businessman Sir Trevor Chinn, among others. Some wondered whether these donations might clash with her desire to be seen as Labour's champion of the working class and of the unions. On 4 March, Long-Bailey gave the journalist Andrew Neil an interview in which she challenged Sir Keir Starmer about the source of some of his donations. 'I think there's always an assumption that you don't get nothing for nothing in this world,' said Long-Bailey. 'And those who donate to your campaign will expect to be repaid in some way in the future.'[6] If Long-Bailey felt the same interpretation could have been applied to Rayner's campaign, she kept quiet about it.

On 4 April, after three rounds of voting, Rayner was announced as Labour's new deputy leader. She had achieved 228,944 votes – that is to say 52.6 per cent of the available votes. By most people's reckoning, it had been a fairly low-key contest, not least because it had been run in parallel with the far more prominent battle for the Labour leadership. In that election, Long-Bailey had been crushed by Sir Keir Starmer, who had won in the first round having received 275,780 votes (56.2 per cent of the available vote) to her 135,218 votes (27.6 per cent). This, of course, meant that Starmer would have as his deputy a woman who had not voted for him to be the leader, just as their predecessors Jeremy Corbyn and Tom Watson had not backed each other either. Some believed the omens were not good.

Among the first tasks facing Rayner in her new role was to assist Starmer in tackling antisemitism. In his acceptance speech, he had promised to 'tear out this poison by its roots'.[7] Straight away, he held a video conference with Jewish leaders – also attended by Rayner – in which he said that an independent complaints procedure would be established to review every case of antisemitism that had been linked to the Labour Party, which had been under investigation by the Equality and Human Rights Commission (EHRC) for the past eleven months. The issue was nothing less than a quagmire from which, as we shall see, Rayner herself could not escape.

By the time of Rayner's and Starmer's elections, life for everybody in Britain had changed markedly. Most people were far less interested in the future of the Labour Party and far more concerned about a potentially lethal new disease called Covid-19. Britain was in lockdown and the planned Labour conference that was to have been held in London to announce the new leader and deputy leader had been cancelled, meaning that the results came through electronically. In fact, just a week before, Rayner herself had come down with the symptoms of Covid-19 and had been lying low. And a day after Starmer and Rayner had assumed their new positions, Boris Johnson was taken to hospital suffering from Covid-19 and had to spend three nights in intensive care. He was considered lucky to survive.

In June, Rayner disclosed that she and Starmer had discussed what would happen if he were to be struck down by the virus. 'One of the first conversations we had was, if something happened to Keir, we've got to put the mechanisms in place for me to lead the party – and what happens if Boris doesn't make it through the next forty-eight hours? Not what I expected to be discussing,' she told *The Guardian*.[8] Whether or not any of their predecessors ever had such a conversation so early on is unknown, but the fact was that at the age of forty Rayner was now as close to power as she had ever been. Indeed she was, in theory, just one step from becoming leader of the opposition.

Within days of her victory, Starmer had reshuffled the shadow Cabinet. Corbyn-supporting MPs including Richard Burgon, Barry Gardiner, Ian Lavery and Jon Trickett were sacked. Long-Bailey was given Rayner's old job as shadow Education Secretary while Rayner took on four new titles: deputy leader of the Labour Party; chair of the Labour Party; shadow First Secretary of State; and national campaigns coordinator for the Labour Party. Starmer had also made clear that she would deputise for him during Prime Minister's Questions. Yet she soon told *The Guardian* of her desire to add a fifth title to this impressive collection by becoming a member of the Privy Council, the group of senior politicians who advise the monarch and receive sensitive security briefings, among other things. The reason that she wanted to be elevated to this rank, she said, was 'so that Tories who'd look down on people like me have to call me the Right Hon. Pregnant mum at sixteen, no qualifications'. She added: 'I'm the Right Hon. and so are all other women in those circumstances, thank you.'[9] Jeremy Corbyn, a staunch republican, had become a Privy Councillor soon after his election as Labour leader in 2015, but only with some reluctance. Yet here was Rayner openly lobbying for an invitation to this cornerstone of the British establishment, supposedly because Conservative MPs whom she felt looked down on her would have to show her greater respect. Not only did this further set her apart from the Corbyn wing of the party, but her behaviour is said to have angered Starmer, who had been a knight of the realm since 2014 and a Privy Councillor since 2017. As he knew very well, however, Rayner now had her own elected position within the Labour Party and he could not ignore her even if he wanted to. She was appointed to the Privy Council in February 2021 and sworn in as a member in July 2021.

From this point Rayner's hands were close to the levers of power within the Labour Party, but what did she want to do with it? In many respects this was not an easy question for her to answer, given how devastatingly disruptive Covid-19 had been to almost every aspect of every person's life. Politics was thrown into turmoil just as everything else was. Parliament barely functioned. As the role of Labour deputy leader is so undefined it was – within obvious limits – for her to decide how she would use her new status. She could focus her attention on rebuilding a party that had been left badly damaged by the 2019 election result, in which it lost dozens of seats in what had long been considered solid Labour-voting areas, or on campaigning for the causes in which she believed.

She appointed a team of MPs to assist her, which showed that part of her objective would be to build up the progressive outlook that is so important to a strand of Labour. During the deputy leadership campaign she had subscribed to a transgender rights charter, the Labour Campaign for Trans Rights, and in doing so called on Labour to expel 'transphobic' members including what she called 'transphobic organisations such as Woman's Place UK, LGB Alliance and other trans-exclusionist hate groups'. In keeping with this vision, Rayner asked her fellow MP Marsha de Cordova to further develop Labour's equality and inclusion offering. Separately, Kim Johnson and Navendu Mishra were appointed parliamentary private secretaries to Rayner; and Tulip Siddiq was given a role based on development of the party. Sam Tarry, who had run Rayner's campaign, was asked to continue as her campaigns and organisation supremo as part of her aim to improve Labour's culture and practices. *The Guardian* reported that she had also introduced unconscious bias training 'throughout the Labour Party'.

The killing of George Floyd – a 46-year-old American who died after a police officer who arrested him outside a shop in Minneapolis in May 2020 knelt on his neck for nine minutes – was another early cause which Rayner and Starmer took up. They marked Floyd's death by 'taking a knee' together, a show of solidarity with the campaign group Black Lives Matter which represented Floyd's cause in Britain. Rayner and Starmer made this gesture in an empty room in Parliament, photographing the occasion and sending the picture out over Twitter. They no doubt felt this was a positive photo opportunity, both for themselves and for the racial justice campaign. Yet in an indirect way, somebody for whom Floyd's death had the opposite effect – and one that nobody could have foreseen – was Rayner's friend, Rebecca Long-Bailey.

Shortly after Rayner and Starmer 'took a knee', Long-Bailey retweeted an interview that the actress and Corbyn supporter Maxine Peake had given to the *Independent*, commenting: 'Maxine Peake is an absolute diamond.' In the article, Peake discussed Floyd's killing and said: 'The tactics used by the police in America, kneeling on George Floyd's neck, that was learnt from seminars with Israeli secret services.'[10] Starmer sacked Long-Bailey immediately, linking her approval of Peake's interview with the perceived antisemitism that had plagued Labour since 2015. In doing so, he swept aside one of the last remnants of Corbynism from his team and one of Rayner's key allies. 'Keir never committed in his campaign to appointing Becky,' says one observer.

> Becky had said she would appoint Keir if she won the leadership, so Keir was pushed into appointing Becky and then he sacked her at the first opportunity. He sacked all the Corbynite members of the shadow Cabinet pretty much immediately. Things moved fast. The relationship between Becky and Angela was pretty difficult because they had been close for a long time.

It was assumed that Long Bailey's sudden departure from the shadow Cabinet would be a significant loss to Rayner. As fellow north-west MPs, each had helped the other to navigate the shark-infested waters of national politics since the summer of 2015. In fact, they had begun to drift apart, and by July 2020 – the month after Long-Bailey's sacking – they were no longer flatmates. Friends were told that Rayner wanted to spend more time with her children. This change in circumstances had repercussions for the public purse, though. As flatmates, Rayner and Long-Bailey paid £1,050 each per month in rent, which they were allowed to claim back from Parliament on top of council tax, utility bills plus telephone and internet charges. From August 2020, Rayner took on a new south London flat that cost £2,500 per month to rent. By contrast, Long-Bailey chose to stay in a hotel whenever she was in London – usually on two or three nights per week – at a lower cost. Her frugality may have been a reflection of the fact that strict limits had been imposed on how many MPs were allowed in the Commons Chamber at any one time, leaving many of them to return to their constituencies on a semi-permanent basis. Hybrid Parliament sittings did not lapse until August 2021, but it was not until April 2022 that Long-Bailey began to rent a flat in London again. It cost £1,500 per month to rent – £12,000 per year less than Rayner's choice.

By the time Rayner and Long-Bailey were no longer sharing a flat, talk in Westminster and in Fleet Street had turned to an individual other than Long-Bailey who had become a significant presence in Rayner's life. In July 2020 it was reported by the *Sun on Sunday* that Angela and Mark Rayner had separated. Neither of them commented on their break-up publicly, but, by then, friends of the couple were aware that Rayner had bonded with Sam Tarry, her campaign chief. In October 2020, the *Sun on Sunday* published the first story confirming that they had formed on what was described as a 'close friendship'.[11] It remains unclear whether Sir Keir Starmer knew at that time that two of his MPs had developed feelings for each other, but anonymous messages about Rayner and Tarry began to be sent to national newspapers.

Evidence of Rayner's and Tarry's relationship did not enter the public consciousness until January 2022 when the *Sun on Sunday* published a recently taken photograph of them leaving her £30,000-a-year taxpayer-funded flat one morning and getting into a taxi together. Tarry's shoelaces were undone and a toothbrush appeared to be sticking out of his overcoat pocket.[12] As the article alongside the photograph referred to Tarry as Rayner's 'lover', there seemed little doubt that their romance was official and some months later a notice of home rights on the marital home was granted in favour of Mark Rayner under the Family Law Act 1996. A source was quoted in the newspaper as saying: 'They've been seeing each other for a long while and have tried to keep it under wraps. But many in the Labour Party know of their relationship.' This would, presumably, have included Sir Keir Starmer.

What is perhaps more intriguing is that, throughout this time, there was alarm bordering on paranoia in select Labour circles that the extramarital affair of a senior party figure other than Rayner was in danger of being exposed. Most damagingly, the male politician at the centre of the claims is said to have enjoyed a long-standing relationship with a woman that had lasted until after his own wife was pregnant with their first child. The politician's lover, who is herself a public figure, then went on to have a child of her own. She left the name of her child's father off her child's birth certificate. This led to concerns that the Labour politician was in fact the child's father, but there was no evidence to support that.

CHAPTER 10

SCUM

The carnage wreaked upon Britain by lockdown was shattering, affecting everybody in the country in one way or another. Angela Rayner was no exception. She told Times Radio of a friend of hers with six children who had struggled after the restrictions were first imposed. 'I gave her my car because I had a second car,' Rayner said. 'It's only an old Golf. But I went round and paid the insurance and gave her the car because she could get to work then and she was literally crying her eyes out.'[1] Friends were not the only ones whom she was willing to help. She told *The Guardian* that she had thought of returning to care work but 'found her skills out of date' so she volunteered with the homeless instead.[2] In her capacity as an MP, she also proved a doughty defender of her constituents' interests, taking aim at the government from as early as April 2020 – the month after lockdown began – for not considering the impact on those who were 'stuck in inadequate accommodation' with 'no back garden … nowhere to go'.[3] And in May 2020 she urged Rishi Sunak to keep the furlough scheme running for as long as necessary and not 'pull the rug from under people's feet'. Yet by September 2020 she was exasperated, blaming Boris Johnson's 'failure and incompetence' for causing '15,000 deaths in our care homes due to coronavirus'.[4] And in October 2020, she described him as 'the biggest idiot Prime Minister we've ever had' for his handling of the pandemic. The reason for her anger soon became apparent.

Two weeks later, on 21 October 2020, she attended Parliament to speak in a hastily arranged Opposition Day debate on econom- ic support for areas with greater Covid-19 restrictions that has, in its way, gone down in parliamentary history. 'I start by placing on record my thanks to the staff at Stepping Hill Hospital in Stockport who recently cared for my aunt, who died of coronavirus last week,' she told MPs.

> I speak today not just as a Member of this House, or just as a Mancunian, but as someone like the many others across our city and our country who have in the past few weeks lost loved ones to this terrible virus. That, more than anything, is why I come here wanting the Government not to fail but to succeed, because lives literally depend on it.[5]

Four MPs – one from the SNP and three from the Conservative Party – were quick to express their condolences at her loss but, after an hour, the mood in the Chamber changed. A fellow Greater Man- chester MP, Chris Clarkson of the Conservative Party, rose to speak. He criticised the Mayor of Manchester, Andy Burnham, for having declined the offer of a £60 million government support package on the basis that it represented only 92 per cent of the figure Burnham had apparently wanted to secure. Clarkson then reminded MPs of the 'opportunism' shown by the Labour MP Kate Green, who had said at a Labour Party conference fringe event a few weeks previ- ously that Labour activists should use the Covid-19 catastrophe to lobby for more money for schools and 'don't let a good crisis go to waste'. Clarkson commented: 'I know [Green] thinks this is a good crisis that the Labour Party should exploit, and I know she speaks for a lot of her frontbench colleagues when she says that. We just need to see it in the support-U-turn-oppose approach that has characterised their hindsight-heavy behaviour.'

Female Labour MPs could be heard heckling, but Clarkson tried to speak over them. Suddenly, he stopped, turned to Rayner and asked: 'Excuse me, did the honourable lady just call me "scum"?' The Deputy Speaker, Dame Eleanor Laing, roared 'Order!' several times as she sought to control the Chamber. With an icy look in her eye and a grave tone of voice she then addressed Rayner herself. 'From the front bench we will *not* have remarks like that. Not under *any* circumstances, no matter how heartfelt it might be – not at all.'

Showing no sign of being perturbed, Rayner requested permission to speak. She stood and said to Laing: 'I think one of the things I'd ask your guidance on is [Clarkson] saying things about the front bench which is [sic] inaccurate in their speech and I'd ask them to withdraw it.' Laing made clear that it was not for her to rule on inaccuracy and Clarkson resumed. 'Thank you, Madam Deputy Speaker,' he said: 'And thank you for your guidance. To clarify, I asked [Rayner] if she called me [scum] – that is what I heard.'

He was not wrong. Others who had heard her casting the slur in Clarkson's direction soon pounced on her conduct, including the Conservative MP Katherine Fletcher, who also hails from the north-west. She said:

As Mancunians, we agree that being fair is most important, after being proud of who we are and where we come from. Is it in order for a senior member of the Labour Front Bench, the hon. Member for Ashton-under-Lyne, to call out repeatedly 'scum' when my hon. Friend the Member for Heywood and Middleton was talking, and then fail to retract it or apologise? Today, she has shamed Manchester and shamed this House. She should apologise.[6]

The Commons Chamber has always been known for its tendency to rowdiness and some MPs more than others have been noted for their use of questionable expression in it. In the 1970s, when Margaret Thatcher was the Education Secretary, backbench Labour MPs would sometimes chant 'Ditch the bitch' when she spoke in the Chamber. Yet it is not likely that one MP has called another 'scum' before – and certainly not recently. Indeed, in the twenty-first century, MPs tend to be far more circumspect, not least because social media platforms can be used to highlight their behaviour so rapidly.

Rayner had made no mention of regret an hour after she called Clarkson 'scum', by when Labour had lost the vote by 261 votes to 340, and so he fired off a letter asking her to retract and apologise for the comment. He posted his letter on Twitter, where the episode had begun to attract considerable attention. She could hardly refuse his request. Early that evening, she issued the following short statement: 'I apologise for the language that I used in a heated debate in Parliament earlier.'[7]

Many on the Tory benches felt this was mealy mouthed and some said so at the time, but little more of any consequence was said about it for the next twelve months or so. Still, there was plenty of debate about what the remark revealed about Rayner, who was later described along with her Labour colleagues by Rod Liddle in the *Sunday Times* as 'semi-house-trained'.[8] The year before, she had complained of receiving online abuse and had posted a message on Facebook saying: 'We have to stop the personal attacks and be kinder to each other.'

What do Tory MPs think of the incident a few years on? Andrew Mitchell, who first sat in the Commons in 1987, is sanguine. 'When Angela used the word scum, I didn't rise to it at all,' he says.

> It was slightly OTT, but it was just Angela. It wasn't in my view an offensive comment, which it could easily have been coming from someone else. You might say that's patronising, but what little I knew of her at the time suggested that any such comment, in spite of the word used, was not meant to be venomous.

Others remain dismayed about it – but oddly happy as well. One prominent backbencher says: 'Angela Rayner is one of the best electoral assets the Conservative Party has. She only has to open her mouth to turn off the Labour vote. This shows why.'

Having settled into her post as deputy leader of the Labour Party, Rayner was seen by some to have assumed the status of an attack dog, rarely passing up any opportunity to challenge the government's record and often making herself available to provide a quote for journalists if asked. She was assiduous in this endeavour. Yet because she and Starmer had taken over their respective leadership positions in the unique circumstances of a lockdown, Covid-19 dominated politics. This required a careful, and often diplomatic, balancing act on their part as they tried to adopt a tone of constructive criticism in what was a time of national emergency.

Outwardly, Labour politicians were keen to advance the idea that Rayner and Starmer had formed a genuine partnership of equals. Yet just as Starmer's early months as Labour leader were an uphill battle as he sought to resuscitate the party's fortunes, so there were tensions underneath the surface between him and his deputy as well. Starmer's promise to remove the stain of antisemitism from Labour placed him on a collision course with the left wing of his organisation. Many of its members continued to coalesce around Jeremy Corbyn, a man from whom Starmer was increasingly keen to distance himself. According to one insider, Rayner, by contrast, had been happy to maintain her relationship with Corbyn since she had become Labour's deputy. 'Angela and Jeremy got on well all the way through,' confirms a friend. 'He was always supportive of her and vice versa from the time she became an MP. It was a warm friendship. That continued until Jeremy's suspension from the party in October 2020.'

Corbyn's removal was triggered by his response to the publication of the Equality and Human Rights Commission's report into antisemitism in the Labour Party, on 29 October 2020. As mentioned in Chapter 9, this inquiry had been launched in May 2019 in response to allegations made by the Campaign Against Antisemitism and the Jewish Labour Movement. The EHRC found that, under Corbyn, Labour had been responsible for 'unlawful' acts of harassment and discrimination, failures in leadership and a poor record of handling antisemitism complaints. In a statement, the EHRC said its analysis pointed to 'a culture within the party which, at best, did not do enough to prevent antisemitism and, at worst, could be seen to accept it'.[9] An unlawful act notice was served on Labour, meaning that it had to produce an action plan within six weeks. Ultimately, the EHRC would continue monitoring the Labour Party until January 2023.

Within minutes of the report surfacing in October 2020, Corbyn released a statement in which he expressed his belief that the scale of the problem under his leadership had been 'dramatically over-stated for political reasons'.[10] He refused to apologise and so the whip was withdrawn. For some, it is notable that on the day the report was published, Rayner told BBC Radio 4's *World at One*: 'Jeremy is a thoroughly decent man, but he has an absolute blind spot and a denial when it comes to some of these issues.' What was perceived as her continuing support for him even at that time has led some Jewish members of the Labour movement to conclude that she has never fully grasped the seriousness of the matter. This is a charge that Keir Starmer has also faced. Even today, certain Labour figures continue to wonder why Rayner and Starmer campaigned twice – in 2017 and 2019 – to get Corbyn into 10 Downing Street at the same time as allegedly harbouring such serious suspicions about their leader's attitude to the Jewish community. In October 2020, however, the problem for Rayner was that within hours of the EHRC's report being published, she was publicly accused of having expressed antisemitic views herself.

Starmer called 29 October 2020 'a day of shame' for Labour and he said sorry to the Jewish community as a result of the findings of the EHRC report. For Rayner, there was no such quick fix. She was one of fifteen of Corbyn's allies in the parliamentary party against whom other complaints were either submitted to Labour – and in Rayner's case resubmitted – by the Campaign Against Antisemitism. Diane Abbott and Rebecca Long-Bailey were two other prominent names on the list.

The CAA's complaint against Rayner sprang from the article she had written about her visit to Auschwitz, which, as mentioned in Chapter 5, was published originally in the *Morning Star* in January 2015, four months before she was first elected to the House of Commons. In it, she referenced a book called *The Holocaust Industry* written by an American political scientist called Norman Finkel-stein. This book posits the highly inflammatory notion that some members of the Jewish community exploit the Holocaust for polit-ical and financial advantage. In her 2015 article, Rayner had praised Finkelstein's book as 'seminal'. She had also made the observation: 'My previous visit [to Auschwitz] was in 2003 and I couldn't help but notice the increased commercialism and tourism related to the Holocaust era in the Kraków region.'[11] In January 2018 she reposted on Facebook a link to her 2015 article to mark Holocaust Memo-rial Day. Ten months after that, in November 2018, her Facebook post was exposed by a Twitter account called The Golem, which fights antisemitism. Rayner was forced to make an apology at that time, saying there had been 'a genuine misunderstanding in what was always intended to be a message of solidarity with the Jewish community'.[12] The fact that her words were being linked to antisem-itism yet again, in 2020, was obviously unhelpful to her. The irony is that Rayner is thought to have asked somebody else to write the *Morning Star* article for her in 2015. There are also questions about whether she had ever read Finkelstein's book in sufficient detail to be able to form the judgment that it is 'seminal'. Nonetheless, she had put her name to the enterprise.

Separately, a second complaint against Rayner was made to the Labour Party at the same time by a Labour Party member. It relat-ed to her *Jaws*-inspired Twitter post, referred to in Chapter 8, in which she stated that opponents of Corbyn and Labour would need a 'bigger smear' if they were to succeed in undermining the party. The Labour Party promised to consider both of the complaints.

Four weeks later, no doubt keen to show that she wanted to make amends for having possibly offended the Jewish community, Rayner addressed a conference staged by the Jewish Labour Movement at which she reportedly said: 'Our members need to get real about this. If they don't think antisemitism is within the Labour Party and that there are problems now, then there's really no place for them in the Labour Party.' She went on: 'People need to understand what our Jewish community have been through. We should have a bit of humility … We should be listening and aware of how hurt and upset people are … If I have to suspend thousands and thousands of members, we will do that.' She also called Corbyn's reaction to the EHRC report 'totally unacceptable', saying:

Any attempts to minimise or downplay the extent of antisemi- tism are part of the problem. This is the issue. I knew this would happen. It is a matter of public record now that I contacted Jeremy to try and get him not to say what he said, and to apologise and withdraw it afterwards. Because I don't think Jeremy really quite gets how upsetting it is.[13]

She has not described him in public as 'a thoroughly decent man' since.

A week before Christmas, in response to the EHRC report, Labour unveiled its Action Plan for Driving out Antisemitism. In a jointly written introduction, Starmer and Rayner said they had 'made rooting out antisemitism our number-one priority', and wanted to 'change the processes, structures and the culture of the Party to ensure Jewish people feel safe to return to their political home.' An independent investigation process for complaints of antisemitism, Islamophobia, racism, sexual harassment and other forms of discrimination, in which the leadership would have no locus, was to be established. Lawyers would advise on antisemitism hearings. 'We will not hesitate to sanction those who breach our rules and regulations,' Starmer and Rayner wrote. 'Social media guidelines will be strengthened and candidates wishing to represent the Party will undergo greater due diligence checks.'[14]

All of this sounded meaningful and was clearly intended to heal the wounds inflicted on the Jewish community during the Corbyn era, yet there was some scepticism two months later, in February 2021, when it came to light that both of the investigations involving Rayner had been abandoned. The *Jewish Chronicle* reported that Labour sources believed the threshold for disciplinary action against her had not been met. At the time Gideon Falter, Chief Executive of the Campaign Against Antisemitism, put out a statement in which he said:

> It is still business as usual for the Labour Party when it comes to antisemitism. Our complaint against Angela Rayner was never acknowledged by Labour. The Party also did not confirm that it was investigating, and now it has tried to drop the investigation without a word ... The investigation of our complaint against Angela Rayner has been a sham and we will be re-introducing the complaint to the independent disciplinary panel when it is set up.[15]

Rayner had not escaped being drawn into the greatest internal scandal to engulf the Labour Party in recent years, but, as far as the official record is concerned, she emerged from it unscathed.

• • •

The year 2021 looked to be significant as far as Rayner's political career was concerned. In early May, local council elections would be held in England; there would be ballots for the London Assembly and Mayor; in the Scottish and Welsh parliaments; for seven 'metro mayors'; and for Police and Crime Commissioners. A Westminster by-election in Hartlepool would also be held following the resignation of the Labour MP Mike Hill, who was found guilty of breaching Parliament's sexual misconduct policy. As the newly appointed chair of the Labour Party, and as its national campaign coordinator to boot, Rayner would be intimately involved in the party's attempt to sell its offering to voters. This was a heavy responsibility and one in which she knew she could not always rely on her boyfriend, Sam Tarry, for support. Having been appointed as Labour's shadow Transport Minister at the beginning of January, Tarry had less time to help her. Instead, she worked with two experienced Labour campaigners, Simon Fletcher and Anneliese Midgley.

To ensure that Rayner's task could be completed to the best of her abilities, it was considered vital that she and Starmer were in lockstep at all times. Yet there is plenty of evidence to suggest that relations between them were not always harmonious. Discipline is important to Starmer. Yet where he is generally thought to choose his words carefully, Rayner has often shown herself to be impetuous. For example, she was lambasted in January 2021 for claiming during an interview on Radio 4's *Today* programme that teachers were more likely to catch Covid than other members of society. She said they should receive the newly launched vaccine as a matter of urgency as soon as the four top priority groups named by the Joint Committee on Vaccination and Immunisation had received it. Indeed, she asserted it was 'a fact' that all key workers, including teachers, were 'more at risk of infection and death'.[16] Critics seized on her proposal, pointing out that if it were followed, a teacher in their twenties would be inoculated before somebody in their sixties, even though age was thought to be a major risk factor. Because the Office for National Statistics had already made clear that death rates for teachers were 'not statistically significantly raised' compared with non-teachers, Starmer was forced into the humiliating position of having to admit that there was 'no scientific evidence' to back up Rayner's theory and that she was therefore wrong. One Labour source told the *Daily Telegraph* they thought her interview had been a 'car crash'.[17]

The following month a similar error was pointed out by the City editor of the *Daily Mail*, Alex Brummer. He asked why Rayner had tweeted regularly about the government having pumped '£22 billion' into the coffers of the services company Serco's 'failed Test and Trace' scheme. Serco may not have been a saintly organisation, Brummer wrote, but Rayner was guilty of 'a shameful perversion of the truth'.[18] Its Test and Trace contract had in fact been worth £350 million in the past financial year – not £22 billion. Indeed, its global revenues for the year 2020 were £3.9 billion. 'Just 1 per cent of Serco's profits of £163 million, up one-third on the previous year, came from pandemic work,' Brummer calculated. He said the 'false news' peddled by Rayner was enough to 'make one question how Sir Keir Starmer can allow such a loose cannon to hold high office in a reformed post-Corbyn party'.[19] Even if Starmer did not read Brummer's column, he could not ignore the point. The independent organisation Full Fact later published a research paper on similar claims that Rayner, among other Labour MPs, had made about Serco. It found them to be incorrect.[20] These two matters further fuelled the perception that Rayner was prone to pontificating on subjects without having done the required research.

Expenses claims published early in 2021 showed that Rayner, who had boasted of 'standing up for working people', had spent £1,600 of public money on twenty-three first-class tickets between London and her Manchester constituency over the previous twelve months, triggering questions from journalists about why standard class wasn't good enough for her. It also came to light that she had spent £2,367 of taxpayers' money on Apple computer items and a new chair. MPs had been told they were allowed to claim up to £10,000 on new equipment for home offices for themselves and their staff, but Rayner was singled out for criticism because of her decision to spend £249 on one pair of personalised AirPod Pro headphones. 'A reasonably-priced pair of headphones would have been sufficient,' raged *The Sun*, which had uncovered the figures. 'If she wanted top-of-the-range personalised Apple AirPod Pros, at £249, then why should you pay for them? It's pure greed.'[21] Once again, Starmer was said to be perplexed by her ability to score an own-goal, not least because Rayner admitted later that year that she had lost the headphones.[22]

Her blundering continued into early March. Following the election of Labour's new leader in Scotland, Anas Sarwar, she was publicly ridiculed for saying on Twitter that he was 'the first ever ethnic minority leader of a political party anywhere in the UK'.[23] Benjamin Cohen, the founder of *Pink News*, was one of the first to point out that she might want to cast her memory back six years. 'I guess Jews don't count, Angela?' Cohen asked sarcastically. Then he reminded her: 'You were first elected in a general election fought by a Jewish Labour leader.'[24] This was a reference to Ed Miliband, but Cohen could just as easily have mentioned Michael Howard, who led the Tories between 2003 and 2005, or, come to that, Benjamin Disraeli, the nineteenth-century Conservative Prime Minister.

More seriously, in late March 2021, a new internal Labour Party battle involving Rayner broke out over the selection process of its nominee for the post of Mayor of Liverpool. In December 2020, Labour's original candidate, Joe Anderson, the incumbent mayor, had been arrested on suspicion of conspiracy to commit bribery and witness intimidation. It was decided that an all-female shortlist should be opened to find his replacement. Three Liverpool councillors – Wendy Simon, Ann O'Byrne and Anna Rothery, who was endorsed by the now-disgraced Jeremy Corbyn – made it onto the ballot paper and were due to be voted on by party members. But at the eleventh hour, the process was suspended by the party in London and then restarted. All three shortlisted candidates were told they would not be allowed to stand. Ultimately, another candidate altogether, Joanne Anderson, was adopted instead. The left was furious, with John McDonnell tweeting that the 'fiasco leaves the Labour bureaucracy wide open to charges of sheer incompetence or a political stitch-up or both. If there was a problem with any candidate it should have been dealt with earlier or is the problem the socialism of a possible winner?'[25] Rayner and her team were widely blamed, ensuring that tensions between her and Starmer simmered as the local election campaign got underway.

It was not as though she was entirely passive at this point, however. In an April 2021 article marking the first anniversary of Starmer's leadership, *The Times* was briefed that Rayner felt as though she had had her 'wings clipped' by him and that he had sidelined her in favour of his 'tight-knit circle of Camden allies'. One of her supporters told the paper: 'At some point Keir is going to have to stop taking it for granted that Angela will placate the Left and be grateful for all the loyalty she has shown.'[26] It was also made clear to the paper that she wanted a more prominent role in the party and would welcome the chance to increase her media profile. This was not the prelude Starmer needed to the following month's local elections, especially as Labour was expected to perform badly. For Rayner, worse was to come.

When May's election results rolled in, it was clear that the political hole in which Labour found itself was getting deeper. The Conservative Party achieved the best results in England, gaining eleven additional councils and 234 new councillors. Labour lost control of ten councils and lost 326 councillors. Most worrying for Starmer was that after nearly fifty years as a Labour-held parliamentary constituency, the Tories also won Hartlepool, securing more than 50 per cent of the vote on a sixteen-point swing. It was only the second time since 1982 that the governing party had gained a seat in a by-election. One year after Starmer's arrival, the Labour Party appeared to be in reverse gear.

The morning after the polls closed, Starmer promised to take responsibility for the disastrous outcome, but it was soon apparent that he wanted Rayner to be made to pay as well. Before all the results from across the UK were declared, he sacked her as chair of the Labour Party and as national campaigns coordinator. To the fury of her and her team, she is said to have learned of her dismissal from journalists, who were apparently briefed about a raft of shadow Cabinet changes before Starmer had even discussed them with the individual MPs concerned. Starmer's office disputed this, accusing Rayner and her inner circle of fanning the flames by relaying the story themselves. They considered it noteworthy, for example, that Andrew Fisher, who had been Jeremy Corbyn's policy chief, was among the first to tweet the news.

That weekend, leaks appeared in the press about the fact that she was said to have insisted on travelling first class when using the train during the campaign. Rayner's team was forced to counter-brief that she had not travelled in standard class because of safety fears following the abduction and murder of Sarah Everard in March 2021. It was also claimed to journalists that Rayner had not, in fact, played any part in developing an election strategy for Labour's campaign despite being its campaigns coordinator. The *Sunday Times* reported that Lord Mandelson, Tony Blair's former spin doctor who had become close to Starmer's operation, had 'asked Rayner following a meeting of Labour MPs and peers to explain what the party's campaign message was' and found that 'she was unable to do so coherently'.[27] One Labour MP told *The Sun* bluntly: 'Her presentations on Zoom were incoherent and embarrassing.' It was also suggested that her working relationship with Starmer had ceased to function because she did not get on with his close aide Baroness Chapman of Darlington.

Some within Labour believed that Starmer felt he could only turn the party's fortunes around if he undermined and ultimately eliminated every last trace of the Corbyn era from its public face. This would include marginalising Rayner. Labour's thrashing during a campaign with which she was inextricably linked represented a legitimate excuse to put that plan into action, it was felt, and he acted accordingly. After all, there was no reason why she could not be Labour's deputy leader from the backbenches. As Labour descended into a new civil war, however, MPs on the left including Jon Trickett, Diane Abbott, John McDonnell and Andy Burnham backed Rayner. Many said she had been made a 'scapegoat'.

With the party apparently turning in on itself, the future of Starmer's own job was openly discussed. Labour's rules stated that to remove him would take the backing of at least forty Labour MPs – 20 per cent of the parliamentary party. By contrast, Rayner in fact looked safer than he did for a period, particularly because her position as the elected deputy Labour leader was out of Starmer's reach. It has even been claimed that some of those who were closest to Rayner began testing the water at this point in preparation for her to try to oust Starmer. She certainly fought back. By the Sunday morning, three days after the local elections, shadow Scotland Secretary Ian Murray appeared on Sky News and tried to broker peace by informing viewers that, far from being demoted, Rayner was about to receive a 'significant promotion'. Within hours, it was indeed confirmed that as part of a wider shadow Cabinet reshuffle, she had negotiated for herself a new post of her design, with two new job titles to replace the old ones.

Labour's difficulties so amused Boris Johnson that he could not resist mocking Starmer when they faced each other a few days later in the Chamber of the House of Commons. During a discussion about jobs that some politicians had done before entering Parliament, Johnson touched on the fact that the Conservative MP Katherine Fletcher is a qualified safari ranger who has worked in Africa. He used this fact to make a joke at Starmer's expense. 'She [Fletcher] knows that in any pride of lions, it is the male who tends to occupy the position of titular, nominal authority, while the most dangerous beast, the prize hunter of the pack, is in fact the lioness,' Johnson jeered. 'That is a point that I am sure [Starmer] bears in mind as he contemplates his right hon. Friend the Member for Ashton-under-Lyne, the deputy leader, shadow First Secretary of State, shadow Chancellor of the Duchy of Lancaster and shadow Secretary of State for the Future of Work.' Then he warned with a chuckle: 'Though the more titles he feeds her, the hungrier, I fear, she is likely to become.'[28]

Even though one of Rayner's new jobs – shadow Secretary of State for the Future of Work – meant that she would be shadowing a government job that did not actually exist, the implication of

Johnson's jibe was clear enough. An impression gained ground that Starmer did not get on with his deputy and was in a sense being held hostage by her. She was in effect shackled to him thanks to his party's constitution. And if the situation was viewed from a certain angle, he now appeared to be weaker than her. In what amounted to a promotion, she was able to demand from him two new job titles – as well as having the Future of Work brief she was now also the shadow Minister for the Cabinet Office and Chancellor of the Duchy of Lancaster – and then receive them. The sense that Starmer was on the back foot was compounded later that day when he was forced to sack his parliamentary aide and close friend Carolyn Harris after she was caught spreading rumours about Rayner on WhatsApp.

The next day, Rayner gave a typically forthright interview to the BBC in which she acknowledged that Starmer had not yet managed to capture the attention of the electorate. 'What I heard on the doorstep is they [voters] didn't know what Keir Starmer stood for. So that's what I think our challenge is,' she said.[29] She was similarly plain-talking with ITV News, explaining that Labour 'got the tone wrong' during the elections and sounded 'patronising' to voters. When asked about the reshuffle from which she seemed to have done quite well, she said: 'Everyone knows I'm quite a trade union negotiator, and a robust talker, and Keir is very frank with me and I've really enjoyed the fact we've had that constructive, open relationship. I'm pleased that will continue.'

Some in the Labour Party believe that Rayner may have overplayed her hand at this point. 'Carolyn Harris was absolutely devoted to Keir,' reports one senior source.

She had spent a lot of time badmouthing Angela. Angela called it out and Keir removed Carolyn – not because he was particularly close to Angela but because he doesn't expect anyone to behave like that in the workplace. I think Keir thought: 'I'm going to let Angela have a win here, because we're in the wrong,' but in a funny sort of way Angela mishandled it, because it went straight to her head. Some in the PLP were thinking: 'You're trying to rub Keir's nose in it.'

This perception of Rayner's disloyalty was only underscored when she told Politico's 'Westminster Insider' podcast that even she might have voted for the 'authentic' Boris Johnson, adding that Starmer does 'cheese me off'.[30] It is not as though she was alone in laying into the leader, however. Tony Blair wrote an uncompromising piece for the *New Statesman* in which he condemned the 'woke left' and acknowledged that Starmer was 'struggling to break through with the public'. He said the party needed to embark on a 'complete deconstruction and reconstruction. Nothing less will do.'[31]

In between the interviews Rayner gave, two insights into her political beliefs emerged. These came courtesy of her own hand, and some felt they illustrated in part why Labour had lost its link to the Red Wall after the Tories had so successfully hoovered up its vote. That week, police officers were called to the Pollokshields area of Glasgow to assist officials who were trying to deport two illegal immigrants. Hundreds of people gathered to protest at what they saw as an injustice. After a lengthy stand-off, the two men were released. Rayner tweeted: 'Solidarity with the people of Glasgow today.' This was taken as proof that she had come down on the side of the law-breakers, not the law enforcers who have traditionally been held in high regard by many Labour supporters. Wasn't this exactly the sort of thing Tony Blair had warned against? Separately,

Sun on Sunday columnist Tony Parsons pointed out a few days later that as tensions had escalated between Israel and Palestine that week, with both sides attacking each other, a 'gormless' Rayner had tweeted: 'Eid Mubarak to all. I want to especially keep in the worlds conscious [*sic*] the Palestinians who are suffering terrible injustices during this joyous occasion.'[32] Parsons seethed: 'The innocent are suffering on BOTH sides of this tragedy. Extremists on BOTH sides are stoking the flames. And this pitiful Labour Party are still spouting their woke student clichés.'

All of this affected the perception of Starmer's position as leader. By the end of the week, Andy Burnham and Yvette Cooper were being spoken of as possible replacements. One ally of Starmer recalls hearing that Rayner was also gearing up to make a leadership pitch at this point.

> When Keir was on the back foot as leader, some people around
> Angela started asking: 'Is she going to run for leader?' but it soon
> became apparent that there wasn't going to be a base of support for
> her in the party. I think that was a bit of a shock to her. I think her
> supporters thought the PLP would say: 'She's the only one who can
> do this,' because this is what tends to happen with deputy leaders.
> She got a bit of a shock when she realised how thin her base was,
> even among people who were socially close to her.

Did a desire to shore up her position with the left lie behind her declaration around this time to Times Radio that '100 per cent' Jeremy Corbyn 'would have done a better job' than Boris Johnson when it came to dealing with the Covid crisis?[33]

After Labour's dismal showing at the polls in May, two further electoral tests followed for Starmer in quick succession. His opponents, both within Labour and outside it, believed this was when the screw would be turned. The first, on 17 June, was the Chesham and Amersham by-election following the death of the Conservative MP Cheryl Gillan. Although it had been a Tory stronghold for decades, Labour was expected to achieve a respectable result. At the 2017 general election, it had come second with more than 11,000 votes; and in 2019 it had come third with more than 7,000 votes. In the event, this by-election result was significant for two reasons. First, to widespread amazement, the Liberal Democrats won the ballot with a swing against the Tories of more than 25 per cent, arguably proving that there is no such thing in politics as a 'safe seat'. Second, Boris Johnson's humiliation was shared by Starmer after Labour polled just 622 votes – 1.6 per cent of the total cast – even though the party had more members than that in the area at the time. Its candidate, Natasa Pantelic, came fourth and lost her deposit. This abysmal performance raised fresh doubts about Starmer's future.

Two weeks later – and less than two months after the debacle at Hartlepool – Labour found itself defending another northern seat at a by-election, this time in the West Yorkshire constituency of Batley and Spen after the sitting MP, Tracy Brabin, had stood down after winning the West Yorkshire mayoral election. Labour had a tight majority of 3,500 and poll after poll suggested that it would lose. Starmer's hopes rested on the shoulders of Kim Leadbeater, the younger sister of the late Jo Cox, who had been murdered five years previously. Leadbeater had only recently rejoined the Labour Party and there was uncertainty as to whether she was a sufficiently strong candidate when the stakes were so high. The sense of mutiny in the air surged when Diane Abbott said that it would be 'curtains' for Starmer if Labour lost.[34] Mischievous newspaper reports suggested that Rayner, who was campaigning in Batley and Spen, was still weighing up a move against him depending on the outcome. Journalists were even told that she would be supported in this endeavour by three left-wing trade unions – the Transport Salaried Staffs' Association, Aslef, and the Communication Workers Union. If Rayner or her band of supporters had secretly been hoping that Leadbeater would lose, she would have been disappointed, for Leadbeater beat the Tory candidate, Ryan Stephenson, by 323 votes.

This wafer-thin victory and its consequences could be said to serve as an adequate reflection of the state of Starmer's leadership at that time. Somehow, he had managed to cling to his position, bolstered by the fact that there was no obvious alternative candidate whom MPs were united in backing. This, of course, meant that Rayner was also forced to remain in her post as deputy leader. Lord Mandelson was notably quick out of the blocks after the Batley and Spen result was known, pointing out to her via a BBC interview that over the previous eight weeks she had been 'egged on by people who are serving their own factional purposes and interests' and that 'she should realise that these are not her friends'.

In accepting the fact that her own assumed ambitions to lead Labour would for the time being have to be put to one side, she also had to confront the bitter truth that she did not enjoy as much support from within her parliamentary party as she had perhaps believed. One Labour veteran who has worked with her closely is adamant that she had a popularity problem at this point, saying:

If Keir had stood down for any reason [in 2021], the person who would have occupied that space of being the slightly left-leaning, acceptable face of radical industrial politics would have been Lisa Nandy. She'd have walked it. And everyone who backed Angela for the deputy leadership in 2020 would have swung in behind Lisa.

In any case, it would soon be clear that May 2021, when the Tories snatched Hartlepool from Labour, had been Boris Johnson's political high-water mark. The political tide was beginning to turn against him and his party. Repeated failures on their part, internal rows, sleaze accusations and a series of self-inflicted political wounds meant that the governing party was about to find itself entering what has come to be known as the 'death spiral'. Hastening this sense of decay was exactly the sort of work to which Angela Rayner was suited. Despite Labour's poor performances at the ballot box that spring, some of which had been attributed to her, she had shown herself to be a survivor. Her focus would now be fixed on trying to bring down Johnson and his government.

CHAPTER 11

JOHN PRESCOTT IN A SKIRT

After the fractious spring and early summer of 2021, it was re-ported that Keir Starmer's office was worried Angela Rayner might kick up a 'stink' at Labour's annual party conference in Brighton in September. There was even talk of Starmer lessening the possibility of any trouble by shortening her speaking slot or picking an awkward time of day for her to address the conference hall. In the event no amount of planning on Starmer's part could have spared his blushes, for it was an unscripted anti-Tory rant on which Rayner embarked during a fringe meeting on the first day of the gathering that caused a publicity storm that overshadowed proceedings. It put Starmer's nose out of joint, but it also had far more profound consequences for her personally.

That Saturday had begun well for Rayner, with Times Radio broadcasting a lengthy interview in which she spoke in some depth about her upbringing and her political future. *The Times* published a 4,000-word companion piece complete with a fashion photo shoot. 'If I felt that it was the right thing to do for the party and the right thing for the country, then I would step up and do it,' Rayner revealed when asked about her ambitions to lead Labour.

As for running the country, she said: 'If Boris Johnson can be Prime Minister, I think I could definitely do a better job than him, because I've been up close and personal and I've seen it.'[1] All this suggested that her political aspirations were fully charged just in time for the most important event in the Labour Party's calendar.

In the afternoon, she was hailed by members as she began her opening address, in which she denounced 'Tory sleaze' and championed workers' rights. If she sounded angry when talking about these perceived injustices, *The Observer* reported the next day that she had been 'furious' with Starmer because he had insisted on clogging up the conference with a vote on changing the rules surrounding the election of future leaders – a diversion that Rayner did not welcome and a policy to which she was opposed. (These measures eventually passed, albeit narrowly and in watered-down form.) This briefing to a Labour-supporting newspaper would only serve to remind the electorate of the tensions between herself and Starmer, which were, by now, openly discussed.

The turbulence began that evening when she attended a meeting for north-west Labour members. At about 9.15 she was recorded tearing into the Conservatives. 'I'm sick of shouting from the sidelines and I bet youse lot are too,' she said. Then, amid yelps and applause from supporters, she was heard saying: 'We cannot get any worse than a bunch of scum, homophobic, racist, misogynistic, absolute pile of [inaudible] banana republic, vile, nasty, Etonian [inaudible] piece of scum.'[2] The *Daily Mirror* broke the story of her tirade and it was immediately picked up by most media outlets. When Sky News challenged her the following day, her line of defence was that in the heat of the moment she had fallen into the 'street language' of her youth. 'It's a phrase that you would hear very often in Northern, working-class towns that we'd even say it jovially to other people,' she claimed. She then trained her fire on Boris Johnson, who in 1998 had referred in the *Daily Telegraph* to 'tank-topped bumboys' and in 2018 in the same publication had stated that Muslim women wearing burkas 'look like letter boxes'. Rayner continued: 'If the Prime Minister wants to apologise and remove himself from those comments that he's made that are homophobic, that are racist, that are misogynistic, then I will apologise for calling him scummy.'[3] Not everybody agreed with her logic. Senior colleagues including Ed Miliband and Lisa Nandy distanced themselves from her.

Starmer was also clearly unimpressed when asked about the incident on the *Andrew Marr Show* on BBC1. 'Angela said those words, she takes a different approach to me,' he said stiffly. 'It's not language that I would have used.' He revealed that he would speak to her but he said he would not force her to apologise. His response was seen as inadequate both by the Conservative Party, which quickly tried to make political capital out of the situation, and perhaps by the BBC political correspondent Adam Fleming, who asked rhetorically: 'Keir Starmer is not able to say to Angela Rayner: "You should apologise for these comments," even though he himself would not have made them. Is that because he doesn't have the strength to do that? Because she has her own mandate directly elected by the party?' Looked at one way, Rayner had once again put Starmer on the back foot, even though he was not the one who had been injudicious.

Despite Rayner's apparent indifference to the repercussion of her outburst, there were plenty of other people within the Labour movement who were angry with her. They believed that if the party was to have a hope of regaining power, it would need to moderate its tone and convince Tory voters that Labour was not intent on waging anything resembling a class war. They also questioned the point of Rayner preaching her class politics to the converted – unless it was part of a calculated effort on her part to improve her standing in their eyes as a leader-in-waiting. Former Labour MP Lord Austin was one who expressed outrage. 'Decent working people in places like Dudley don't wander around calling each other 'scum' as a term of endearment,' he wrote in *The Sun*. 'They will be appalled – by her saying it in the first place and then claiming they speak like that.' He added:

> It's not the first time, but she gets away with it because middle class people in politics are so out of touch. They either think this is how ordinary working people behave or they are worried about being called snobs if they call her out. Either way, it's deeply patronising.[4]

It wasn't just that some Labour politicians found the comments offensive. The episode came at an unhelpful time for the Labour Party, which needed to be seen to exert pressure on the government as problems piled up around the country. The UK's debt mountain had ballooned to a sixty-year high of £2.2 trillion. The Bank of England had warned that inflation was predicted to reach 4 per cent by December – twice its official target. Energy prices were rising. Under-employment was affecting food and fuel supplies. And the term 'cost of living crisis' had entered common parlance. Starmer's office believed that if Rayner had not been so careless, more media coverage might have been devoted to how Labour proposed to tackle these pressing matters. Instead, her refusal to say sorry had become the central plotline of a soap opera she had created.

When Rayner was photographed pensively smoking a cigarette

outside the conference centre, it was hoped that she might have been contemplating the wisdom of her decision to publicly label the Tories 'scum' for the second time in eleven months. But when her parliamentary colleague Emily Thornberry proclaimed that 'there may have been drink partaken' before Rayner's broadside, it was clear that the longer she left her apology, the more damaging the row might become.[5] Yet she appeared to be unrepentant, and on the last night of the conference she was to be found singing karaoke duets at a party with Andy Burnham and Jonathan Ashworth. It was only as the conference ended that she expressed anything close to regret. 'That's me,' she said. 'I'm bombastic and I apologise if it offended the public in the way in which I expressed it.'

Four weeks later, however, she suddenly changed her tune. In a Facebook post on 28 October, she explained why. On that day, a member of the public called Benjamin Iliffe was sentenced to fifteen weeks in prison, suspended for eighteen months, after pleading guilty to malicious communications. Twelve days previously, on 16 October, he had sent Rayner a threatening and abusive email in which he told her to 'watch your back and your kids'. He was swiftly arrested and charged. Huntingdon Magistrates' Court heard that Iliffe believed that Rayner's propensity to cast a slur had contributed to the murder of the Conservative MP Sir David Amess, committed the day before Iliffe wrote to Rayner. A probation officer said that Iliffe

informed me that following the death of Sir David Amess MP, he felt angry at [Rayner] who – he states – described a member of the Conservative Party previously … as 'scum'. He stated he wanted to vent, and felt that somebody needed to tell her she was partially responsible for the attack following her use of language.[6]

Iliffe's account, together with the death of a close friend, apparently forced Rayner to reconsider her recent conduct. 'I have also reflected on what I said at an event at Labour Party conference,' she wrote. 'I was angry about where our country is headed … but I would like to unreservedly apologise for the language I used. I will continue to speak my mind. But in the future I will be more careful about how I do that and in the language that I choose.' By July 2022, a total of eight people had been detained in what had come to be called Operation Octant, a Greater Manchester Police investigation focussed on abuse and threats aimed at Rayner. Panic alarms had been installed at her house and, she told the *Daily Mirror*, her children were given a police escort when going to school.[7]

•   •   •

In November 2021, things were going wrong for Boris Johnson's government. This was most obvious in the case of Owen Paterson, a former Tory Cabinet minister who had returned to the backbenches. Having been found guilty by the Parliamentary Commissioner for Standards, Kathryn Stone, of breaking lobbying rules, he faced a thirty-day suspension from the House of Commons – a penalty that would almost certainly lead to a by-election in his North Shropshire constituency. In what turned out to be a self-inflicted wound that would never quite heal, Johnson agreed to hold a special parliamentary vote whose outcome was designed to block Paterson's suspension and change the rules so that he could appeal the commissioner's decision. This scheme triggered such indignation across the Commons that it had to be dropped. Paterson resigned his seat, where he had a 23,000 majority, on 5 November. In the following month's by-election the Liberal Democrats won on a 34 per cent swing against the Tories.

The damage to the Conservative Party and to Johnson's authority from the Paterson episode was significant, marking the start of a nosedive in both of their fortunes. But for Rayner, the Tories' chaos represented an opportunity. The day before Paterson quit the Commons, Starmer was unable to appear at Prime Minister's Questions because he was thought to have Covid-19. It fell to Rayner to stand in for him. She had fulfilled this role once before, a year earlier, and by this point was considered to be a capable frontbench performer. This was a chance to shine, to make up for her recent 'Tory scum' comments, and to outclass Starmer, whose advocacy skills have never been regarded by everybody as first-rate.

One person who has long admired Rayner's Commons performances is the former Tory MP Lord Soames, who stood down as an MP in 2019. 'She's got presence,' explains Soames. 'She's brilliant at the despatch box. The House loves that she's fiery. Not many MPs have the ability to stand there and be funny and mischievous, but she does.' Others say it is not just that Rayner can acquit herself well in this context, it is also that when Boris Johnson was Prime Minister, he was noticeably diffident when debating with her. As one seasoned observer who knows him remarks:

Boris found it hard to deal with her in the Commons because she comes from a totally different background to him. That is a formidable weapon that she could use. He was scared of seeming snobbish or misogynistic, so he always had to think carefully about what he said to her. She inhibited him in a way that no male opponent did.

Their exchange that day was a case in point. Rayner quizzed Johnson on the Paterson debacle, saying: 'It is one rule for everybody else and another rule for the Conservatives.' She added:

I know Donald Trump is the Prime Minister's hero, but I say to him in all seriousness that he should learn the lesson that, if he keeps cheating the public, it will catch up with him in the end. While the Conservatives are wallowing in sleaze, the rest of the country faces higher bills, rising costs and damaging tax rises.[8]

Despite this onslaught, Johnson was a model of flattery in his reply. And the irony is that it was Starmer who came off worst – even though he wasn't present. 'I enjoy my conversations with the right honourable lady, in spite of the insults and party political points that she directs towards the government,' he said.

I do not want to cause any further dissension on the opposition benches, but I think you will agree, Mr Speaker, that she has about a gigawatt more energy than the right honourable and learned Member for Holborn and St Pancras [Keir Starmer]. I am just putting that out there.

If this barb punctured Starmer's ego, it might have contributed to his decision to conduct a wide-ranging shadow Cabinet reshuffle a few weeks later. Unlike six months previously, he had no plan to tinker with Rayner's position, but he did make a raft of changes to the rest of his team. These included inviting Yvette Cooper to return to the front bench as shadow Home Secretary; David Lammy's promotion to shadow Foreign Secretary; Lisa Nandy moving to the post of shadow Levelling Up Secretary; and Wes Streeting's appointment to shadow Health Secretary.

These announcements, seen as a triumph of the party's moderate wing with one or two exceptions, caught many off guard, and none more so than Rayner. She was due to give a speech that day about Tory sleaze and standards in public life and, while publicising it on Times Radio, was asked what she knew about a forthcoming reshuffle. She said: 'I don't think there's any focus on that at the moment … We've been holding governments to account and that's what we're focusing on at the moment, not internal.' When asked whether Starmer would have let her know about any potential reorganisation, she said: 'I reckon that Keir would tell me first, yeah.'[9] Starmer had done no such thing. Journalists knew about it before she did. The first she heard of it was when she was about to deliver her speech at the Institute for Government in central London. Then, while her speech was underway, news of the changes was made public. This left Rayner having to field questions about a restructuring that she knew nothing about instead of the topic at hand. Her attack on the Tories was blunted and her advisers were left wondering why the Labour leader had chosen that precise moment to unveil his new team. Rayner's spokesman did not try to hide her ignorance, saying: 'She was not aware of the details of the reshuffle and she was not consulted on the reshuffle.'[10] Once again, questions were asked about the state of her working relationship with Starmer. Were they still on speaking terms, some wondered, after raised voices were heard later that day when they met in his Westminster office?

What seemed to have turned into a game of tit-for-tat continued a few days afterwards with the publication of an interview Rayner had given to *Grazia* magazine, in which she said of Starmer: 'I'm always trying to bring him out of his shell a bit more because, as you've probably guessed, I'm a bit more… spicy.'[11] It is impossible to know how calculated this assessment of his character was on her part, but it was unlikely to enhance his personal standing among voters. Until this point, polls showed consistently that even though the Tories' lead over Labour had shrunk, Johnson was still ahead of Starmer when people were asked who of the two of them would make the best Prime Minister. Relations appeared to be so bad between them that Starmer was forced to explain himself: 'There is no personal issue between me and Angela,' he said. 'We're friends, we get on, we talk a lot. We bring different things to the table. The two of us make each other stronger. She's politically astute and invaluable to me as a deputy.'[12] Rayner's team was far from convinced.

Amid these internal clashes, Rayner pressed on with her project of challenging the Conservatives' record. She and her advisers were convinced that the charges of sleaze would stick if they were repeated enough times, and they wasted no opportunity. By early December, she had sent ten letters requesting investigations into their activities in the space of a month. Her flurry of communications included asking for the parliamentary standards' commissioner to open an inquiry into Boris Johnson's recent rent-free holiday in a Spanish villa owned by the Tory peer Lord Goldsmith; for an assessment to be made of the Health Secretary Sajid Javid's shareholding in an artificial intelligence company; and for the independent adviser on ministers' interests, Lord Geidt, to look into whether Jacob Rees-Mogg had broken parliamentary rules by failing to declare £6 million of loans from Saliston Limited, a company he owns, to himself. Her last letter in this burst of scrutiny was to the head of the civil service, Simon Case. A series of questions about allegations of parties in 10 Downing Street during the previous year's lockdown were put to him.

In this show of dogged determination, Rayner was ably assisted by Jack McKenna, her head of communications and speechwriter, who had worked for her since 2020. He had been an aide to Jeremy Corbyn for several years before moving across to work for her. On 5 December, it was reported that McKenna had been suspended by the Labour Party. He was alleged to have briefed a journalist about a row between Ian Murray, the shadow Scotland Secretary, and Claire Ainsley, Labour's head of policy, regarding whether one of Murray's aides was going to be dismissed from their post. In doing so, he had supposedly breached personal data rules. In fact, McKenna successfully turned the tables on his accusers. He received compensation from the Labour Party a year later by proving that he himself had been the subject of 'misleading and unauthorised leaks' to the media before he had been officially informed of his suspension.[13] He left the Labour Party in November 2022 with what was described as a 'clean record' and a substantial sum of money. But in December 2021, when the original charge was levelled against him, Rayner and others took his suspension as a further sign of Starmer's office seeking to undermine her position in his quest to moderate the party. 'Jack was very close to Angela,' confirms an ally. 'Knocking him out removed one of the biggest supports she had. The brute politics of it certainly made it seem like quite a hostile move.'

By then, Boris Johnson's mounting political problems were providing a useful distraction from this row. The *Daily Mirror*'s series of stories about parties having been held at 10 Downing Street a year previously, when much of Britain was in lockdown, had become the chief concern of most Westminster journalists. Downing Street did not deny these allegations, with a spokesman instead maintaining that 'Covid rules have been followed at all times', but the pressure was ratcheted up when the Metropolitan Police was asked to investigate them. At Prime Minister's Questions on 8 December 2021, Labour MP Catherine West asked Johnson if there had been a party in Downing Street on 13 November 2020. To this, Johnson replied: 'No, but I am sure that whatever happened, the guidance was followed and the rules were followed at all times.'[14] In doing so, he committed himself to what sounded like a specific position. This would turn out to be unwise. At the same session of PMQs, Starmer raised with Johnson the matter of a video of Allegra Stratton, the government's COP26 spokesman, which had been unearthed by ITV News showing her joking about a party having been hosted at Downing Street in December 2020. He asked if Johnson had the 'moral authority' to lead the country. Johnson had said at the start of the session that he was 'furious to see that clip' and had already asked the Cabinet Secretary Simon Case – to whom Rayner had by then written – to 'establish all the facts and report back as soon as possible.'[15] This response quickly unravelled. Stratton resigned later that day, and the following week Case had to recuse himself from his inquiry after it was claimed that he had attended one of the parties he had been tasked with investigating. He was replaced by another senior civil servant, Sue Gray.

In the run-up to Christmas 2021 the 'Partygate' allegations grew, as it was claimed that dozens of public servants had been present at events in official buildings during 2020, breaching Covid regulations in the process. They included Johnson himself, who was accused of having taken part in a 'virtual Christmas quiz' on 15 December 2020; Johnson's communications chief, Jack Doyle; more than twenty Treasury staff; Department for Work and Pensions staff; and

Shaun Bailey, the Conservative London Assembly member who had apparently gone to a party at Conservative Campaign Headquarters when he was the party's London mayoral candidate.

By this point it was increasingly obvious that just two years after winning an eighty-seat Commons majority, the Conservative government was vulnerable on several fronts. It wasn't just sleaze accusations or 'Partygate' that put it in an increasingly precarious position. There were also questions to be asked about the planned rise in National Insurance, together with broken promises on social care. Rayner ended the year by giving an interview to the *Daily Record* in which she talked about Labour now being a government-in-waiting and discussed her own potential role in that future administration. 'I'm John Prescott in a skirt, me,' she said, referring to the man who was deputy Labour leader between 1994 and 2007. 'I like to think I look better in a skirt, but I do consider myself to be like him. I wear my heart on my sleeve. I think that is a very northern thing.' When it came to her relationship with Starmer she said:

> Imagine having to deal with me all the time. I am lively. But Keir and I also work well together. He is much more cautious than I am, more forensic. I'm bombastic, a bit more reactionary. Any relationship is going to be bumpy. He calms me down and deals with my rough edges, and I like to think I make him a bit more spicy.

She discussed herself in self-regarding terms, too, saying '[Andy Burnham] is the king of the North but I'm the Queen' and she did not dampen speculation that she might one day try to become the Prime Minister. 'Do you think the United Kingdom is ready for that?' she asked, adding: 'Try before you buy. Put Keir in as PM and me as deputy, then see how good I am. I reckon I will be good at it. If people are happy then maybe I'll have a go after him.'[16]

By the turn of 2022, the sense of momentum that Labour had been lacking for several years had returned, as opinion polls suggested that it had taken a six-point lead over the Conservatives. This progress continued on 19 January when, to the delight of Starmer, Christian Wakeford, the Conservative MP for Bury South, defected to the Labour Party minutes before Prime Minister's Questions began. Rayner was perhaps less enthused about Wakeford's arrival on the Labour benches, however. WhatsApp messages from the previous May were soon leaked, showing that when he had found out Rayner had been tipped to become the new shadow Chancellor of the Duchy of Lancaster he had commented: 'Fuck me, that will be one to watch for the giggles.' The following week came further politically advantageous developments for Labour when it was announced that the Metropolitan Police had launched a criminal investigation into whether the law was broken in Downing Street by parties having been held there during the 2020 lockdown. These included a surprise gathering in a Downing Street stateroom during the afternoon of 19 June 2020 to mark Johnson's fifty-sixth birthday, which was organised by his future wife, Carrie. This move was considered necessary after Scotland Yard received evidence from Sue Gray's ongoing inquiry. The plot was thickening, as far as Johnson was concerned.

Amid these developments, Rayner put herself at the centre of the scandal by using media interviews to call repeatedly for Johnson's resignation. Her prominence in the debate as Labour's political battering ram did not escape people's attention, though not all of the coverage she received was taken in the spirit she might have hoped. This prompted her to tweet: 'I've been on the media this morning so

my accent and grammar are being critiqued. I wasn't Eton educated, but growing up in Stockport I was taught integrity, honesty and
decency. Doesn't mater [*sic*] how you say it. Boris Johnson is unfit
to lead.'[17] Having compared herself a few weeks previously with
John Prescott, who was notorious for mangling his syntax, several
northerners hit back. For example, journalist Colin Brazier, who
was born in Bradford, wrote a piece for the online magazine *Spiked*
in which he argued that Rayner was guilty of 'crass class-baiting'. He
wrote:

> Many people will agree that the prime minister isn't fit to lead.
> But what about the other implicit idea within that tweet: the
> notion that to understand or use good grammar, you have to be
> posh? Or that somehow grammar is not just a mark of privilege,
> but pointless, too?[18]

Angela Levin, an author, agreed tweeting: 'You don't have to have
gone to Eton to speak well. It's easily done. Some working-class
people, however, exaggerate their grammatical mistakes and / or
their accents deliberately to make a point.' And Iram Ramzan, a
self-declared 'gobby Northern lass' from Oldham, wrote in the *Mail
on Sunday* that she had 'winced' when she had heard Rayner demanding on Radio 4's *Today* programme: 'Was you there or not at
the party?'[19] Even if this criticism was difficult for Rayner to take,
it did show that she was by now so prominent a figure in British
politics that even seemingly trivial matters involving her were considered worthy of comment.

By the end of January, Sue Gray had finished her 'Partygate' investigation, but, because the Metropolitan Police had begun its own
inquiry by then, publication of her findings was delayed and a short

summary was published instead. In light of this, Johnson apologised to the Commons, but his grip on power was weakening. By the end of March, the Met had begun issuing fines to Downing Street officials who had been found to have breached lockdown rules, thereby proving that Johnson had technically misled Parliament when he had spoken about the issue in December 2021. Johnson received a £50 fine himself on 12 April, making him the first Prime Minister to have been found to have broken the law while in office. His offence related to his attendance of his surprise birthday party on 19 June 2020. By the end of May, Sue Gray's report was published in full. It was not as compromising for Johnson personally as Labour might have expected, yet five weeks later, on 7 July, he stood down following a series of resignations from his Cabinet. Still Rayner persisted, calling him a 'coward' for jumping before he was pushed into fighting a potential by-election and rebuking him for having 'no respect' for those who had voted Tory in 2019.

Arguably, Johnson had become a key figure in Rayner's political life, providing her with the material she needed to further her own career as Labour's most potent prosecutor. And, as mentioned in Chapter 8, some find it hard to forget that she and Johnson are not entirely dissimilar characters, who may even like or respect each other on some level. As her rant at Brighton showed, he was capable of bringing out the worst in her. Yet she could not hide her respect for him. In July 2022, she was asked on LBC which of the candidates who were standing to replace him as Tory leader she feared. 'I'm quite happy with any one of them,' she said.

> Because the one thing, and I kind of could see it … [Boris] had this, like, Teflon coating … It's like a little magic where he was able to get through to the public and get through to places that I

actually don't see any of the five candidates that are standing for the Conservative leadership having at the moment... Boris had so much going for him. He got an eighty-seat majority and the country was really behind him ... and he just squandered all of that good will.

Throughout this time, it had not all been plain sailing for Labour. In tandem with the various inquiries into the Partygate scandal, Starmer's party found itself caught in a similar controversy now commonly known as 'Beergate', of which Rayner was an integral part. In the middle of January 2022, Starmer was accused of 'brazen hypocrisy' for his criticism of Johnson's lockdown 'partying'. A picture which had originally been published in *The Sun* the previous spring, and was then largely forgotten, resurfaced in the *Daily Mail*. It showed Starmer on the evening of 30 April 2021 standing in an office normally used by the Labour MP Mary Foy at Durham Miners Hall with a bottle of beer in his hand chatting to several colleagues. At that time, lockdown restrictions banned people from socialising inside with somebody from another household.

The picture – a still taken from thirty-four seconds of footage secretly filmed through a window by a Durham University student called Ivo Delingpole – was captured while Starmer was in the north of England during the local election campaign. Delingpole recorded it at 10 o'clock at night. An unidentified woman could be seen with her back to the camera. When this was put to Labour in January 2022, the party used the same defence that Johnson had relied on, namely that Starmer was at a work 'meeting', had stopped for a break, and then carried on working. Initially, a spokesman also denied that Rayner was present, telling the *Daily Mail* that she 'wasn't there'. This denial was apparently made without Rayner's knowledge. In early February, Durham Police looked into whether any breach had occurred and concluded that it had not.

Two months later, however, in April 2022, shortly before the local elections, some digital detective work proved that Rayner had in fact been at the Durham event, and Labour was forced to admit as much. The party claimed that its previous denial of her attendance was a 'mistake' made in 'good faith'. Starmer told reporters:

> Whether Angela Rayner was there or not makes absolutely no difference. There was no breach of the rules; the matter's already been looked into. I know what's going on here. We're a few days away from local elections, and Conservative MPs are trying to throw as much mud as possible.[20]

He added there was a 'huge contrast' between the Durham event and lockdown parties in government buildings – for which the police had already issued in excess of fifty fines. Yet many Conservatives were perplexed as to how Starmer could have forgotten that Rayner was with him in Durham. They were equally surprised that she had not volunteered her presence at the event sooner.

On 6 May 2022, Durham Police confirmed that 'following the receipt of significant new information over recent days', an investigation 'into potential breaches of Covid-19 regulations relating to this gathering' was being conducted.[21] It soon transpired that seventeen people had been present. A copy of Starmer's schedule was also obtained by journalists. It showed that the plan had always been for him and his team to have some food that night. The relevant entry read: '20.40 – 22.00 Dinner in Miners Hall with Mary Foy.'[22] A takeaway curry was eaten on the premises. Labour insisted it was a work event.

On 9 May, Starmer announced that he would resign as Labour leader if he received a fine. He made this announcement after seeking four legal opinions as he dealt with the crisis. Rayner made the same pledge. Some thought this was a huge and unnecessary gamble. Others wondered whether their threat to quit had politicised the situation, because Durham Police's decision would in effect be about the future leadership of the parliamentary Labour Party, not just whether its leader and deputy leader had breached lockdown rules. Both Starmer and Rayner received a questionnaire from Durham Police on 31 May, which they returned on 17 June. On 8 July 2022, a month after Johnson's resignation as Conservative leader and Prime Minister, Durham Police concluded that the gathering they had attended in April 2021 was 'reasonably necessary' for work purposes, and that no fixed-penalty notices had been issued over it. Starmer and Rayner were cleared. By then, however, Rayner had found herself caught up in an entirely separate, and arguably more damaging, wrangle. Indeed, the publicity that it generated is likely to linger for longer in the collective memory than that triggered by Beergate.

CHAPTER 12

DEPUTY PRIME
MINISTER-IN-WAITING

On 24 April 2022, in the midst of the Beergate controversy, an altogether different story about Rayner appeared on page 5 of the *Mail on Sunday*, one which offered the public a glimpse into her private conduct. The article itself surprised some readers, outraged others and perhaps amused the rest, who took it in the spirit in which it was intended. But, ironically, it was not the salacious suggestion the story contained that proved to be so revealing of Labour's deputy leader. Rather, her reaction to the piece, and what was taken as her willingness to manipulate channels of the media, were felt by many to show a side of her character that they had not perhaps identified with her previously. The fact that Rayner's response to this article arguably almost cost the journalist who wrote it his career was a reflection of how high the stakes were for a time.

Under the headline 'Stone the crows! Tories accuse Rayner of *Basic Instinct* ploy to distract Boris', the story, written by the newspaper's political editor Glen Owen, centred on the claim that Rayner 'likes to put Boris Johnson "off his stride" in the Chamber by crossing and uncrossing her legs when they clash at Prime

Minister's Questions'. It continued: 'Tory MPs have mischievously suggested that Ms Rayner likes to distract the PM when he is at the despatch box by deploying a fully-clothed parliamentary equivalent of Sharon Stone's infamous scene in the 1992 film *Basic Instinct*.' One unnamed MP was then quoted as saying: 'She knows she can't compete with Boris's Oxford Union debating training, but she has other skills which he lacks. She has admitted as much when enjoying drinks with us on the [Commons] terrace.'[1] The piece made clear that Rayner's office denied the allegation, calling it 'categorically untrue'. A Labour source also said: 'Just when you think the Conservative Party can't get any lower they outdo themselves. The Conservatives clearly have a problem with women in public life.'

Shortly after 8 o'clock on the morning it was published, Rayner took to Twitter and over 300 words decried the piece. 'Women in politics face sexism and misogyny every day – and I'm no different,' she asserted. 'This morning's is the latest dose of gutter journalism courtesy of @MoS_Politics.' She continued:

Boris Johnson's cheerleaders have resorted to spreading desperate, perverted smears in their doomed attempts to save his skin. They know exactly what they are doing. The lies they are telling. The potted biography is given – my comprehensive education, my experience as a care worker, my family, my class, my background. The implication is clear. But it is the PM who is dragging the Conservative Party into the sewer – and the anonymous Tory MPs doing his bidding are complicit. He and his cheerleaders clearly have a big problem with women in public life. They should be ashamed of themselves. I won't be letting their vile lies deter me. Their attempts to harass and intimidate me will fail. I've been open about how I've had to struggle to get where I am today. I'm proud of my background, I'm proud of who I am and where I'm from – but it's taken time. I hope this experience doesn't put off a single person like me, with a background like mine from aspiring to participate in public life. That would break my heart. We need more people in politics with backgrounds like mine – and fewer as a hobby to help their mates. Thank you to so many of you for your messages of solidarity and support. For calling this out for what it is. You are making a stand in the name of decency – against those who would further coarsen, cheapen and debase our politics to benefit their own interests. We all deserve so much better.[2]

Within hours, thousands of sympathetic social media users began to make their feelings known. Most damagingly for the *Mail on Sunday*, Boris Johnson appeared to be among them. A statement posted on his Twitter account read: 'As much as I disagree with Angela Rayner on almost every political issue I respect her as a parliamentarian and deplore the misogyny directed at her anonymously today.'[3] Rayner thanked him for these sentiments. Scotland's First Minister, Nicola Sturgeon, added her voice to the chorus of critics, tweeting: 'Solidarity from across the political divide to Angela Rayner on this. It's a reminder of the deep misogyny women face every day.'[4]

Owen, personally, faced a far coarser reaction. After a photograph of him taken twenty years previously surfaced online, one Twitter user compared the dimple on his chin to a 'cat's arsehole'. The Labour MP Diane Abbott weighed in as well, stating that she found it 'interesting' that Owen felt able 'to judge female MPs by their looks' – even though he had done no such thing.[5] Another Twitter user even claimed to detect 'strong rapist energy' in Owen just by looking at his picture. These were among the less hostile messages about him that were written. Yet few, if any, of those who chose to involve themselves in the debate seemed to understand that Owen was merely the messenger. He had not made the claim himself – apparently, Rayner had done that. And, as his story showed, a group of Tory MPs had told him as much.

It is unlikely that, by this point of what turned out to be a seven-day cycle of recrimination, anybody associated with the production of the story thought it had been presented as carefully as it might have been. *Basic Instinct* probably seemed like an obvious cultural reference point to have used, but it soon became clear that, as with any piece of journalism in the social media era, facts and objectivity are often overlooked by those with strong opinions. The next day, the speaker of the House of Commons, Sir Lindsay Hoyle, told the Commons that he believed the article was 'misogynistic and offensive' and he said he was going to arrange a meeting with the editor of the *Mail on Sunday*, David Dillon. Hoyle also held a meeting with Rayner that evening. Separately, a Conservative MP called Caroline Nokes wrote to Hoyle asking him to consider revoking Owen's parliamentary pass, a measure that would mean he would be unable to do his job. Meanwhile Sir Keir Starmer told the ITV programme *This Morning* that parliamentary culture could be 'sexist and misogynistic' as he confirmed that Rayner would be the next British Deputy Prime Minister if he was in 10 Downing Street. He described her as a 'fantastic and formidable woman' and a 'brilliant politician.'[6]

The following morning, a trouser-suited Rayner gave an interview to another ITV show, *Lorraine*, in which she said she had asked the *Mail on Sunday* not to publish the story and disclosed that she had had to explain its contents to her teenage sons. She also said she had become worried about how the public would perceive her.

I just thought: 'Is that what people expect and think about what I do?' All I worry about when I'm at the despatch box is doing a good job and being able to do justice to my constituents and the work that I'm doing. So I was just really crestfallen.

She added that she felt the story was 'steeped in classism' that put women off achieving more in their careers.

The tide only appeared to turn after three days, in light of Hoyle's summons to David Dillon. Suddenly, Hoyle was seen in some quarters of the media as having cast himself in the role of censor. Dillon declined to see him, pointing out that freedom of the press would become a thing of the past 'if journalists have to take instruction from officials of the House of Commons, however august they may be, on what they can report and not report'. What most people did not know at that point was that Owen had in fact run a 'clean' version of the story he had been handed. The full version included a graphic joke that Rayner had told her fellow MPs.

The *Mail on Sunday*'s sister title, the *Daily Mail*, reported that three months earlier, in January 2022, Rayner had given an interview to 'The Political Party', a podcast hosted by a comedian called Matt Forde. During it, she had volunteered that her appearance at Prime Minister's Questions that month had drawn comparisons with Sharon Stone, the star of *Basic Instinct*. On the podcast, she made a comment about 'giving the PM a flash' and joked that it had resulted in an internet meme appearing of her crossing and uncrossing her legs. She could be heard laughing about this as she and Forde discussed it.[7] This certainly proved that she had joked about the *Basic Instinct* line in public before.

Then more details came to light of the origins of Owen's story, beginning with Rayner's chat with the group of Tory MPs on the

House of Commons terrace. One source with knowledge of the occasion explains: 'Angela Rayner laughed – and got a laugh out of everyone there – by saying "I just make sure I give him a flash of my ginger growler". That's what she said and that's what Glen Owen was told.' Owen apparently assumed that there would be no outrage about repeating Rayner's joke in a sanitised form because Rayner herself had told others about it. Yet upon publication there was widespread fury about the article – whether real or confected – not least from Rayner herself.

On 1 May, Owen's colleague, Dan Hodges, was able to report a fuller version of the background to this storm, interviewing the Tory MPs to whom Rayner had told the joke on the Commons terrace. There were four of them. Each confirmed that they had heard Rayner talk about her 'ginger growler' while they were having a cigarette break with her in January 2022. Some were able to remember at what point they had joined in the conversation. 'In response to what everyone recognised was a racy but light-hearted aside, Rayner's colleagues laughed, and carried on smoking. Then they all went their separate ways,' Hodges wrote. He added that he believed Rayner had been genuinely embarrassed about the prospect of the incident being reported in full in the *Mail on Sunday*, which may have explained her attempt to cover up her joke. Instead of shrugging it off in the manner some would have expected of her, Hodges mused, 'she tried to leverage the moment by painting herself as a victim of Tory sexism and classism. And that represented a false deflection.'[8]

Whether or not Hodges' theory is correct, some facts cannot be ignored. Although more than 6,000 complaints were made to the Independent Press Standards Organisation (IPSO) about the *Mail on Sunday*'s report, it was announced on 5 May 2022 that all of them had been rejected because Rayner had not complained herself and neither had any of her representatives. In fact one week later, Rayner – or perhaps one of her representatives – did lodge a complaint with IPSO questioning the *Mail on Sunday*'s accuracy but, ultimately, she did not pursue it. IPSO contacted her on several occasions in an effort to help her to achieve the outcome she said she wanted, to no avail. The case was closed in November 2022.

Special mention must go to Guto Harri, who was at the time Boris Johnson's press chief. 'Guto threw Glen Owen under a bus by tweeting on Boris Johnson's behalf and effectively condemning him,' says a source. 'It was a cynical piece of positioning on his part, which he took without even bothering to check the background. He later rang Glen to apologise and claimed he had had to move quickly because things were getting out of hand.' To what extent Rayner deliberately massaged the situation into that excited state by alerting thousands of keyboard warriors to a newspaper story that turned out to be based on a comment that four MPs say they heard her make is a question that only she would be able to answer.

●　●　●

Given the difficulties Boris Johnson faced at that point in his premiership, the Conservatives' results in the local elections on 6 May 2022 were not as bad as some had predicted, even if they were not good either. The Tories lost 487 seats, mainly in the south, yet Labour hardly distinguished itself, gaining only 108 seats and failing to recover lost ground in the north. The Liberal Democrats performed best, picking up 224 seats. Labour did succeed in taking overall control of the most councils, however, including three in London – Wandsworth, Westminster and Barnet – which were highly prized and had been under Tory control for decades. This allowed the perception to persist that the Tory Party was ailing and Labour was on the march. Opinion polls reflected as much.

But in fact, at that time, tensions were mounting in Labour over how the party would respond to the possibility of three days of rail strikes, which were due to take place in June. The strikers were planning to inflict the worst industrial action on Britain's railways for thirty years in their quest for pay increases. Despite Rayner's strong links to various trade unions – some of which had supported her financially – and notwithstanding her boyfriend Sam Tarry backing the strikes, she initially stayed quiet. Her neutrality angered many in the Labour movement. Her history and her recent attendance as the guest speaker at the 125th anniversary dinner of the Transport Salaried Staffs' Association (TSSA) suggested that she, like Tarry, was in fact in favour of the strikes, but her refusal to take a public position fuelled a whispering campaign that she lacked the courage to say so. The consequence of this awkward stance was plain for all to see. For example, when the BBC asked her whether her sympathy would be directed towards commuters or picketing union members, she said: 'I am hopeful that they won't get to that point, but I will probably be one of those commuters as well that will be in that situation.' It was not exactly a definitive answer. One Labour MP told the *Daily Telegraph*: 'It makes her look unprincipled because it is so different to what she has said in the past and what she said she is. One has to assume that Keir's people have had a conversation with her.'[9] Starmer appeared to be equally reluctant to get involved in the dispute, claiming to be on the side of the public but consistently failing to criticise those who had vowed to strike. The most he felt able to do was plead with his front bench not to join the picket lines. To his enemies, this neatly captured the perils of Labour accepting millions of pounds from trades unions.

Then, on 21 June, the first day of the walkout, Rayner broke ranks with Starmer by declaring her support for the strikers. 'Workers have been left with no choice,' she tweeted. 'No one takes strike action lightly. I will always defend their absolute right to do so for fairness at work. The PM needs to do his own job. His Government caused this. Now they must solve it.'[10] Starmer's authority was also challenged by the shadow Transport Secretary, Louise Haigh, who refused to criticise Tarry – a shadow Transport Minister who was close to many high-profile union bosses, notably Manuel Cortes, the hard-left general secretary of the TSSA – for having joined a picket line in London manned by members of the RMT. At the end of the week, having sided with the workers, there was some amusement when Rayner was seen at Glyndebourne drinking champagne and watching a performance of *The Marriage of Figaro*. It wasn't just the surprise that this self-declared socialist had decided to attend one of the smartest events of the summer season, it was also that her spokesman was forced to admit to the *Daily Telegraph* that she had travelled to the East Sussex venue by car rather than risking the journey by train.[11]

At the end of July, Starmer's drive to present the Labour Party as a more moderate force intensified, as he admitted he was going to abandon his aim to renationalise the railways. As this had been one of the key pledges he had made in 2020 when he won the Labour leadership, left-wing MPs and unions were furious. Starmer explained that Britain had to 'take a pragmatic rather than an ideological approach' to spending given the state of the economy, but there was no small amount of confusion when Louise Haigh, the shadow Transport Secretary, appeared not to accept his words, tweeting that despite Starmer's statement, Labour was 'committed to public ownership of rail'.[12][13]

The sense of chaos intensified when Rayner retweeted Haigh's message, while Tarry said the party's policy was 'bringing our rail networks back into the hands of the British public'.[14] On 27 July, Tarry joined a picket line at Euston Station in central London, once again defying Starmer's wishes. He told Channel 4 News: 'If I lose my job for standing shoulder-to-shoulder with rail workers, then so be it.'[15]

The next day, Starmer called his bluff by sacking him from his frontbench post. At the time, the reason provided for the dismissal was that Tarry had given unauthorised interviews and had made up Labour policy on public sector pay 'on the hoof'. A Labour spokesman explained:

> This isn't about appearing on a picket line. Members of the front bench sign up to collective responsibility. That includes media appearances being approved and speaking to agreed frontbench positions. As a government-in-waiting, any breach of collective responsibility is taken extremely seriously and for these reasons Sam Tarry has been removed from the front bench.[16]

His close friend Manuel Cortes, the TSSA general secretary, said he felt ashamed of the party. 'Whatever excuses the Labour Party makes about the reasons for Sam being sacked, the reality is that Sam has shown solidarity with his class and we applaud him for that,' he said. 'If they think they can win the next general election while pushing away 7 million trade union members, they are deluded.'[17]

Three weeks previously, however, Tarry's constituency party at Ilford South had threatened to deselect him, and it was surmised by some that Tarry had staged his sacking from the front bench in order to achieve the status of a martyr and so win favour locally. Tarry denied this, saying that he believed there needed to be a 'fundamental recalibration' of the relationship between Labour and the trades unions.[18] The upshot was that Starmer had removed a second key political ally from Rayner's orbit in the space of less than twelve months, following Jack McKenna's dismissal the previous December.

When Tarry was asked by *The Times* if he thought that Starmer had a worse relationship with the unions than Tony Blair, he shot back: 'I think far, far worse. I think there is a complete lack of dialogue, a complete lack of understanding and a complete lack of culture, and I think that is really hamstringing his leadership.'[19] To many in the Labour Party, it was ironic that it was the Conservative Party, and not Labour, that was at that time locked in a leadership contest, for Labour's splits seemed to be far more radical and ideological than the Tories'. Ten days later, during a visit to Scotland, Rayner commented that Starmer had been 'completely within his rights' to sack Tarry, who was deselected by his constituency party soon afterwards.[20] Few thought she really meant it. Her critics also noted that when Tarry's friend, Manuel Cortes, was subsequently dismissed from his post at the TSSA for gross misconduct following an inquiry into sexual harassment and bullying within the union, Rayner, who is normally so vocal in defending women's rights, apparently made no public comment.

At the Labour conference in Liverpool that September, Rayner and Starmer contradicted each other again when asked about their reaction to the Tories' latest idea, contained in the mini-Budget of the new Chancellor, Kwasi Kwarteng, to cut the basic and top rate of income tax. Rayner said that she would axe both cuts. Yet just thirty minutes later, Starmer told Sky News that he backed the cut on the basic rate, paid on earnings between £12,571 and £50,270, from 20p to 19p in the pound. Ultimately this argument was academic because Kwarteng was soon sacked by the short-lived Prime Minister Liz Truss, and the policy was reversed anyway, but the episode emphasised an explicit difference of opinion between the Labour leader and his deputy, just as there had been over the rail strikes. It was noted, too, that Rayner did not mention Starmer during her opening speech to the conference, in which she reaffirmed her commitment to workers' rights – and that he did not mention her when he addressed the conference either. Yet other shadow Cabinet members were publicly praised by him, including Ed Miliband and Rachel Reeves. For all the optimism on display at Liverpool, there was a lasting feeling among Westminster observers that the Labour Party still lacked the unity and discipline that would be required to earn it a stint in power. The party was ahead in the opinion polls, but many wondered whether this lead was attributable to the government's problems rather than the merits of Labour.

Rayner was prepared to acknowledge as much in an interview with the *Financial Times* six weeks later. Even though, by then, Truss's premiership had come to an end and Rishi Sunak had been installed in 10 Downing Street, she seemed to recognise that Labour still faced a long road back to government. 'We've changed. People are willing to listen. But the idea that people are running out of their doors saying, "yay, Labour" is not where they are,' she said. 'They don't want us to get ahead of ourselves.'[21] This interview attracted attention for other reasons, as well. Over the three-course lunch and bottle of Chablis that she and the interviewer consumed, she confessed that she 'didn't have a particularly strong view either way' about Brexit. If this seems a surprising attitude for a senior politician to take on one of the defining issues of the era, it is consistent with her non-ideological approach to politics. She also disclosed that she had a £320,000 mortgage and that in 2010 she borrowed £5,600 to have a breast enhancement operation. Many were staggered by such honesty from an MP, even if not every *Financial Times* reader wanted to know the intimate details of why she had chosen to have the cosmetic surgery. 'I had my boob job on my 30th birthday,' she said.

> I'd lost six stone thanks to my personal trainer, but my boobs just looked like two boiled eggs in socks. You know, like basset hound ears. You can't be thirty and have a chest like an 84-year-old granny. I had spent about fourteen months losing my baby weight, I was seventeen stone after I had my children.

When Starmer was interviewed by *The Times* a week later, he said of Rayner: 'I'm not saying we agree on everything, but we are very fond of each other and there's something core there about looking out for each other.'[22] Those with a full understanding of their working relationship were sceptical about this apparent warmth.

By Christmas 2022, Britain was veering towards what appeared to be a General Strike, as thousands of public sector workers insisted on pay increases in order to keep pace with the rising inflation that was chewing through their finances. Border Force staff, civil servants, nurses, teachers, paramedics, postal workers and rail workers all planned industrial action that would likely cripple Britain throughout the winter. It was apparent to many that the underlying intention of these trade union-backed walkouts was to bring down the Conservative government. Sunak was of the view that giving in to their demands would embed inflation in the system and he got to work on introducing anti-strike legislation that would compel unions to offer minimum service levels when any strike was held. Amid this turbulence, Rayner congratulated Mick Lynch, the General Secretary of the National Union of Rail, Maritime and Transport Workers (RMT) for doing 'a good job' for those who were going to strike and described him as an 'incredibly reasonable man' and not an 'evil villain'. She also lashed out against Sunak's 'militant' government.[23]

At the same time, speculation that Rayner was being overlooked by Starmer in favour of his shadow Chancellor, Rachel Reeves, began to show up in the news pages. As part of Labour's push for government, in which it was being advised by Lord Mandelson, it was seen as vital to present itself as a moderate, centre-ground party of economic competence and responsibility. Reeves, an Oxford-educated former Bank of England economist, soon came to be seen by Starmer and his allies as a safe pair of hands, not least in the company of business leaders. Her deep Labour pedigree might also help explain her elevation to the status of the leader's de facto number two in preference to the unpredictable Rayner: Reeves's husband, Nicholas Joicey, was Gordon Brown's speechwriter when he was Chancellor; her sister Ellie and brother-in-law John Cryer were parliamentary colleagues; and John's parents Bob and Ann Cryer had also been Labour MPs. Certainly it was not seen as an accident that Reeves introduced Starmer when he made his first public speech of 2023. The following week Rayner cut a slightly humbler figure when speaking to Sky News: 'I never hold back on what my views are, and I never would,' she said. 'And I wouldn't sacrifice those principles and be dishonest with the public. But yeah, I have to compromise as part of the team. There's things I don't always get.'[24] That week she went on to give a 3,500-word interview to the *Sunday Times* about her life in which she heaped praise upon her leader. 'Nothing about him gets on my nerves,' she said.[25]

Questions about her future persisted as the threat of another shadow Cabinet reshuffle loomed. While the summer of 2023 was dogged by talk of which shadow ministers faced dismissal, Rayner embarked on a tour of the north-east of England, supported by the *Daily Mirror*, so that she could reconnect with everyday people and understand their concerns better. She also spent part of August in Scotland, where she was interviewed at the Edinburgh Festival by the comedian Matt Forde. It is hard to believe that she was not aware that the stories she told him would end up in the pages of most national newspapers. She spoke of having recently returned from a holiday in Spain where she had enjoyed vodka-fuelled rave sessions lasting more than twelve hours. She said that her vaping habit meant that her children call her the 'Vape Dragon'. She also described a cocktail called Venom – comprising a bottle of vodka, a bottle of Southern Comfort, ten bottles of the alcopop WKD Blue, and a litre of orange juice – which she made if she ever had a party. She said:

> If you're ever having a crowd of you at home get that out and everyone will have a good time. I invited my two youngest kids' head teacher from primary school and he had to take his wife home because she'd had some Venom. One of my local councillors – I found her curled up in the dog's bed with the dog.

Inevitably, Forde also asked her about her relationship with Starmer. She said the difference between them was that she was 'more

bombastic and in-your-face' while he was 'the ultimate civil serv-
ant/public servant.'[26] Not for the first time, Starmer's team struggled
to imagine Rachel Reeves saying anything like this.

Her next stop was Liverpool, where she addressed the TUC
conference. In her speech she said that she was able to make a
'cast-iron commitment' that a future Labour government would
introduce a new Employment Rights Bill within its first 100 days
of entering office that would make it easier for unions to organise
in the workplace, simplifying the statutory recognition process,
allow electronic balloting and boost collective bargaining. She also
vowed to repeal Sunak's minimum service strike laws, calling them
'spiteful and bitter'. If these measures were to be enacted, there are
fears among Labour's opponents that industrial action on a scale
not seen since the 1970s could return to Britain courtesy of Angela
Rayner.[27] When the BBC asked her that month if it was true that
her posts as Shadow First Secretary of State, Shadow Chancellor
of the Duchy of Lancaster and shadow Minister for the Future of
Work were under threat, Rayner replied: 'The important thing is
that I will be the Deputy Prime Minister and I will be the deputy
leader of the Labour Party, so actually the important job is around
supporting Keir as the leader.' Some interpreted this as her trying
to force Starmer's hand by bouncing him into giving her that post.
Others wondered if she knew already where her future lay. Nobody
had to wait long to find out whether she would prosper or not.

On 4 September, the shadow Cabinet reshuffle was announced.
Starmer confirmed – again – that Rayner would become his Deputy
Prime Minister if Labour won power and he was in 10 Downing
Street. Rayner was also appointed as the shadow Secretary of State
for Levelling Up, Housing and Communities, replacing her friend

Lisa Nandy, who was demoted from that post. In a series of moves that confirmed that the Blairite wing of the Labour Party had regained control, another of Rayner's left-wing friends, Jonathan Ashworth, was also sidelined. Starmer's new chief of staff Sue Gray, the former civil servant who had been in charge of investigating Boris Johnson over the Partygate scandal, was said to have played a major part in the reshuffle. *The Guardian* reported that she had even been involved in negotiations with Rayner about her new responsibilities.

Yet some felt let down by the consequences of these changes to the shadow Cabinet. 'Angela was in something of a political alliance with Lisa Nandy and Jonathan Ashworth around the shadow Cabinet table, and I'm told they suggested to her: "Can you please hold this alliance together because we think we're going to be pushed aside?" and Angela then jettisoned them,' says one Labour figure.

> So behind the scenes, they were very unhappy about this reshuffle because she sold them out. That goes on all the time. The most sophisticated operators do that as well. But it lends itself to the fact that ultimately Angela is a loner and I'm not quite sure where her project is going to go.

Despite the confidence that Rayner could now justifiably feel, thanks to her elevation to shadow Deputy Prime Minister, some who attended that month's Labour Party conference in Liverpool were bemused when she decided to take a phone call from her mother while giving an interview to Channel 4 News. Rayner apparently decided to pick up her phone mid-interview because she was worried something was wrong. It was not. Her mother rang to congratulate her on the speech she had given. But the fact that she had not switched her phone off before the interview began, and that she then put the phone on loudspeaker to speak to her mother while on camera, and finally put footage of the incident onto her social media feeds, did not convince everybody that the call was genuine. Some, indeed, wondered whether she was seeking attention and they wondered why anybody in her position might need to arrange such a stunt, if that is what it was.

Less than nine years after arriving in the House of Commons, then, Angela Rayner had gone from novice MP to being promised the second most powerful political position in Britain in what was expected to be Starmer's last reshuffle before the next general election. By any standards, this was a remarkable feat. When, in November 2023, it was announced that she and Sam Tarry had split up, questions were asked privately by some cynics about whether she had exercised pragmatism by ending the relationship, thereby ensuring that any battles he would have to fight in future could not be linked to her. She would also have more time to devote to mastering her brief.

A senior Labour source says:

Keir has a very meritocratic way of running things. Whereas other politicians don't particularly look for capability – they look for loyalty or oratory or organisational skills – Keir looks for straight-bat policy delivery. That's why Angela's new brief is interesting. He's essentially given her the ball to see whether she runs with it or not. He has a track record of getting rid of people who don't perform. If Angela doesn't perform, there will therefore be a precedent for getting rid of her. He's basically said to her: 'Have this job and let's have a look at how you do with it.' At the back of his mind he'll be thinking the same of every shadow Cabinet member. It's obviously more significant with Angela because he's applying the same measure to her as he is to everyone else, despite the fact she's got her own mandate from the membership. It'll be very interesting to see what happens next.

EPILOGUE

As 2023 drew to a close, one of the last published interviews which Angela Rayner gave was to the fashion and lifestyle magazine *Vogue*. It was noteworthy on several levels. 'Once she hit puberty, she experienced period poverty before there was even a name for it,' the magazine declared. It then quoted Rayner as saying:

> We didn't really have sanitary products at home. If there were any, it was those huge ones [they had in the early 1990s], these bad boys that were way too big for my tiny frame. We called them surfboards. I used to go to school and get loads of toilet paper and just stuff that in. I made it into a ball.'[1]

It is hard to imagine any other politician of any era speaking in this way to the media about a bodily function, but these few sentences alone were sufficient to secure coverage of the interview across other parts of the media. According to some of the online comments that her words inspired, it is fair to say that not everybody who read them felt it was either desirable or necessary for Rayner to have been so graphic. Yet there is no doubt that she has made herself conspicuous.

At the same time, it is difficult to ignore the fact that there are precious few of the 650 MPs in Westminster to whom *Vogue* would devote several pages. Some would argue that politics needs all the help it can get if it is to remain relevant in people's lives – especially among younger generations – and a figure such as Rayner giving a candid interview to *Vogue* is useful in that regard.

This tension perhaps goes to the heart of who Angela Rayner is and what she wants to achieve. Such is the nature of the media industry today that some politicians have become semi-celebrities as well. Rayner is surely among them, whether she likes it or not. This status may have its merits, helping to ensure that politics reaches more people, but it does prompt questions about how wearing two different hats in public can affect an MP's priorities.

It is sometimes said that those with a big ego, or those who have the greatest need for attention, can suffer from a higher level of insecurity or doubt about whether others like them or admire them. Rayner has been described as a 'loner'. But two contributors to this book who worked closely with her in the past are certainly prepared to accept that she has marketed herself, and they wonder what this says about her character. 'If we assume that all politicians are in some way self-regarding, Angela's at the high end of the spectrum,' says one.

> She's not a narcissist – she doesn't flip over into thinking the entire world revolves around her. But she hasn't found a balance and she isn't fully mature yet. Perhaps she's over-compensating for a lack of self-esteem. This may relate to her childhood. If you've got a keen sense of who you are, you have the ability to see the absurdity of it all – the transient nature of serving in a political post and so on. It's easy to be seduced by the power of politics.

Lots of politicians fall apart in those circumstances. I don't know if she'll get through it.

The other adds: 'I wonder whether, at root, despite all appearances to the contrary, she is just unsure of herself. There's so much bravado it's difficult to work out who the real Angela Rayner is.'

Might these insights explain Rayner's apparent willingness to shock or surprise – whether by discussing period poverty with *Vogue*; by shouting 'Scum!' at a Tory MP in the Commons Chamber; by mentioning her cosmetic surgery to the *Financial Times*; by recounting details of her drinking sessions to an audience at the Edinburgh Festival; or by taking a phone call from her mother while giving an interview to Channel 4 News?

If her readiness to attract attention is partly attributable to a need to be liked, it may surprise some people to learn that Rayner is more popular across the House of Commons than she would perhaps care to admit. For example, Andrew Mitchell, who has served in the Cabinets of David Cameron and Rishi Sunak, says breezily that he and some of his Conservative colleagues get on with her quite well. 'Everyone will claim to you that Angela is their best friend or their worst enemy, because politics is like that,' Mitchell says.

I know her a bit. I do like her. I can't say we're bosom buddies. Everyone always thinks Labour and the Tories tear chunks out of each other. But there is this other side of politics that people don't see – people working together – and I think more of that goes on behind the scenes than people realise. I've seen her getting on well with various Tory MPs.

The only Conservative politician whom Rayner has been prepared to say publicly that she gets on well with is the grandson of Sir Winston Churchill, Lord Soames, who was in the Commons from 1983 until 2019. 'From the first time I saw Angela she was quite obviously a kindred spirit,' Soames says.

> She was really fun and engaging and then I heard about her background and I really admired her. The moment I saw her I knew she'd be at the top of the Labour Party in a short period of time. She's unbelievably good company. She's much shrewder than she lets on. Every now and again she bogs it, as she did with the Tory scum comment, but she knows she doesn't need to say that sort of thing anymore. She is a friend.

Indeed, theirs is a friendship that Rayner seems keen to maintain. 'She sometimes sends me these wonderful texts,' he adds. 'She sent me one at New Year from Churchill's nightclub in Manchester, where she was dancing with some friends.'

Of more importance are Rayner's own beliefs. As this book has shown, she is clearly motivated to try to improve the lot of others and she has developed progressive instincts in areas such as education, employment rights and social justice. She calls herself a socialist and a firm believer in the trades union movement. And yet her politics are often hard to place. She seems to have no strong view on Brexit. She says she is not and never was a Corbynite, but she served in Jeremy Corbyn's shadow Cabinet for almost four years and tried to get him elected to 10 Downing Street twice. Neither is she easily described as 'soft-left' or 'centrist', yet she has never been shy about praising Tony Blair and Gordon Brown. She has often remarked that 'ideology never put food on my table', but one former colleague is none the wiser, despite being in her company over a period of years. 'Does she actually want to try to recreate those conditions where kids who've had pretty traumatic childhoods can find a path through?' they ask.

> I believe that's her mission, but I don't know, is the honest truth. She just likes the attention. The fact that I can't make my mind up on what drives her and what she wants to do is telling in itself. On benign days I think: 'You're doing your best.' On some days I just think: 'You're being utterly ridiculous.'

Another former colleague is blunter. 'She plays a supportive role for Keir Starmer, who's ripped up all that Jeremy Corbyn stood for. She's a political opportunist. She went where the power was going. She's a politician. That's what they do.'

Those who have worked closely with her say she is not brim-full of new ideas. Her talent, apparently, lies in promoting the ideas of others. 'She is someone who can run with a notion,' says another politician.

> So if she's seized with a sense of injustice or there's something she wants to do, she will pursue it with great persistence and be vocal about it. That's a good quality in all MPs, especially backbenchers. But when you're in those kinds of jobs where there are 150 decisions a day to make and you're weighing up matters that are laced with nuance and complexity, the ability to fixate on a single issue is a plus and a minus. It's a good quality that she's prepared to run with some things, but it may get her into trouble in future if she's in government.

The fact is that over the past couple of years Starmer has devoted a considerable amount of time to washing away what he now seems to regard as the stain of the Jeremy Corbyn era. Most obviously, he has eliminated Corbyn himself from the Parliamentary Labour Party; he has done his best to keep those on the hard left from being adopted as Labour candidates; and he has excluded the Corbynite wing from the most powerful roles in the party. The one person he has been unable to dislodge, but who ultimately owes her position to Corbyn, is Rayner. In many ways, she can be seen as the last remaining monument to Corbyn's leadership inside the Parliamentary Labour Party, despite her insistence that she is not a Corbynite. As we have seen, following her emergency elevation to the shadow Cabinet in June 2016 she successfully raised her public profile so that by the spring of 2020 she was ready to secure the deputy leadership. Nobody knows this better than Starmer, and it places him in a difficult position. It is worth asking the questions: had Corbyn not been deserted by most of his front bench in June 2016, and had he not needed to promote Rayner then, would she really have been a serious candidate for the deputy leadership straight after the 2019 general election? Or might her political career have matured some years later, perhaps in a post-Starmer Labour Party? History cannot be rewritten, though, and Starmer's balancing act must be maintained. On the one hand, he needs to keep Rayner onside for the sake of party unity and in order to appease the trade unions, a group to which she is closer than he is. At the same time, it is generally known that there are Labour MPs other than Rayner whom Starmer would have chosen as his second-in-command had he been able to do so. The Labour Party's constitution prevented him from doing this. Its rules also ensure that he cannot dismiss her.

Some also wonder if there is a strain between the accounts of her childhood that she airs regularly in the media and how much her life has changed in adulthood over the past ten or so years. People have questioned if this shift in circumstances has caused her priorities to shift in turn. She is a supporter of gender self-identification; she has spoken in favour of menopausal women being able to take a leave of absence from their job; and she believes in a legal right to work from home. Not everybody endorses these policies, however, which are usually more closely linked with the concerns of the metropolitan middle class rather than the working-class, Red Wall voters whose interests she claims to represent.

She has also suggested that she is in favour of more tax rises, notably in the area of savings and investments. Yet some voters already struggling under the highest tax burden on record – including her constituents, or those in Stockport where she grew up – might have a different view, especially if they reflect on the fact that Rayner has not done badly out of taxpayers herself. She managed to get onto the property ladder aged twenty-six courtesy of the right-to-buy scheme, but, as detailed in Chapter 4, questions remain over how long she was a full-time resident in the council house that she was ultimately able to purchase and therefore whether she was entitled to benefit from the entirety of the rise in its value, as she appears to have done.

Would Red Wall voters rather she offered inspiration and answers instead of calling for more taxes? One Labour figure says:

In my political career I've spent plenty of time talking to working-class women in the north of England. The idea that they want Angela to keep discussing how she flunked out of school at sixteen is not true. They want her to be more aspirational. They want her to say: 'Don't make the mistakes I made.' It's difficult, because to go from being a single mother of sixteen to the deputy leader of the Labour Party is one hell of a journey. But how do you then build on that foundation? How do you make yourself someone different? What are the lessons for other people? That's what they want to hear from her. I'm not sure we've heard that bit yet.

Her relationship with Sir Keir Starmer also remains a concern. 'It's not a close relationship,' says a friend of both of them. 'There are few social aspects to it. I think she will want him to appreciate her, and he will appreciate her if she does her job properly because he just expects people to do their job and he plays with a straight bat.' Another ally warns that their recent history – in which Starmer was seen to have undermined Rayner – is in danger of being forgotten. 'At every point she's been underestimated or patronised,' says this person.

It's always men who do it, be they Tory MPs or civil servants. She uses that to win. It's impressive. Keir's doing well in the polls now and their relationship is better as a result of that, but he wasn't doing well in the polls for quite some time. The only thing that's changed is that the Tories have thrown away their lead, but Keir hasn't become a different person overnight. He just happens to be twenty points ahead in the polls through little agency of his own.

What would a Starmer–Rayner government be like? And would she be a good minister? 'If Labour win, it's that first twelve months,' says a former Labour Cabinet minister.

Will she get any legislation through in the first 100 days? How will she build a team? What will she do if a junior minister is involved in some scandal? How will she handle all of that? What's the permanent secretary going to report back to the Cabinet Secretary about her work ethic? I don't even know if she knows she's going to be judged on that stuff. You never know what it's like until you've experienced it. I don't think she has a good grasp of the structure, the system and how the government machine operates. Then again, neither did Tony Blair in 1997. But she'd be a novice Cabinet minister, and that's sink-or-swim time.

Her friend Lord Soames is less sceptical. 'I don't know how she'd be running a department, but, as a fixer, I think she'd be very good,' he says.

If Starmer makes it to Number 10, I think he would run a serious and high-minded administration and he'd need an Angela figure. This is not meant to sound patronising, but she's very good at translating to the membership the sort of stuff that they may not see as important but is. She'll never be PM, but she'd be a brilliant deputy PM.

Another ex-colleague adds:

I'd guess in a Keir government she'd push her social justice measures into his overall political framework. She'd be one of a very small number of loyal, more left-facing people in the government, like John Prescott was under Blair. It wouldn't translate into much. She'd be a centre-left political friend.

As we have seen, Rayner has referred to herself as 'John Prescott in a skirt', but more recently she has also drawn comparisons with an altogether more powerful figure from Labour's past: Barbara Castle.

'The thing is, Angela seems to have less influence and power than Prescott had and he didn't have much under Blair and Brown,' says a former colleague. 'It depends what a Keir government would be like and how much she would become a lightning rod for opposition to things Keir would do that most on the left wouldn't like.' In Britain's two-party system, the Conservatives and Labour have to be political coalitions, and must have internal arguments, otherwise voters do not get the representation they deserve. This is where Rayner could make a real difference. But would Starmer allow it? One former colleague is sceptical:

> Barbara Castle was an ally of Harold Wilson, historically. They associated with the Bevanite left. She had some autonomy not just because she was popular but because there were different parts of the Labour movement that had access to levers of power in a way that they don't at the moment under Keir. What's unclear now is whether there is any space for independent political bases under Keir's regime. Even under Blair there was some toleration or acceptance that Labour was a party with different wings and traditions and they were all part of the broad church. There was a limited acknowledgement that an aeroplane needs two wings to fly. Keir's not really allowing that. I see her as more of a Prescott figure than a Castle figure, but even Prescott had more autonomy than Angela does. Her autonomy, such as it is, comes from the media and a bit of trade union support. She's identified with the unions, the workplace and working-class issues more than Keir is.

All of this, of course, depends on Starmer winning a majority. And the size of that majority would presumably dictate how much power Rayner is able to exercise. This person adds: 'If it's a narrow majority, left-wing MPs would have more power in Parliament. That was seen as a reason for Starmer to get rid of them. The bigger the parliamentary majority, the less important that is. That's why Blair could afford to ignore the Socialist Campaign Group.' Angela Rayner is an unusual politician, but she is not unique. Beneath her tough exterior many, including her political opponents, say she is warm and engaging in person. As some of her Labour colleagues, including Wes Streeting, would be the first to point out, she is not the only member of the House of Commons to have had a complicated upbringing, but it has left its mark on her. She is a product of her experiences, though when she has spoken of her past she has sometimes caused alarm among some commentators. In September 2021, she gave an interview to *The Times* in which she spoke about 'political chaos'. She told the newspaper: 'The trauma, the screaming, the unpredictability – this is my bread and butter.' She continued: 'I think it's strange when people are nice. I find taking compliments more difficult than taking abuse. I've never had that love and affection, so I don't crave it. That's really sad, because I see how people can be fulfilled by those things. And I can't.'[2] These words prompted author and journalist Douglas Murray to write: 'I don't think there's anything normal about Angela Rayner. That comment shows she is not a remotely normal person. And it is indeed sad.'[3] She is clearly committed to the causes she promotes and she has shown herself to be a successful campaigner and a remarkably capable politician. But when it comes to serving in government, she is entirely untested. Whether she has the aptitude for ministerial responsibility is something we may all see soon enough. One thing we do know: she will have no shortage of self-belief.

NOTES

INTRODUCTION

1 Barbara Ellen, 'Less of the backstory, Angela Rayner, it's beginning to wear a bit thin', *The Observer*, 15 May 2021, available at https://www.theguardian.com/commentisfree/2021/may/15/less-of-your-backstory-angela-rayner-show-us-your-political-credibility

GIRL GUIDE

1 'What I Wish I'd Known: Angela Rayner', Times Radio, 27 September 2021, available at https://www.thetimes.co.uk/podcasts/what-i-wish-id-known

2 'At Lunch with… Angela Rayner MP', BBC Sounds, 17 October 2017, available at https://www.bbc.co.uk/sounds/play/p05k6qns

3 Kiran Stacey and Pippa Crerar, '"I love campaigning – it's like playtime": Angela Rayner on her rising appeal', *The Guardian*, 6 October 2023, available at https://www.theguardian.com/politics/2023/oct/06/i-love-campaigning-its-like-playtime-angela-rayner-on-her-rising-appeal

4 'Political Thinking with Nick Robinson: The Angela Rayner One', BBC Sounds, 18 May 2018, available at https://www.bbc.co.uk/sounds/play/p067kbxv

5 Friedrich Engels, *The Condition of the Working-Class in England in 1844 with preface written in 1892*, translated by Florence Kelly, (London: Swan Sonnenschein & Co., 1892)

6 Hansard, HC debate, 18 June 1985, vol. 81, cols 169–83

7 Times Radio, 2021

8 BBC Sounds, 2017

9 'Grangela: Labour's Angela Rayner is grandmother at 37', BBC News, 22 November 2017, available at https://www.bbc.co.uk/news/uk-politics-42078457

10 'Full Disclosure with James O'Brien: Angela Rayner', Global, 23 September 2021, available at https://podcasts.apple.com/gb/podcast/angela-rayner/id1454408831?i=1000536441288

11 BBC Sounds, 2017

12 Global, 2021

13 Times Radio, 2021

LITTLE SHADOW

1 Stephen Moss, 'Labour's Angela Rayner: "Ideology never put food on my table"', *The*

Guardian, 28 July 2017, available at https://www.theguardian.com/politics/2017/jul/28/angela-rayner-shadow-education-secretary-interview

2 Toby Helm and Michael Savage, 'Angela Rayner: "I'm not okay with a school system that allows you to fail or be chucked out"', *The Observer*, 21 September 2019, available at https://www.theguardian.com/politics/2019/sep/21/angela-rayner-labour-ofsted-education-interview

3 Barry Hines, *A Kestrel for a Knave* (London: Michael Joseph, 1968)

4 *Kes* (1969), directed by Ken Loach, Great Britain: Woodfall Film Productions, Kestrel Films

5 Times Radio, 2021

6 Global, 2021

7 BBC Sounds, 2018

8 Ibid.

9 Iain Dale, Jacqui Smith, *The Honourable Ladies: Volume II: Profiles of Women MPs 1997–2019*, 1st edition (Biteback: London, 2019)

10 'Angela's Childhood in Poverty', Times Radio, 4 September 2020, available at https://www.youtube.com/watch?v=6BIcY9Mijms

11 'In full: Labour deputy leadership candidate Angela Rayner on her "traumatic" childhood', ITV News, 24 February 2020, available at https://www.youtube.com/watch?v=aGwSP-Hu3rs

12 Global, 2021

13 Times Radio, 2020

14 *The Observer*, 2019

15 Oliver Milne, 'A quick guide to shadow education secretary, Angela Rayner, for teachers', *The Guardian*, 5 July 2016, available at https://www.theguardian.com/teacher-network/2016/jul/05/quick-guide-shadow-education-secretary-angela-rayner-teachers

16 Owen Bennett, 'Angela Rayner Talks The Reality Of Poverty, Tories Misunderstanding Her And How Tony Blair Changed Her Life', *Huffington Post*, 19 January 2017, available at https://www.huffingtonpost.co.uk/entry/angela-rayner-labour-tony-blair_uk_587f8e70e4b005cc588b7224

17 Times Radio, 2020

18 Times Radio, 2021

19 'From a council estate to the Houses of Parliament', UNISON, 21 February 2017, available at https://www.unison.org.uk/news/article/2017/02/from-a-council-estate-to-the-houses-of-parliament/

20 BBC Sounds, 2018

21 'Father of boy Labour's Angela Rayner gave birth to as a 16-year-old schoolgirl', Read Sector, 18 May 2021, available at 'https://readsector.com/father-of-boy-labours-angela-rayner-gave-birth-to-as-a-16-year-old-schoolgirl/

22 Global, 2021

23 ITV News, 2020

THE SAMARITAN

1 Dale, Smith, 2019

2 ITV News, 2020

3 Rosie Kinchen, 'The Magazine Interview: the shadow education secretary, Angela Rayner, on raising a blind son and becoming a grandmother at 37', *Sunday Times*, 14 January 2018, available at https://www.thetimes.co.uk/article/the-magazine-interview-the-shadow-education-secretary-angela-rayner-on-raising-a-blind-son-and-becoming-a-grandmother-at-37-voqwd6tgw

4 Decca Aitkenhead, 'Angela Rayner: I overshare. Keir Starmer undershares', *Sunday Times*, 18 February 2023, available at https://www.thetimes.co.uk/article/angela-rayner-i-overshare-keir-starmer-undershares-nwvxx97xh

5 Read Sector, 2021

6 Political Thinking with Nick Robinson: The Angela Rayner Deputy Leader One', BBC Sounds, 29 October 2022, available at https://www.bbc.co.uk/sounds/play/m001dmh

7 'Angela Rayner MP and Julia Gillard: In Conversation', Kings College London, 28 June 2023, available at https://www.kcl.ac.uk/news/angela-rayner-and-julia-gillard-in-conversation-1
8 ITV News, 2020
9 Angela Rayner, 'Education Gave Me A Vital Second Chance That Too Many People Still Don't Get', *Huffington Post*, 12 November 2019, available at https://www.huffingtonpost.co.uk/entry/labour-education_uk_5dca8440e4b0fcfb7f6c53fa
10 Kings College London, 2023
11 Global, 2021
12 'Pleased to Meet You – Angela Rayner', UNISON, 23 November 2012, available at https://www.unisonmanchester.org/campaigns/pleased-to-meet-you-angela-raynor
13 BBC Sounds, 2018
14 Ibid.
15 Global, 2021
16 BBC Sounds, 2018
17 ITV News, 2020
18 Times Radio, 2021
19 Kate Mossman, 'Angela Rayner: "The Tories fear me because I say it how I see it"', *New Statesman*, 23 February 2022, available at https://www.newstatesman.com/long-reads/kate-mossman-interview/2022/06/angela-rayner-interview-conservatives-fear-me

UNIONISED

1 Global, 2021
2 Demetrious Matheou, 'He spoke to me as a human being, not as a scally off the estate', UNISON, 11 February 2020, available at https://magazine.unison.org.uk/2020/02/11/he-spoke-to-me-as-a-human-being-not-as-a-scally-off-the-estate/
3 BBC Sounds, 2018
4 Ibid.
5 UNISON, 2020
6 Global, 2021
7 Mark King, 'A working life: the union official', *The Guardian*, 17 February 2012, available at https://www.theguardian.com/money/2012/feb/17/working-life-union-official-unison
8 Angela Rayner, 'Speech to Congress 2016', Trades Union Congress, 13 September 2016, available at https://www.tuc.org.uk/speeches/angela%C2%A0rayner-mp-speech-congress-2016
9 *The Guardian*, 2012
10 'Angela Rayner: "Normally I say, 'play the ball not the man'. But Boris was literally the ball and the man"', *Financial Times*, 11 November 2022, available at https://www.ft.com/content/ec7bf67e-5261-41a2-a9a1-c4581d471b87
11 '100 women on 100 years of voting', *The Observer*, 28 January 2018, available at https://www.theguardian.com/politics/2018/jan/28/100-women-on-100-years-of-womens-vote-suffrage
12 'Wait for council homes getting longer', *Manchester Evening News*, 14 November 2005
13 Vicky Spratt, 'Labour will consider changing right-to-buy council houses policy to stop social homes being lost', *The i*, 16 November 2023, available at https://inews.co.uk/news/labour-consider-changing-right-to-buy-council-houses-policy-stop-social-homes-lost-2753799
14 Times Radio, 2021
15 *The Guardian*, 2012
16 Ibid.

'IN MY OWN LITTLE NORTHERN WAY'

1 https://www.manchestereveningnews.co.uk/news/women-candidates-vie-ashton-mp-7518937
2 Jennifer Williams, 'All-woman Labour shortlist announced for Ashton-Under-Lyne and Failsworth seat', *Manchester Evening News*, 8 August 2014, available at https://www.

manchestereveningnews.co.uk/news/greater-manchester-news/all-woman-labour-shortlist-announced-ashton-under-lyne-7578406

3   'Red on red: Dirty tricks against "alcoholic" Labour PPCFake [sic] leaflet of candidate snorting sambuca with hospital tube', Guido Fawkes, 2 October 2014, available at https://order-order.com/2014/10/02/red-on-red-dirty-tricks-against-alcoholic-labour-ppcfake-leaflet-of-candidate-snorting-sambuca-with-hospital-tube/

4   Jennifer Williams, 'New Labour candidate: We need real people with life experience to bring common sense to Parliament', *Manchester Evening News*, 8 September 2014, available at https://www.manchestereveningnews.co.uk/news/greater-manchester-news/new-labour-candidate-need-real-7736452

5   Angela Rayner, 'Inside the factory of genocide', *Morning Star*, 27 January 2014, available at https://www.manchestereveningnews.co.uk/news/greater-manchester-news/all-woman-labour-shortlist-announced-ashton-under-lyne-7578406

6   Angela Rayner (2015), Facebook, available at https://www.facebook.com/AngelaRaynerMP/photos/pb.100044226349967.-2207520000/911726388859183/?type=3&locale=en_GB

7   https://www.facebook.com/photo/?fbid=911645152200640&set=pb.100044226349967.-2207520000

8   'Margaret Beckett: I was moron [sic] to nominate Jeremy Corbyn', BBC, 22 July 2015, available at https://www.bbc.co.uk/news/uk-politics-33625612

9   Tim Carr, Iain Dale, Robert Waller, *The Politicos Guide to the New House of Commons*, 1st edition (London: Biteback, 2015)

10 Charles Yates, 'MP used House of Commons paper to complain about not being able to buy £195 Star Wars shoes', *Daily Mirror*, 8 November 2015, available at https://www.mirror.co.uk/news/uk-news/mp-used-house-commons-paper-6794276

THE DIVA

1   Frances Perraudin, 'Reshuffle was like multidimensional game of chess, says Jeremy Corbyn', *The Guardian*, 7 January 2016, available at https://www.theguardian.com/politics/2016/jan/07/jeremy-corbyn-reshuffle-like-multidimensional-game-of-chess

2   Hansard, HC debate, 25 May 2016, vol. 611, cols 620–25

3   'Jeremy Corbyn must quit now for his party and his country', *The Mirror*, 27 June 2016, available at https://www.mirror.co.uk/news/uk-news/jeremy-corbyn-must-quit-now-8298423

4   BBC Sounds, 2018

5   Mark Ellis, 'Teachers strike: Thousands of schools shut as NUT members stage colourful walkout over funding', *Daily Mirror*, 5 July 2016, available at https://www.mirror.co.uk/news/uk-news/teachers-strike-thousands-schools-shut-8350983

6   Angela Rayner, 'The Tories Are Harking Back to a Mythical "Golden Age" of Grammar Schools', *Huffington Post*, 27 July 2017, available at https://www.huffingtonpost.co.uk/angela-rayner/grammar-schools_b_11196098.html

7   Angela Rayner, 'May talks of a "one nation" party but dreams of a one party nation', LabourList, 13 September 2016, available at https://labourlist.org/2016/09/angela-rayner-may-talks-about-a-one-nation-party-but-dreams-of-a-one-party-nation/

8   Conor Pope, 'Corbyn puts focus on winning power to deliver "socialism of the 21st century"', LabourList, 28 September 2016, available at https://labourlist.org/2016/09/corbyn-puts-focus-on-winning-power-to-deliver-socialism-of-the-21st-century/

RISING STAR OF THE YEAR

1   Owen Bennett, 'Angela Rayner Talks The Reality Of Poverty, Tories Misunderstanding Her And How Tony Blair Changed Her Life', *Huffington Post*, 19 January 2017, available at https://www.huffingtonpost.co.uk/entry/angela-rayner-labour-tony-blair_uk_587f8e70e4b005cc588b7224

2   Todd Fitzgerald, 'Jeremy Corbyn says two Labour rising stars tipped to take his job could

"absolutely" be future leaders', 10 February 2017, available at https://www.mirror.co.uk/news/politics/jeremy-corbyn-says-two-labour-9791157

3   James Lyons, 'Secret Labour search for Corbyn heir', *The Times*, 12 February 2017, available at https://www.thetimes.co.uk/article/secret-labour-search-for-corbyn-heir-mkmskppr6

4   'Election: Theresa May urges voters to "strengthen my hand"', BBC News, 25 April 2017, available at https://www.bbc.co.uk/news/uk-wales-politics-39698499

5   Freddie Whittaker, 'Angela Rayner: Full text of Labour Conference 2017 speech', Schools Week, 26 September 2017, available at https://schoolsweek.co.uk/angela-rayner-full-text-of-labour-conference-2017-speech/

6   Fraser Nelson, 'Look down on me at your peril: I'll eat you alive', *The Spectator*, 6 January 2018, available at https://www.spectator.co.uk/article/why-isn-t-angela-rayner-a-tory/

7   Tom Peck, 'Labour Minister: We must have controls on immigration', *The Independent*, 28 September 2016, available at https://www.independent.co.uk/news/uk/politics/labour-front-bench-we-must-have-controls-on-immigration-a7334641.html

BETRAYAL

1   Rosie Kinchen, 'The Magazine Interview: the shadow education secretary, Angela Rayner, on raising a blind son and becoming a grandmother at 37', *The Times*, 14 January 2018, available at https://www.thetimes.co.uk/article/the-magazine-interview-the-shadow-education-secretary-angela-rayner-on-raising-a-blind-son-and-becoming-a-grandmother-at-37-voqwd6tgw

2   Matt Finnegan, *Betrayal* (Independently published: 2019)

3   Simon Walters, 'Angela's clashes: Labour star Rayner's former chief aide is paid £20,000 over an unfair dismissal claim – then writes a novel about a murderous MP with some very coincidental parallels', MailOnline, 17 January 2020, available at https://www.dailymail.co.uk/news/article-7900839/Angelas-clashes-Labour-star-Rayners-former-aide-paid-20-000-unfair-dismissal-claim.html

4   BBC Sounds, 2018

5   Ibid.

6   Sally Weale, '"End education snobbery. There's no out-of-work brickie or sparkie"', *The Guardian*, 18 September 2018, available at https://www.theguardian.com/education/2018/sep/18/end-education-snobbery-labour-angela-rayner

7   'Keir Starmer is outnumbered as Labour seeks its Maggie: Women will lead the charge to replace Jeremy Corbyn if the party crashes to defeat in the general election', *Mail on Sunday*, 8 December 2019, available at https://www.dailymail.co.uk/news/article-7768073/Women-lead-charge-replace-Jeremy-Corbyn-party-defeated-general-election.html

8   James Tapsfield, Split between Corbyn and McDonnell is exposed as Labour leader slams tax cut for 32m Brits just a day after his shadow chancellor talked up the plans', MailOnline, available at https://www.dailymail.co.uk/news/article-6340235/Split-Corbyn-McDonnell-exposed-Labour-leader-slams-tax-cut-32m-Brits.html

9   'Labour conference: Starmer says EU remain option on the table', BBC News, 24 September 2018, available at https://www.bbc.co.uk/news/uk-politics-45622161

10   'Rayner: New referendum "undermines democracy"', BBC News, 13 December 2018. Available at https://www.bbc.co.uk/news/av/uk-politics-46562209

11   Jessica Elgot and Rajeev Syal, 'Unite leader warns Labour against backing second EU referendum', *The Guardian*, 5 December 2018, available at https://www.theguardian.com/politics/2018/dec/05/unite-leader-warns-labour-against-backing-second-eu-referendum

12   Sienna Rodgers, 'Rayner calls for "kinder" politics following attacks over Blair tweet', Labour List, 4 March 2019, available from https://labourlist.org/2019/03/rayner-calls-for-kinder-politics-following-attacks-over-blair-tweet/

13   *Financial Times*, 2022

14 Geoff Barton, "'Don't get angry about the LGBT row…'", *TES Magazine*, 21 March 2019, available at https://www.tes.com/magazine/archive/dont-get-angry-about-lgbt-row

15 Josh Halliday, 'Labour whip to rebuke MP who backed school protest in Birmingham', *The Guardian*, 9 June 2019, available at https://www.theguardian.com/politics/2019/jun/09/labour-mp-criticised-for-siding-with-birmingham-school-protesters

16 Rowena Mason, 'Esther McVey unfit to be an MP after LGBT comments, says Labour', *The Guardian*, 3 June 2019, available at https://www.theguardian.com/politics/2019/jun/09/labour-mp-criticised-for-siding-with-birmingham-school-protesters

17 Toby Helm and Michael Savage, 'MPs tell Jeremy Corbyn: get a grip or lose general election', *The Observer*, 29 June 2019, available at https://www.theguardian.com/politics/2019/jun/29/mps-tell-jeremy-corbyn-get-grip-or-lose-election-antisemitism

18 'Labour votes to abolish Britain's private schools', *The Economist*, 26 September 2019, available at https://www.economist.com/britain/2019/09/26/labour-votes-to-abolish-britains-private-schools

19 *The Guardian*, 2019

20 Freddie Whittaker, 'Angela Rayner: Full text of Labour Conference 2019 speech', Schools Week, 22 September 2019, available at https://schoolsweek.co.uk/angela-rayner-full-text-of-labour-conference-2019-speech/

21 'General election 2019: Under-30s question politicians in TV debate', BBC News, 9 December 2019, available at https://www.bbc.co.uk/news/election-2019-50722313

THE PROGRAMME

1 Sienna Rodgers, 'Rayner launches deputy leadership bid with bold "win or die" warning', LabourList, 6 January 2020, available at https://labourlist.org/2020/01/rayner-launches-deputy-leadership-bid-with-bold-win-or-die-warning/

2 Quentin Letts, 'Get the bevvies in! Labour's gorging itself on spending: QUENTIN LETTS on yesterday in Parliament', MailOnline, 5 Jul7 2017, available at https://www.dailymail.co.uk/news/article-4666146/Labour-s-gorging-spending-writes-QUENTIN-LETTS.html

3 Andrew Sparrow, 'Labour leadership: NEC decides contest to last three months, with result announced Saturday 4 April – as it happened', *The Guardian*, 6 January 2020, available at https://www.theguardian.com/politics/live/2020/jan/06/labour-leadership-jess-phillips-clarifies-brexit-stance-saying-she-cant-see-party-backing-remain-at-next-election-live-news

4 Kate Proctor, 'Angela Rayner: I'm a socialist but not a "Corbynite"', *The Guardian*, 6 January 2020, available at https://www.theguardian.com/politics/2020/jan/06/angela-rayner-launches-campaign-to-become-deputy-labour-leader

5 ITV News, 2020

6 Heather Stewart, 'Keir Starmer: Andrew Neil and Long-Bailey keep up donation pressure', *The Guardian*, 4 March 2020, available at https://www.theguardian.com/politics/2020/mar/04/keir-starmer-andrew-neil-and-long-bailey-keep-up-donation-pressure

7 'Labour leadership: Sir Keir Starmer's acceptance speech', BBC News, 4 April 2020, available at https://www.bbc.co.uk/news/av/uk-politics-52164949

8 Gaby Hinsliff, 'Angela Rayner: "Boris Johnson needs to get up off his backside and lead"', *The Guardian*, 20 June 2020, available at https://www.bbc.co.uk/news/av/uk-politics-52164949

9 Ibid.

10 Alexandra Pollard, 'Maxine Peake: "People who couldn't vote for Labour because of Corbyn? They voted Tory as far as I'm concerned"', *The Independent*, 25 June 2020, available at https://www.bbc.co.uk/news/av/uk-politics-52164949

11 Ryan Sabey, 'RAYN MAN Labour deputy Angela Rayner strikes up close friendship with married MP after split from husband', *The Sun*, 10 October 2020, available at https://www.thesun.co.uk/news/12898761/angela-rayner-close-friendship-married-mp/

12 Ryan Sabey and Isaac Crowson, 'SCUM BACK TO MINE Labour deputy Angela Rayner

spotted leaving flat with married MP lover', *The Sun*, 22 January 2022, available at https://www.thesun.co.uk/news/17410123/angela-rayner-married-mp-lover/

SCUM

1   Times Radio, 2021
2   Gaby Hinsliff, 'Angela Rayner: "Boris Johnson needs to get up off his backside and lead"', *The Guardian*, 20 June 2020, available at https://www.theguardian.com/politics/2020/jun/20/angela-rayner-boris-johnson-needs-to-get-up-off-his-backside-and-lead
3   Peter Walker, 'Matt Hancock warns of tougher UK lockdown if too many break rules', *The Guardian*, 5 April 2020, available at https://www.theguardian.com/world/2020/apr/05/matt-hancock-warns-tougher-uk-lockdown-too-many-break-rules
4   'Johnson needs to fulfil promise to fix social care – Labour', *Jersey Evening Post*, 18 September 2020, available at https://www.jerseyeveningpost.com/morenews/uknews/2020/09/18/johnson-needs-to-fulfil-promise-to-fix-social-care-labour/
5   Hansard, HC debate, 21 October 2020, vol. 682
6   Ibid.
7   'Angela Rayner apologises for "scum" remark in Commons', BBC, 21 October 2020, available at https://www.bbc.co.uk/news/uk-politics-54638267
8   Rod Little, 'Hard luck, Corbyn. Barnet judged you by the anti-semitic, thuggish company you keep', *Sunday Times*, 6 May 2018, available at https://www.thetimes.co.uk/article/hard-luck-corbyn-barnet-judged-you-by-the-antisemitic-thuggish-company-you-keep-7g59d7csv
9   'Investigation into antisemitism in the Labour Party', Equality and Human Rights Commission, Equality and Human Rights Commission, October 2020, available at https://www.equalityhumanrights.com/sites/default/files/investigation-into-antisemitism-in-the-labour-party.pdf
10 Jeremy Corbyn (2020), Facebook, available at https://www.facebook.com/330250343871/posts/my-statement-following-the-publication-of-the-ehrc-reportantisemitism-is-absolut/10158939532253872/
11 *Morning Star*, 2015
12 Joe Millis, 'Angela Rayner apologises for quoting from "Holocaust Industry" book', *Jewish News*, 28 November 2018, available at https://www.jewishnews.co.uk/labour-figure-invited-to-board-chanukah-event-praised-holocaust-industry-book/
13 Sienna Rogers, 'Rayner warns "thousands" of Labour members may be suspended from party', LabourList, 29 November 2020, available at https://labourlist.org/2020/11/rayner-says-thousands-of-labour-members-may-be-suspended-from-party/
14 'Action plan: Driving out antisemitism from the Labour Party', Labour Party, 17 December 2020, available at https://labour.org.uk/wp-content/uploads/2020/12/Labour-Party-EHRC-Action-Plan.pdf
15 Lee Harpin, 'Labour drops Rayner antisemitism complains probe', *Jewish Chronicle*, 11 February 2021, available at https://www.thejc.com/news/labour-drops-rayner-antisemitism-complaints-probe-x7oyusqu
16 'Angela Rayner challenged over claims teachers at "greater risk" from Covid-19', BBC, 28 January 2021, available at https://www.bbc.co.uk/news/av/uk-55841838
17 Harry Yorke and Camilla Turner, 'Angela Rayner urged to retract teachers are "more at risk of catching Covid" claim', the *Daily Telegraph*, 28 January 2021, available at https://www.telegraph.co.uk/politics/2021/01/28/angela-rayner-urged-retract-teachers-risk-catching-covid-claim/
18 Alex Brummer, 'Labour's false narrative: Angela Rayner's attacks on Serco over Test and Trace are a shameful perversion of truth', This is Money, 26 February 2021, available at https://www.thisismoney.co.uk/money/comment/article-9300743/ALEX-BRUMMER-Labours-false-narrative-Sercos-Test-Trace.html
19 Ibid.

20 'The government did not give £37 billion to Serco', Full Fact, 14 September 2021, available at https://fullfact.org/health/37-billion-serco-social-care/

21 Jonathan Riley, 'Air Head: Labour's deputy leader Angela Rayner claimed £249 personalised Apple AirPods on expenses', The Sun, 28 February 2021, available at https://www.thesun.co.uk/news/14191884/labour-angela-rayner-apple-airpods-expenses/

22 'Rayner admits she's lost her taxpayer-funded airpods', Guido Fawkes, 22 November 2021, available at https://order-order.com/2021/11/22/rayner-admits-shes-lost-her-taxpayer-funded-airpods/

23 Angela Rayner, Twitter, 27 February 2021, available at https://twitter.com/AngelaRayner/status/1365622984757686272

24 Benjamin Cohen, Twitter, 27 February 2021, available at https://twitter.com/benjamincohen/status/1365655216331325448

25 John McDonnell, Twitter, 23 February 2021, available at https://twitter.com/johnmcdonnellmp/status/1364220643512700928

26 Eleni Courea, Henry Zeffman and Patrick Maguire, 'A year on, and Keir Starmer is feeling the strain', The Times, 3 April 2021, available at https://www.thetimes.co.uk/article/a-year-on-keir-starmer-is-feeling-the-strain-s5scj8mnm

27 'Sidelined Rayner fears a first-class stitch-up', Sunday Times, 9 May 2021, available at https://www.thetimes.co.uk/article/sidelined-rayner-fears-a-first-class-stitch-up-tgf96zg8c

28 Hansard, HC debate, Vol. 695, cols 7–12

29 Harry Yorke, 'Sir Keir Starmer's closest parliamentary aide quits after claims she spread rumours about Angela Rayner', Daily Telegraph, available at https://www.telegraph.co.uk/politics/2021/05/11/sir-keir-starmers-closest-aide-quits-claims-spread-rumours-angela/

30 'Meet Angela Rayner – Labour's deputy leader on winning back the North', Westminster Insider Podcast, 14 May 2021, available at https://podcasts.apple.com/be/podcast/meet-angela-rayner-labours-deputy-leader-on-winning/id1544479523?i=1000521660756

31 Tony Blair, 'Without total change Labour will die', New Statesman, 11 May 2021, available at https://www.newstatesman.com/politics/uk-politics/2021/05/tony-blair-without-total-change-labour-will-die

32 Angela Rayner, Twitter, 12 May 2021, available at https://twitter.com/angelarayner/status/1392594431728132100

33 Alastair Lockhard, '"Jeremy Corbyn would have done better" Rayner ridiculed after "deluded" assessment', The Express, 28 May 2021, available at https://www.express.co.uk/news/uk/1442643/Jeremy-Corbyn-Angela-Rayner-Labour-Party-coronavirus-Boris-Johnson-latest-vn

34 Jessica Elgot, 'Losing byelection would be "curtains" for Starmer, says Diane Abbott', The Guardian, 19 May 2021, available at https://www.theguardian.com/politics/2021/may/19/losing-byelection-would-be-curtains-for-keir-starmer-says-diane-abbott

JOHN PRESCOTT IN A SKIRT

1 Rachel Sylvester, Alice Thompson, 'Angela Rayner: "I find it difficult feeling happy"', The Times, 24 September 2021, available at https://www.thetimes.co.uk/article/angela-rayner-i-find-it-difficult-feeling-happy-rkhsz6jqd

2 Rowena Mason, 'Angela Rayner stands by labelling of Tories as "scum"', The Guardian, 26 September 2021, available at https://www.theguardian.com/politics/2021/sep/26/angela-rayner-stands-by-remarks-calling-tories-scum

3 Alan McGuinness, 'Angela Rayner doubles down on "scum" comments – as minister criticises "absolutely appalling" attack', Sky News, 26 September 2021, available at https://news.sky.com/story/labour-conference-deputy-leader-angela-rayner-doubles-down-on-tory-scum-comments-12418461

4 Ian Austin, 'Decent working class people will be appalled by motormouth Angela Rayner branding the Tories "scum"', The Sun, 26 September 2021, available at https://www.the-sun.com/news/3738841/angela-rayner-branding-tories-scum-appalling/

5 Tony Driver, '"Drink may have been partaken": Labour colleague defends Angela Rayner over Tory

"scum" comments', *Daily Telegraph*, 27 September 2021, available at https://www.telegraph.co.uk/politics/2021/09/27/drink-may-have-partaken-emily-thornberry-defends-angela-rayner/

6   'Man who emailed Rayner felt she was "partially responsible" for Amess death', *Shropshire Star*, 28 October 2021, available at https://web.archive.org/web/20211129094833/https:/www.shropshirestar.com/news/uk-news/2021/10/28/man-who-emailed-rayner-felt-she-was-partially-responsible-for-amess-death/

7   Laura Conner, 'Labour's Angela Rayner says sons need panic buttons and police escort after death threats', *Daily Mirror*, 5 February 2022, available at https://www.mirror.co.uk/news/politics/labours-angela-rayner-says-sons-26148979

8   Hansard, HC debate, 3 November 2021, vol. 702, cols 896–9

9   'Tensions reignite in Labour Party as Starmer blindsides Rayner with reshuffle', *Shropshire Star*, 29 November 2021, available at https://www.shropshirestar.com/news/uk-news/2021/11/29/tensions-reignited-in-labour-party-as-starmer-blindsides-rayner-with-reshuffle/

10 'Angela Rayner appears blindsided as Sir Keir Starmer launches Labour reshuffle during speech', ITV, 29 November 2021, available at https://www.itv.com/news/granada/2021-11-29/angela-rayner-appears-blindsided-as-sir-keir-starmer-launches-labour-reshuffle-during-speech

11 Gaby Hinsliff, 'Labour's Angela Rayner: "I'm Always Trying To Bring Keir Out Of His Shell A Bit More"', *Grazia*, 30 October 2021, available at https://graziadaily.co.uk/life/in-the-news/labour-deputy-leader-angela-rayner-interview-grazia/

12 Ryan Sabey, 'Furious Angela Rayner raged at Labour leader Sir Keir Starmer for keeping her in the dark over his reshuffle', *The Sun*, 4 December 2021, available at https://www.thesun.co.uk/news/16940918/angela-rayner-rage-keir-starmer-labour-reshuffle/

13 Rowena Mason, 'Angela Rayner's former aide "given significant payout" after media leaks', *The Guardian*, 11 November 2022, available at https://www.theguardian.com/politics/2022/nov/11/labour-angela-rayner-jack-mckenn-former-aide-payout-after-leaks

14 Hansard, HC debate, vol. 705

15 Ibid.

16 John Ferguson, '"I'm John Prescott in a skirt": Labour deputy Angela Rayner on being passionate and outspoken', *Daily Record*, 19 December 2021, available at https://www.dailyrecord.co.uk/news/scottish-news/im-john-prescott-skirt-labour-25733844

17 Angela Rayner, Twitter, 12 January 2022, available at https://twitter.com/AngelaRayner/status/1481202592826986497?lang=en

18 Colin Brazier, 'No, Angela Rayner, speaking well is not just for posh people', *Spiked*, 13 January 2022, available at https://www.spiked-online.com/2022/01/13/no-angela-rayner-speaking-well-is-not-just-for-posh-people/

19 Iram Ramzan, 'Angela Rayner, I am also a gobby Northern lass who didn't go to a posh school. But that's no excuse for bad grammar', MailOnline, 15 January 2022, available at https://www.dailymail.co.uk/news/article-10406507/IRAM-RAMZAN-Angela-Rayner-gobby-Northern-lass-Thats-no-excuse-bad-grammar.html

20 'Angela Rayner was at a lockdown event with Starmer', BBC, 29 April 2022, available at https://www.bbc.co.uk/news/uk-politics-61271050

21 'Durham Constabulary Press Statement', Durham Police, 6 May 2022, available at https://web.archive.org/web/20230607055448/https:/www.durham.police.uk/News/News-Articles/2022/May/Durham-Constabulary-Press-Statement.aspx

22 James Tapsfield and Glen Owen, 'Ministers lash Keir Starmer's "double-standards" as leaked memo demolishes his Beergate story showing curry WAS pre-planned – while Labour leader's allies up the stakes by branding him "Mr Rules" amid full-blown police probe', MailOnline, 8 May 2022, available at https://www.dailymail.co.uk/news/article-10794221/Ministers-lash-Starmers-double-standards-leaked-Beergate-memo.html

DEPUTY PRIME MINISTER-IN-WAITING

1   Glen Owen, 'Tories accuse Angela Rayner of Basic Instinct ploy to distract Boris: MPs claim

Labour deputy leader likes to put PM "off his stride" by crossing and uncrossing her legs at PMQs', MailOnline, 23 April 2022, available at https://web.archive.org/web/20230521062906/https://www.dailymail.co.uk/news/article-10746873/Tories-accuse-Angela-Rayner-Basic-Instinct-ploy-crosses-uncrosses-legs-PMQs.html

2 Angela Rayner, Twitter, 24 April 2022, available at https://twitter.com/AngelaRayner/status/1518126832272486400?lang=en-GB

3 Boris Johnson, Twitter, 24 April 2022, available at https://twitter.com/BorisJohnson/status/1518169693638561792

4 Nicola Sturgeon, Twitter, 24 April 2022, available at https://twitter.com/NicolaSturgeon/status/1518131858684395522?lang=en

5 Diane Abbott, Twitter, 26 April 2022, available at https://twitter.com/HackneyAbbott/status/1518862566189109248?lang=en-GB

6 *This Morning*, Twitter, 25 April 2022, available at https://twitter.com/thismorning/status/1518529595963752449?lang=en

7 The Political Party, 'Show 261 – *Angela Rayner Live*', 26 January 2022, available at https://shows.acast.com/the-political-party/episodes/show-261-angela-raynr-live

8 Dan Hodges, 'The truth about the story Angela Rayner branded a desperate, perverted smear… SHE was the one who told it', MailOnline, 30 April 2022, available at https://www.dailymail.co.uk/debate/article-10771103/DAN-HODGES-truth-story-Angela-Rayner-branded-smear-one-told-it.html

9 Camilla Turner, 'Angela Rayner accused of hypocrisy for not backing rail workers' walk-out', *Daily Telegraph*, 11 June 2022, available at https://www.telegraph.co.uk/news/2022/06/11/angela-rayner-accused-hypocrisy-not-backing-rail-workers-walk/

10 Angela Rayner, Twitter, 21 June 2022, available at https://twitter.com/AngelaRayner/status/1539166668584255489

11 Christopher Hope, 'Exclusive: Labour's Angela Rayner brings a splash of champagne socialism to Glyndebourne', *Daily Telegraph*, 24 June 2022, available at https://www.telegraph.co.uk/news/2022/06/24/exclusive-labours-angela-rayner-brings-splash-champagne-socialism/

12 Ned Simons, 'Keir Starmer "Pragmatic" About Nationalisation Amid Confusion Over Labour's Stance', *Huffington Post*, 25 July 2022, available at https://www.huffingtonpost.co.uk/entry/labour-rail-nationalisation_uk_62de6db2e4b081f3a9017ff7

13 Louise Haigh, Twitter, 25 July 2022, Available at https://twitter.com/LouHaigh/status/1551540867776876544

14 Nick Gutteridge, 'Keir Starmer sparks Labour revolt with U-turn on renationalisation of railways', *Daily Telegraph*, 25 July 2022, available at https://www.telegraph.co.uk/politics/2022/07/25/keir-starmers-u-turn-renationalisation-sparks-fury-among-labours/

15 Channel 4 News, Twitter, 27 July 2022, available at https://twitter.com/Channel4News/status/1552317087548424194?lang=en

16 BBC, 'Keir Starmer sacks shadow transport minister who backed rail strikes', BBC, 27 July 2022, available at https://www.bbc.co.uk/news/uk-politics-62325842

17 Ibid.

18 Joe Middleton, 'Sacked shadow minister calls for Labour to show solidarity with strikes', *The Guardian*, 30 July 2022, available at https://www.theguardian.com/politics/2022/jul/30/sam-tarry-sacked-shadow-minister-calls-for-labour-show-solidarity-strikes

19 Geraldine Scott, 'Union fury after Sir Keir Starmer sacks frontbencher Sam Tarry who joined picket', *The Times*, 28 July 2022, available at https://www.thetimes.co.uk/article/union-fury-after-sir-keir-starmer-sacks-frontbencher-sam-tarry-who-joined-picket-q899loztj

20 Chris Green, 'Angela Rayner says Keir Starmer was "within his rights" to sack her partner, Sam Tarry', *The i*, 9 August 2022, available at https://inews.co.uk/news/politics/labour/angela-rayner-keir-starmer-sack-partner-sam-tarry-1786298

21 *Financial Times*, 2021

22 Rachel Sylvester, Alice Thomson, 'He could be the next PM – but who is the real Keir

Starmer?', *The Times*, 18 November 2022, available at https://www.thetimes.co.uk/article/
keir-starmer-interview-kissed-tory-labour-pm-xcz9dq66f

23 'Angela Rayner: Railway system is crumbling', BBC, 6 December 2022, available at https://
www.bbc.co.uk/news/av/uk-politics-63873455

24 Richard Vaughan, 'Has Angela Rayner been sidelined? Rachel Reeves fast becoming Keir
Starmer's right-hand woman', *The i*, 13 January 2023, available at https://web.archive.org/
web/20230602115116/https://inews.co.uk/news/politics/superglued-together-keir-starmer-
rachel-reeves-lead-bid-labour-party-sound-finance-2081862

25 Decca Aitkenhead, 'Angela Rayner: "I overshare. Keir Starmer undershares"',
The Times, 18 February 2023, available at https://www.thetimes.co.uk/article/
angela-rayner-i-overshare-keir-starmer-undershares-nwvxx97xh

26 Isabella Boneham, 'Angela Rayner admits to "raving" in Spain, heavy drinking and vape
addiction – and shares "lethal" Venom cocktail recipe', Yahoo News, 19 August 2023, available at
https://uk.news.yahoo.com/angela-rayner-admits-raving-spain-103400383.html?guccounter=2

27 'Deputy Labour leader, Angela Rayner's speech to TUC Congress 2023', TUC, 12 September 2023,
available at https://www.tuc.org.uk/speeches/deputy-labour-leader-angela-rayners-speech-
tuc-congress-2023

EPILOGUE

1 "'I've Always Had To Earn My Place": Labour's Deputy Leader Angela Rayner On Child
Poverty, Teen Pregnancy & Going Toe To Toe With Old Etonians', *British Vogue*, 21 November
2023, available at https://www.vogue.co.uk/article/angela-rayner-interview

2 *The Times*, 2021

3 Douglas Murray, 'Elon Musk is right, the far left DOES hate everyone – including
themselves', *The Sun*, 2 May 2022, available at https://www.thesun.co.uk/news/18439768/
elon-musk-far-left-hate/

INDEX